Shame and Philosophy

Shame and Philosophy

An Investigation in the Philosophy of Emotions and Ethics

Phil Hutchinson
Manchester Metropolitan University

© Phil Hutchinson 2008
Softcover reprint of the hardcover 1st edition 2008 978-0-230-54271-6

First published 2008 by
PALGRAVE MACMILLAN
Houndmills, Basingstoke, Hampshire RG21 6XS and
175 Fifth Avenue, New York, N.Y. 10010
Companies and representatives throughout the world

PALGRAVE MACMILLAN is the global academic imprint of the Palgrave
Macmillan division of St. Martin's Press, LLC and of Palgrave Macmillan Ltd.
Macmillan® is a registered trademark in the United States, United Kingdom
and other countries. Palgrave is a registered trademark in the European
Union and other countries.

ISBN 978-1-349-36028-4   ISBN 978-0-230-58318-4 (eBook)
DOI 10.1007/978-0-230-58318-4

This book is printed on paper suitable for recycling and made from fully
managed and sustained forest sources. Logging, pulping and manufacturing
processes are expected to conform to the environmental regulations of the
country of origin.

A catalogue record for this book is available from the British Library.

Library of Congress Cataloging-in-Publication Data
Hutchinson, Phil.
   Shame and philosophy : an investigation in the philosophy of
emotions and ethics / Phil Hutchinson.
      p.   cm.
   Includes bibliographical references and index.

   1. Emotions
(Philosophy)   2. Shame.   I. Title.
B105.E46H88 2008
   128'.37—dc22   2008011120

10   9   8   7   6   5   4   3   2   1
17   16   15   14   13   12   11   10   09   08

Transferred to digital printing in 2009.

Contents

Preface

Emotions research is 'in'. It is no longer the philosophical equivalent of an 'odd backwater', as one philosopher, writing just over 10 years ago, referred to it. The backwater has been discovered—and the developers have moved in. To stretch the metaphor, philosophy of the emotions seems to have been transformed from 'odd backwater' to 'boomtown'. Does this transformation amount to progress? My thoughts on this question will emerge in what follows, if they are not made somewhat clear now by my choice of metaphors. In short, I am cautious (maybe even sceptical) as to the direction in which most of the developers of the former backwater would like to take us. It sometimes feels like a challenge to simply keep pace with the number of new theories emerging; the boomtown, it seems, is beginning to sprawl . . .

Just over 10 years ago, about the same time as the philosophy of the emotions was being depicted as an odd backwater (a depiction which seems in retrospect to have triggered, or coincided with, the boom), I decided that I wanted to write on shame. I made the decision after reading Primo Levi's *If This is a Man* and *The Drowned and the Saved*. At that time, as I read Levi, I was unaware of the existence of an area of philosophy devoted to explaining the emotions; of course, it did not take me long to find out that there was, and thus, for me to see that being dragged into all sorts of debates that had not been my initial concern was unavoidable. A few years later I attended the Royal Institute of Philosophy Conference on Philosophy and the Emotions, hosted by my (then) home department at Manchester University. This confirmed to me what had hitherto been suspicions. Lots of arguments took place regarding the merits or otherwise of the various theories that currently dominated the literature. More general arguments took place about the merits or otherwise of the (neo-)Jamesian approach in contrast to the cognitivist (judgementalist) approach (and *vice versa*): The cognitivist approach—after a period of dominance in philosophy of the emotions—was coming under strong attack from adherents to the (neo-)Jamesian approach—an approach which had been bolstered by the recent increased prominence of research in cognitive neuroscience. While, as the reader will deem from the following chapters, I do believe these disputes need to be studied by anyone serious about studying the emotions, they can leave one a little cold if one's initial interest was prompted by a desire to make sense of (and grasp the philosophical/ethical significance of) emotional episodes (such as those reported by Levi). It is important, in allowing oneself to be dragged into such disputes, not to lose one's grip on that which brought one to study the emotions in the first place; that is to say, one should endeavour to keep in mind one's initial purpose.

In this book I do not provide another theory of the emotions (or of shame). I do not add a suburb (however pretty) to the boomtown. I offer, such that one might find it useful, a framework for understanding: world-taking cognitivism. My hope is that this will enable some to gain clarity regarding emotional expression and help them resist the temptations of the boomtown—resist the temptation to think that we need another (only better, more complete) theory of the emotions.

Having submitted the book for publication, I still feel there is much more of worth that might be said about shame. And I hope to contribute something to this end in the future. It continues to strike me—despite a number of publications appearing as this book goes to press—how odd it is that shame gets such little attention. If I persuade readers of little else, I should like to have persuaded them that shame should be accorded central concern by anyone interested in moral psychology.

Acknowledgements

Much of the material which makes up Chapters 1, 2 and 3 of this book first saw light as part of my PhD thesis. I thank my supervisors at Manchester, Harry Lesser and Veronique Pin-Fat, and my examiners, Peter Goldie and Nigel Pleasants, for their very helpful comments. A number of people have read the manuscript (less much of Chapter 4) and taken the time to offer extensive and thoughtful criticism and comment. I would like to mention David Cockburn, Rupert Read and Wes Sharrock; I am indebted to, and thank, each of them. Richard Hamilton read early versions of Chapters 1 and 3; Ulrika Björk kindly read and gave extensive comments on Chapter 2; I should like to thank them both for their comments. I should also like to thank my editors at Palgrave, Pri and Melanie, Dhivya at Integra-India and my former editor at Palgrave, Dan Bunyard, who before leaving Palgrave (nothing to do with my having just submitted the manuscript, I like to think) initially invited me to publish this material. Thanks to Jean Sanders for compiling the index. Of course, I bear sole responsibility for what follows.

I have presented sections of the book at various research seminars and conferences over the past 7 years; these include Åbo Akademi University, Finland; ALWS Conference, Kirchberg am Weschel, Austria; Philosophy Research Seminar, University of Hertfordshire; Lampeter Philosophy Colloquium; British Society for the Philosophy of Science Conference, Glasgow; Royal Institute of Philosophy Conference on Philosophy and the Emotions, Manchester University; Emotions and Self-Knowledge Symposium, Stockholm University; the Human Sciences Seminar, Manchester Metropolitan University; and Mind and Society 10, Manchester. Thanks to all those who raised questions.

I should also like to give thanks in particular to the philosophers at Åbo Akademi University. In addition to inviting me to speak at their conference, Emotions and Understanding, in 2005, they invited me back the following year to deliver a week-long series of lectures and workshops. On the latter occasion, I had the privilege of delivering all of the following material (less much of Chapter 4). I thank Ylva Gustafsson, Lars Hertzberg, Tom Kettunen, Jacek Kornak, Camilla Kronqvist, Olli Lagerspetz, Hannes Nykänen, Tove Österman, Hugo Strandberg and Göran Torrkulla for some of the most stimulating conversations

I have had in any philosophical forum. I have also benefited much from extensive correspondence with (Åbo alumni) Michael McEachrane. The (2005) conference at Åbo also provided me with the opportunity to meet and talk at length with—in addition to some of those already mentioned above—Jack Canfield, Kathleen Higgins, Dina Mendonça, Brian Parkinson, Robert C. Roberts and Robert Solomon; I gained much from my conversations with each of them over the four days of the conference. I am sad that Bob Solomon will not see the book.

I was given (little but much needed) teaching relief at Manchester Metropolitan University (MMU), thanks to a grant from Peter Gilroy at the MMU Research and Enterprise Development Unit and a Promising Research Fellowship awarded by the same unit. Michael Loughlin and Stewart Crehan, my colleagues at MMU, have also been supportive, insisting on occasion that I leave my office and go with them to the pub to talk about film (mainly Herzog), football (mainly Arsenal), music (mainly John Coltrane) and politics (mainly... no; that would be another book, or two, or three) over a drink.

One usually finds a list of friends and family appended to the acknowledgements. In this case I want to emphasise that this book might well not exist if it were not for the genuine support and friendship of the following people at various times over the last 8 years: Helen Caddick, Suchetana Chattopadhyay, Karen Chung, Ian Cross, Mira Dimitrova, Ayo Dove, Dan Firth, John Game, Richard Hamilton, Kacey Harrison, Jenny & Tony Hutchinson and John & Miles Hutchinson, Charlotte Jarman, Greg Lawrence, Frank Lores-Penalver, Steven Marshall, Askala McMorris, Ekua McMorris, Michael Nedo, Ayanna Prevatt-Goldstein, Rupert Read, Philippe Rouchy, Cris Sanchez-Gonzalez, Wes Sharrock, Susan and Michael Wood, and Tom Young. It was Tom Young, along with John Game and Sudipta Kaviraj, who inspired and encouraged me to pursue my academic interests, when I was an undergraduate. I hope that they are not too disappointed. I should also mention Simon Munnery, a late night/early morning conversation with whom, some 10 years ago, started me thinking about shame.

For never failing to put a smile on my face, even at times when I was sure it was not possible, I want to thank Amber, Ebony, Maisie, Mia, George, Samuel and Taitu (sorry this is not as interesting as the books I usually give to you all).

Finally, madeleine kennedy-macfoy... thanks so much.

Introduction

Ethical enquiry takes a number of forms. It can be conducted in the manner of normative moral theorising: theorising as to how we ought to act and/or live. It can be conducted in the manner of metaethical enquiry: enquiring about the nature of value and value claims. It can be conducted in another, more tangential, though, I suggest, equally as important a manner; not directly concerned to theorise as to what one ought to do, nor concerned directly with the metaphysics of value, but rather concerned with questions such as what it means to be human, what place do moral concepts have in our lives, and how are they related to other concepts. This is the sense in which the present work is an ethical investigation; it is offered as a work in moral psychology, though, importantly, one which also seeks to work on the reader's moral sensibilities.[1]

The main title of the book has a double meaning, as no doubt will have been suspected. The first of these is the 'straight', or literal, meaning; here the topic of investigation is 'shame', the emotion, and the investigation is philosophical. The second meaning, though less literal, is no less central to my purpose; here I am suggesting for discussion that philosophy, as a subject, should feel a little ashamed. This, of course, is a deliberately dissentious claim. I mean to suggest that many of us, when doing philosophy, continually acquiesce to the temptation to abstract from personhood, from the world we inhabit, etc. in order to reflect on matters which have direct impact upon, and are directly related to, the person.

Recently there has been a revival of interest in the virtues. We are often told that we now have three approaches to normative ethics from which to choose.[2] This might well be so. What is appealing about virtue ethics is the central place such an approach accords to personhood, character,

1

and the life lived with others. This is the topic, somewhat tangentially addressed, of the present work. It is hoped that the reflection on the emotions, on shame, and on philosophers who have undertook to study them is one that will give rise to one's reflection on the nature of, and conditions for, being a person. One way in which I hope it will be so is by, as the work progresses, increasingly engaging with the emotion of shame as experienced, documented, and reflected upon by survivors of (and one perpetrator of) extreme trauma. This serves to concretise the discussion.

As regards shame, my aim is not to provide a theory of shame but rather a framework for understanding. My philosophical approach is therapeutic; in this regard my objective is purely to facilitate understanding. I will not theorise the substantive content of shame (or the emotions in general). Such content comes from our observation of the phenomena, clearly viewed. The philosophical task I undertake is to provide a framework that facilitates our understanding of the phenomena. I seek no more than to aid the reader to see shame by providing a perspicuous presentation of the phenomena in question; this is what my framework for understanding—the 'world-taking cognitivist' approach—seeks to make possible.

I will not, therefore, be concerned to arrive at a conclusion that offers a substantive theory of the emotions, of shame, or of the person. Indeed, I shall offer no theory of the person. What I seek to show is that shame as an emotion, when understood, can afford us insight into our nature as human animals, our nature as persons. One of the promises of virtue ethics is that the person is 'brought back in'; unfortunately, the promise is not always kept, because in seeking to compete with the other two normative theories, the virtue ethics on show often becomes virtue *theory*, merely one methodological tool among others that can be applied by the theorist faced with a moral dilemma. In what follows, I propose to meditate upon both personhood *and* philosophy's relationship to personhood. I do this through an analysis of the emotions and of shame. 'Signposting' and the explicit stating of aims and objectives will be kept to a minimum; the therapeutic approach to philosophy seeks to facilitate aspect shifts—reorientations in thought—in one's readers. Such reorientations must be *freely* arrived at. The author's—my—task is, therefore, one of *facilitating* such aspect shifts.[3]

This book has a structure that needs some explanation. Chapters 1 and 2 engage with philosophical approaches to emotion, which might well be considered to be at polar extremes. While Chapter 3 works towards a way of understanding emotion through an engagement with, what are most often termed as, cognitive theories of emotion. Chapter 4 begins by addressing some of the current issues in philosophical discussions of the emotions and moves towards conclusion by suggesting future directions of study.

The book will take the form described below.

Chapter 1

Experimental methods and conceptual confusion: philosophy, science, and *What Emotions Really Are*

My reflections on emotions begin with an engagement with a hugely influential book: Paul E. Griffiths' *What Emotions Really Are*. This is done, and takes such a place of prominence, for a number of reasons. Griffiths, in effect, denies philosophers a voice when considering emotion. He seeks to show that philosophical theories of emotion are nothing more than recapitulations of the current stereotype of emotion terms, sometimes stated as being nothing more than recapitulations of our folk psychology of emotions. One needs to meet Griffiths' challenge. Griffiths' book is a prominent, influential, and sophisticated version of philosophical scientism. It can be tempting to see scientism as self-loathing philosophy—philosophy that cannot tolerate acknowledgement of anything genuinely and distinctively philosophical, i.e. philosophy that is not modelled on or reducible to (what are taken to be) the methods of or the results of natural science. Griffiths both denies that (non-scientistic) philosophy can give any insight into the reality of emotion and advocates a science of emotion.

An engagement with Griffiths' work is a pertinent place to begin. I give some time to outlining Griffiths' claims; I then set about identifying the presuppositions which lead him to make those claims. Ultimately, there is in play an eliding of normativity. This leads to a replacement of ordinary talk of 'learning' with talk of 'phenotypes developing'; it leads to a replacement of talk of the place of emotions in people's lives with talk of 'affect programs running on a limited database'. Now, it is easy and may be tempting to sneer at the employment of such language if one is not tempted by scientism; the burden of Chapter 1 is to resist such sneering and rather try to bring us to the realisation that such language plays no more than a rhetorical role. The claim is *not* that authors such as Griffiths, in a somewhat Machiavellian manner, deliberately set out to blind us with rhetoric; rather, the claim is that if we can show such use of language to have no more than rhetorical significance, over and above that which it replaces (and often less significance in terms of making sense of our lives), we might persuade such authors and those persuaded by them to rethink their position.

Griffiths' scientism is founded upon a scientifically determined theory of meaning: his own version of the causal homeostatic theory of natural kind semantics. The chapter ends by identifying the limits of such a theory of language and with a suggestion about concepts, and how we might understand their place in our lives.

Chapter 2

To 'Make Our Voices Resonate' or 'To Be Silent': Shame as Fundamental Ontology

Having engaged with scientism in the philosophy of the emotions, one might recoil. Such recoil might lead one to an engagement with a radically different form of philosophy, a form of philosophy very distant from scientism. Such a form of philosophising might both reject (what are understood as) the methods of the natural sciences as having import for philosophical reflection and might eschew attempts at determining meaning. Giorgio Agamben's work provides the locus for an engagement with such a philosophical position. Agamben situates his work in the post-Heideggerian tradition, and his discussion of shame is embedded in a wider historico-political thesis. His claim is that the individual's awareness of the self is felt as shame. In making this claim he draws upon Aristotle, Derrida, Foucault, Heidegger, Kant, and Levinas and claims that phenomenological support is provided by an analysis of Holocaust survivor testimony, particularly that of Primo Levi and of Robert Antelme.

Such a project initially shows promise, for it is somewhat refreshing to be moved away from the abstractions of scientism. However, such promise is not realised in the final analysis. Levi and Antelme are both garnered as support; unfortunately their own writings do not quite offer the support that Agamben presents them as so doing. Noting this serves as a spring-board to reflection upon Agamben's own philosophical prejudice. While engaging in a mode of philosophising which one might see as standing diametrically opposed to scientism, one finds it to be a mode of philosophising which can similarly elide the person in the name of theory. Ultimately this eliding is driven by a picture of language, which too-readily abstracts from the person's role in language. The eliding is, therefore, structurally conferred.

Agamben's prejudice is, we might say, to be located in his indebtedness to post-structural linguistics. Here, in contrast to the attempts to theoretically determine meaning that we found in scientism, meaning is said to be continually deferred, always—logically—just beyond our grasp. The philosophical task is to make emotional expression intelligible, to elucidate its place in our lives. Agamben's inquiries do not fulfil this task. The cost of this failure is misrepresentation of expressions of shame.

Chapter 3

Emotion, Cognition, and World

Chapters 1 and 2, in engaging with visions of the philosophical task which appear to be polar opposites regarding the understanding of our subject and approach to the subject matter, help to orient me as regards my own enquiries. I want to understand shame as it is expressed by Primo Levi, and other survivors of extreme trauma; to gain some understanding of the place of shame in the lives of people; and to gain some understanding of the nature of the person. Neither the approach recommended by Griffiths nor that advanced by Agamben is sufficient to this task (though one gains much more from the latter of the two). However, in recognising their deficiencies, I am better placed with regard to pursuit of my goal.

Chapter 3 pursues this goal. In Chapter 1, I note how Griffiths focuses his hostility to philosophical accounts of the emotions on an approach to emotions called cognitivism. In Chapter 3, I discuss variants of cognitivism. In the course of doing so, I explore numerous ways in which philosophers of the emotions marginalise the person, through the invocation of sub-personal mechanisms. I suggest that such a denial is borne of having in play a picture of mind and world which is *not*, on reflection, obligatory. This picture underlies traditional cognitivism (what I term 'reason-giving cognitivism'), and it underlies many of the critical remarks offered by critics of traditional cognitivism.

Chapter 3, therefore, sees me pursuing—broadly speaking—two tasks: first I seek to make manifest the pictures, the thought-constraining grip of which leads both reason-giving cognitivists and their opponents to their conclusions; second I seek to offer another way of understanding emotion: (what I term) 'world-taking cognitivism'. World-taking cognitivism, I suggest, avoids the problems to which the other philosophical accounts of emotion are subject. Most importantly, it is a way of understanding emotion in which the person is central, not marginalised by a desire for non-normative explanation (Griffiths; Chapter 1), not marginalised by the search for a fundamental ontology (Agamben; Chapter 2), and not marginalised by the invocation of sub-personal mechanisms (Robinson, Prinz; Chapter3).

Chapter 4

Shame and World

Chapter 4 moves us towards conclusion. I first subject to scrutiny some criticisms of cognitivism not covered in Chapter 3. This is the criticism advanced by John Deigh (and many others) that a commitment to the fact of the intentionality of emotion cannot be aligned with the fact of (non-human) animal emotions. I show that Deigh's 'two facts' do not pose a problem for the approach to emotion I offer here.

I then progress to a more focussed discussion of shame. I pay particular attention to the metaphor of the audience and to the question of heteronomy, as discussed by Bernard Williams (1993). I move towards the concluding section with a discussion of bystanders and the absence of shame.

It is my hope that by this stage the ethical sense of this work, which I discussed above, will have become manifest. It is ethical in the sense of my remarks about the second way in which one might understand the title. Philosophies which proceed to offer explanations which elide the person are all too familiar; as a philosopher one should make every attempt to find a way of describing a situation in a perspicuous manner, before turning to theory. It is also ethical in the sense in which it provides, I hope, a small step on the path to a better understanding of the person and, through the examples garnered, stimulates one's moral sensibilities.

1
Experimental Methods and Conceptual Confusion: Philosophy, Science, and *What Emotions **Really** Are*

Philosophers in the Anglo-American tradition began to take renewed interest in the emotions in the 1960s. Since then the dominant 'research program' in the philosophy of the emotions has been—what is widely, though not uncontroversially, called—cognitivism. Authors such as Anthony Kenny (1963), Robert Solomon (1976, 2003c), Gabriele Taylor (1985), and Peter Goldie (2000)[1] have offered explanations of the human emotions chiefly in terms of the beliefs (thoughts, judgements, evaluations) of the agents; in the early stages this 'project' was seen (often self-consciously) as a corrective to 'feeling theories' of the emotions, particularly those offered and/or influenced by William James (1884) and Carl Lange (1885)—often referred to as the James-Lange theory—which depicted emotions in a manner which led to them being characterised as irrational irruptions into an otherwise rational life. Cognitivism was seen as a corrective to this, in that it set out to rationally explain the emotions. Recently, the post-1960s, dominance of philosophical cognitivism has been subjected to strong criticism.

In his (1997) book *What Emotions Really Are* (*WERA*), Paul Griffiths launches a 'blistering' attack on philosophical cognitivism in the philosophy of emotions.[2] Griffiths refers to cognitivism in the philosophy of the emotions as 'propositional attitude theory' so as to guard against it being confused with cognitive science; the latter being an area of inquiry which he thinks has genuine merit. In this chapter I will follow Griffiths' terminology, if only so as to avoid confusion. (I shall critically examine his choice of the name 'propositional attitude theory' when I examine 'cognitivist' accounts in Chapter 3).

I examine Paul Griffiths' work for a number of (related) reasons: first, because it provides us with a particularly stark and very forthright example of scientism in the philosophy of the emotions, and philosophy in general; second, Griffiths' book has been extraordinarily influential;[3] and third, if Griffiths is correct most of the philosophical work on the emotions undertaken over the last 30 years has told us nothing about what emotions really are. As with regards to 'scientism', this is a term often employed pejoratively; this is not my intention here. Every aspect of Paul Griffiths' book is unabashedly, and somewhat defiantly, scientistic.[4] 'What emotions really are' will be explained by a science of the emotions. Griffiths' book is part (Part 1 of the book) report on the current state of the 'science' of emotions and part (Part 2 of the book) argument for a theory of language which will allow for (improved prospects for) scientific explanation of the emotions.

'What emotions really are', for Griffiths, is not what they mean for the individuals experiencing them; not what an examination of the use of emotion terms might tell us; they are not explained by some combination of the propositional beliefs and the desires of the individual experiencing the emotion; nor are they explained by some combination of the propositional beliefs, the desires, and the attendant feelings of the individual experiencing the emotion. Indeed, neither does it help—as far as Griffiths is concerned—if we include a bit of added narrative; nor if we replace 'beliefs' with 'judgements', 'evaluations', or 'construals'. No; 'what emotions *really* are' is explained by uncovering and scientifically explaining the category to which the concept (putatively) refers.

Griffiths makes many (substantive) claims in his book. I focus my attention on his main philosophical claim. Both his criticisms of propositional attitude theory and his proposals for the future scientific study and explanation of emotion explicitly rest upon his arguments and proposals for a causal homeostatic theory of natural kind semantics. Griffiths' work in the emotions, therefore, stands or falls on the arguments he advances in Chapters 7 and 8 of *WERA*.

This chapter takes the following form:

- Section 1 gives a *précis* of *What Emotions Really Are*. In this section I restrict critical comments of my own to a minimum. It is tempting to engage with the substantive claims Griffiths makes both about the emotions, in Chapters 2 through 6 (Part 1) of his book, and about progress in philosophy throughout his book; however, the temptation is (in the main) resisted. The force behind Griffiths' criticisms of propositional attitude theory and his substantive claims about what emotions *really* are, as noted, arises from his theory of natural kinds.
- Section 2 critically engages the history of natural kind semantics, as that history is presented to us by Griffiths. I begin by looking at Hilary

Putnam's (1975d) account: Griffiths claims to be working within the paradigm initiated by Putnam (and Kripke 1980 [1972]). I question Griffiths' rendition of Putnam; I advance some of my own criticisms of Putnam's position (correctly understood); and I note the criticisms of Putnam advanced by others.

- Section 3 critically engages Griffiths' own theory of natural kinds: the causal homeostatic theory. Griffiths claims his theory avoids the pitfalls to which *he* (see Section 2) found Putnam's to be subject. I question this. Griffiths oscillates between, on the one hand advancing a robustly metaphysical thesis,[5] and on the other hand doing no more than describing the pragmatic nature of our concepts in certain domains.[6]

- Section 4 moves towards conclusion by suggesting that careful reflection upon our concepts not only gives answers to questions, which Griffiths *assumes* only science can answer, but also shows us the conceptual confusions in which Griffiths seems trapped.

1. Précis of *What Emotions Really Are*

1.1. Degenerative research programs

Griffiths' charge is substantial. Not only does he see in propositional attitude theory a resounding and inevitable failure, but also charges its proponents with a systematic antipathy for the results of scientific psychology. The antipathy is 'systematic' because the failure to acknowledge the 'insights' of 'science' is no mere accident or oversight on the part of propositional attitude theorists; rather, it is a result of their methodological orientation. While propositional attitude theory in the philosophy of the emotions has its origins in Anthony Kenny's (1963) *Action, Emotion and Will*, it had still, 27 years later (in 1989), failed to overcome its original difficulties. The conclusion should be that propositional attitude theory is a failed research program (Griffiths 1989; *WERA*: p. 38).

Griffiths' attack is two-pronged. The first prong, we might say, is his identification of a number of substantive failures of propositional attitude theory. These failures are: the inability to account for objectless emotions, reflex emotions, and unemotional evaluations; further charging that the theory cannot provide an explanation for the underdetermination of emotions by judgements, emotional responses to imagination, and physiological responses. Despite some late attempts by some propositional attitude theorists (e.g. Stocker 1987; Nash 1989) to address some of these problems, Griffiths suggests that these substantive problems cannot be overcome by the research program for deep-seated, methodological reasons. This is the second prong of Griffiths' attack. For, one might be tempted to defend the propositional attitude theorists by asking for them to be granted more time in which they might address these substantive problems. However, such a (potential) plea is undercut by the charge that these substantive failures stem from an underlying, fundamental, methodological flaw: i.e. the theory's reliance upon conceptual analysis.

Conceptual analysis as a methodology comes in for a similar two-pronged attack. The first prong is Griffiths' *assertion* that the form of conceptual analysis engaged in by propositional attitude theorists 'is a view which has been very broadly rejected in the philosophy of language' (*WERA*: p. 4); the second prong is the charge that there are flaws in the account of linguistic meaning presupposed by conceptual analysis. Conceptual analysis, we are told, presupposes that a concept can be defined by identifying its rules for correct application; therefore, it should be rejected as a methodology owing to its failure to do more than tell us the current stereotype of a concept. Equating the meaning of a concept with the current stereotype leads to our explanation of (say) 'fear' being no more than a reflection of the current stereotype of fear. The (alleged) problem with this is that stereotypes change as our knowledge of things (or phenomena) grows. Hence, allowing one's explanation of a phenomenon to rest upon the stereotypical understanding of that phenomenon is merely to explain the phenomenon in terms of our current (contingent) understanding of it, and not to explain the phenomenon itself. This is, we are told, as if to define a whale as a fish because people (folk) once thought that whales were fish. Griffiths writes:

> All conceptual analysis will reveal is the current stereotype of fear. To insist that all and only the things that fit this stereotype are examples of the kind is simply to stand in the way of clarifying the concept. It is exactly akin to insisting that whales are fish because people called them so.
>
> (*WERA*: p. 5)

In place of conceptual analysis Griffiths proposes the semantics of natural kinds, conceived by Kripke (1980) and Putnam (1975d), but developed and refined since.[7] Briefly (I come back to this in more detail below), the semantics of natural kinds classifies a term into four components: syntactic marker, semantic marker, stereotype, and extension. An example of these classifications for the term 'whale' might be as follows: syntactic marker—'noun'; semantic marker—'mammal'; stereotype—(something like) 'large, migratory, sea-faring mammal'; extension—what the best current science tells us a whale 'really is'. On Griffiths' understanding we can get by in our day-to-day lives, and be seen as competent users of the language, while only ever knowing the stereotype of a term. However, to really know the *meaning* of a term is to know its extension, and the knowledge of a term's extension is identified with the best current scientific knowledge of the kind. I shall leave to one side, for now, what 'scientific knowledge' might mean here, but, needless to say, what it might mean is central to any account given of the semantics of natural kinds (I shall address this in Section 3.5). For now it is enough to note that for Griffiths conceptual analysis can only alert us to the stereotype of a term; in order for us to know what emotions *really* are we need to know more than the current stereotype.

To recap, Griffiths sets his sights on the dominant philosophical approach to the emotions: the propositional attitude theory. He depicts a number of theorists, whom he claims advance a propositional attitude theory of the emotions, as comprising a research program. He charges the research program with a number of serious substantive failures to explain the emotions, arguing—as he has before (Griffiths 1989)—that these substantive failures are *in themselves* enough for us to conclude that the research program is no longer worth pursuing (it is a terminally degenerate research program). He then submits the further charge that these substantive failures are borne of the research program's methodological reliance upon conceptual analysis:[8] writing that conceptual analysis has been largely abandoned as a research program in the philosophy of language, epistemology, and the philosophy of mind. If, therefore, we want to answer the 'vernacular' question 'what *are* the emotions?' (ibid.: p. 228) we need to do more than identify the stereotype, we need to know the extension of the term. The subsequent chapters of Part 1 of Griffiths' book explore the ways in which—what he takes to be—current science might 'fill out' the extension.

1.2. Alternative approaches: learning from 'science'

Griffiths identifies three distinct phenomena that fall under the vernacular term 'the emotions': affect program emotions; higher cognitive emotions (which in subsequent publications he prefers to call 'complex emotions'); and disclaimed action 'emotions'.

1.2.1. Affect program emotions

'The *affect program* is the coordinated set of changes that constitute the emotional response' (*WERA*: p. 77) and these changes are experienced as psychological events.[9] The leading exponent of this approach is Paul Ekman (1975),[10] whose work builds upon Charles Darwin's nineteenth-century experiments on facial expression. Ekman (and various co-authors) have conducted experiments on human facial expressions across cultures; from these experiments they hypothesise that certain emotion terms are the names of categories of psychological event. The hypotheses, we are told, are confirmed in ongoing experiments whereby people are asked to examine photographs of a number of facial expressions and attribute the emotion being experienced by the person in the photograph. Ekman and his various co-authors claim that these experiments uncover 'six species-typical' human affect programs: surprise, anger, fear, disgust, sadness, and joy (*WERA*: p. 78). Griffiths claims that Ekman's research is complemented and supported by work done on the autonomic nervous system (ANS) by Joseph Schachter (1957), Gary E. Schwartz *et al.* (1981), and Antonio Damasio (1994); these authors' work shows that the arousal of the ANS is differentiated among the emotions in a way that lends support to the hypotheses advanced in Ekman's research. Those emotions which are explained as affect programs are therefore 'restricted to short-term, stereotyped responses, triggered by modular subsystems operating on a limited database' (*WERA*: p. 241).

1.2.2. The higher cognitive emotions

The higher cognitive emotions are, paradigmatically, emotions such as pride, shame, guilt, and remorse (Griffiths includes loyalty and revenge in the list). These differ from the affect programs in that they are 'irruptive motivations' (*WERA*: p. 243). That is to say, the higher cognitive emotions are irruptions in our long-term planned actions, owing to our immediate circumstances. While Griffiths told us that the affect program emotions are 'sources of motivation not integrated into the system of beliefs and desires' (ibid.) thus requiring the introduction of the concept of *mental state*, the higher cognitive emotions *are* (often) integrated into our beliefs and desires. Griffiths largely[11] follows Frank (1988) in seeing in the higher cognitive emotions *apparently* irrational responses to our immediate environment, which enable us to pursue long-term rational goals. So, for example, we believe we should be loyal, owing to current circumstances; therefore, we depart from our goal-directed long-term plans in order to carry out the duties demanded by that loyalty.[12] Those duties, though seemingly irrational in virtue of our long-term plans, might serve a rational purpose in engendering loyalty, trust, and the like in others. Thus long-term rational plans are served after all. This, we might note, relies heavily on the 'findings'[13] of game theory. The higher cognitive emotions, then, are less like reflex responses than the affect program emotions.[14] Griffiths sees the scientific explanation of the higher cognitive emotions as being more troublesome. Current work in evolutionary psychology and game theory *might* combine to provide the answers, but many questions are, at present, pending satisfactory answers. What is clear to Griffiths, however, is that we have enough evidence to establish the existence of a category of emotions distinct from the affect program emotions.

1.2.3. *Disclaimed action emotions*

Disclaimed action is uncovered on examination of the literature on the social construction of emotion[15] (*WERA*: ch. 6). Griffiths divides the social construction of emotion into two models: the social concept model and the social role model. We are told that the social role model has two variants: the disclaimed action version and reinforcement version (*WERA*: p. 143). The disclaimed action version of the social role model is the aspect of social constructionist accounts that Griffiths thinks offers insight into some 'emotion' phenomena; such insight is not afforded by either the affect program theory or the psycho-evolutionary candidate for explaining the higher cognitive emotions. In a disclaimed action, the behaviour of an individual is 'acted' in an attempt to conform to a social role. This differs from the affect program emotions and the higher cognitive emotions in that in the first instance it lacks the professed cross-cultural status of the other two. Examples of such 'culturally specific' disclaimed action are: the state of 'being a wild pig' reported in the Gururumba people of New Guinea (Newman 1964, cited in *WERA*: p. 140); 'running *amok*', which has been documented in South East Asian societies; and 'multiple personality syndrome' (MPS) found in some western societies, as discussed by Ian Hacking (1995).[16] Emotions can be disclaimed actions in the same way that 'being a wild pig', 'running *amok*', and 'multiple personality syndrome' are identified as being. Disclaimed action emotions are a display of behaviour that is socially appropriate in a particular situation. This is learned behaviour, though neither the individual nor society acknowledges this fact. On the contrary, the behaviour is seen as 'a natural and inevitable response to the circumstances and outside the control of the individual' (*WERA*: p. 141).

The disclaimed action emotions are pseudo-emotions on Griffiths' account. They are strategic in that they play on the status accorded to particular emotions in certain circumstances in different societies. If a given situation is acknowledged by society as giving rise to extreme anger, and extreme anger is acknowledged by a society as being worthy of providing mitigation for an act, then we might find anger behaviour acted out within that society in those situations. This anger is not 'real' anger—affect program anger—but rather disclaimed-action-'anger'. Importantly, the suggestion is not that this is a self-conscious, calculated 'aping' of the emotion on the part of the individual, rather it is *caused* by internalised (learnt) beliefs about appropriate action in given situations in certain societies. Griffiths tells us,

> Disclaimed action emotions are modelled on the local cultures' conception of the emotions. They aim to take advantage of the special status that emotions are accorded because of their passivity. Like socially constructed illnesses, disclaimed action emotions are actually very different from the phenomena on which they are modelled. At a psychological level, far from being disruptive of longer term goals, they are 'strategic' devices for the achievement of those goals. Rather than involving isolated modules [affect programs], or special adaptations of higher level cognition [higher cognitive emotions], they are manifestations of the central purpose of higher cognitive activity—the understanding and manipulation of social relations.
>
> (*WERA*: p. 245)

Disclaimed actions are, then, distinct from both affect program emotions and the higher cognitive emotions. What is in question is whether they are to be admitted to the list as a genuine emotion category: i.e. whether they form a natural kind; Griffiths suspects not, though he leaves the question (partially) open.

1.3. Eliminating emotion

Griffiths' discussions in Part 1 of *What Emotions Really Are*, together with his declared philosophical agenda, lead him to conclude that the vernacular term 'the emotions' needs to be eliminated in favour of two natural kind terms corresponding to the two identified categories of emotions. The elimination of the 'folk concept' will better facilitate the induction and explanation of the emotion. We cannot identify the vernacular term 'the emotions' with one of the above kinds of emotional explanation; for if we were to identify the vernacular term 'the emotions' with the affect program emotions we would be forced to exclude the higher cognitive emotions. This would lead to a failure to answer the question.

It strikes me that there is a degree of confusion in play here. Either the concept of 'emotion' employed in the vernacular question 'what is an emotion?' has significance, or it has not. On the one hand he wishes to say it has not, and should therefore be eliminated—because it does not refer to one natural kind, but two, maybe three; while on the other hand he says we cannot answer the question 'what is an emotion' in a way which leaves out a number of concepts which we would ordinarily take to be emotion concepts—i.e. the paradigm cases of higher cognitive emotions: shame, guilt, remorse, &c.—because in doing so we would have failed to have adequately answered the (vernacular) question. Is Griffiths here—in the latter case—saying it is part of what we mean by 'emotion' that we include 'both' higher cognitive *and* affect program emotions in the extension of the term, and thus we would not admit an answer which excluded 'one' of 'these'? It pays also to give thought to the distinction between the higher cognitive emotions and the, so called, disclaimed action 'emotions'. The distinction rests upon two claims: first, that the disclaimed action emotions are consonant with long-term rational goal-directed actions as opposed to disruptive of them, as in the case of the higher cognitive emotions; and second, the claim that these (latter) 'emotions' cannot be genuine because they are culturally indexed. These are the reasons provided for these 'emotions' forming a distinct 'category'. To refuse to accept them as real emotions for these two reasons is to already have in play an account (a substantive conception) of what counts as *real* hereabouts.

Furthermore, the question 'what are the emotions?' is, Griffiths tells us (p. 242), a request for an answer which distinguishes the emotions from other cognitive processes. Given what we have learnt of his project thus far, we might expect Griffiths to hold that there is no possible answer to such a question. However, he informs us that there is, and it is the oft-cited phenomena referred to as the 'passivity' of emotion. He writes:

> What is to be explained by emotional phenomena in general is the way in which they contrast to other cognitive processes. The phenomena referred to as the 'passivity' of emotion are central to this contrast. I am not convinced that all instances of the passivity phenomena can be explained by the modularity of the affect programs. I suggested in chapter 5 that a form of passivity may characterise some emotional responses controlled by higher cognition. These responses

are *irruptive* motivations: motivations not derived from more general goals by means-end reasoning. This class of states has as good a claim to be the referent of the general concept of emotion as the class of affect program states.

(ibid.)

The point here is somewhat obscure. On the one hand he—seemingly approvingly—claims that emotions can be explained in terms of their passivity, i.e. it is this that differentiates them from other cognitive processes; [17] yet on the other hand, he says that the modularity of affect programs cannot explain all instances of such passivity. He seems to assume that this inability on the part of computational psychological explanations of affect programs to explain passivity means we should question the explanatory/epistemic worth of passivity, rather than doubt the explanatory worth of the modularity thesis and the affect programs. Things are made no clearer by what he writes a little further on:

> I have argued that the vernacular concept of emotion **groups together all states, which produce passivity.** Affect programs and the less well understood higher cognitive emotions are both grouped together under the concept of emotion simply because both produce a form of passivity.
>
> (*WERA*: p. 245; my emphasis)

So the vernacular concept of emotion groups together states that produce passivity. This is not enough to save the concept because neither the affect program research alone nor the Psycho-evolutionary research alone can sufficiently explain this passivity. We might ask of Griffiths, why he does not then question his own insistence on a form of reductionist explanation which leads to this problem? It is telling that he does not entertain this question. If my diagnosis in Sections 3 and 4 is correct we shall have a clearer understanding as to why.

So, talk of passivity aside, for Griffiths it is established that we have *at least* two distinct natural kinds falling under the vernacular term 'emotion'. Therefore, he argues that we have no choice but to eliminate the vernacular term. He concludes, echoing—but failing to heed—a point made by Ian Hacking, that concepts do not serve purely epistemic purposes, and thus the concept 'emotion' might continue to be employed *for a time* in the vernacular. However, he is in no doubt that the vernacular term has *no place* in psychology: '[A]s far as understanding ourselves is concerned the concept of emotion, like the concept of spirituality, can only be a hindrance' (*WERA*: p. 247).

1.4. How to respond to *What Emotions Really Are*

The foregoing *précis* of Griffiths' book serves a number of purposes: it serves as an introduction to current issues in the philosophy of the emotions; it serves to clarify the extent to which Griffiths is hostile to the hitherto dominant 'research program' in the philosophy of emotions, and why he is so; and it serves to clarify the theoretical foundations of Griffiths' project. Griffiths is explicit about the fact that he has an agenda. In this respect, as can be seen by the last (quoted) sentence of the previous paragraph, Griffiths ends his book as he began. He makes bold claims in the name of science and does not shy away from bringing philosophers and folk psychologists[18] to task for not taking note of the science to which he gives voice. He insists that any epistemic claims advanced in psychology without due attention paid to both recent work in natural kind semantics—his own, which builds on the work of the 'Cornell Realists', such as Richard Boyd—and the 'scientific' observations of authors such as Damasio, Ekman, Fodor, and Frank are no more than reassertions of folk psychological dogma. How does one respond?

Griffiths' *substantive* taking to task (pp. 28–29) of propositional attitude theory is unoriginal, and will be of little concern to those theorists he targets. This is not surprising. The problems Griffiths identifies are identified by many of those of whom he charges with failure. It is crucial for him, therefore, that he makes his charges about (the philosophy of) language stick. For to accept his claims about the failure of the 'research program' we must accept his claim that propositional attitude theory is *unable* to overcome its difficulties owing to fundamental (essential) commitments. Unfortunately for Griffiths, one is far from obliged to subscribe to his characterisation of the progress made in the philosophy of language.

I also find myself somewhat resistant to Griffiths' invocation of a Fodorian 'computational psychology' throughout *What Emotions Really Are*. As we have seen, Griffiths employs criticisms and appraisals such that arguments have been 'widely abandoned' or others have been 'widely accepted'.[19] Assertions such as these are just not relevant to the appraisal of an argument. Questions of philosophical method are not best settled by engaging in a sort of epidemiology of philosophical theories. I am also somewhat unconvinced that philosophy progresses in a linear manner as Griffiths persistently, often in (a crude rendition of) Lakatosian language,[20] assumes it does.

Therefore, questions as to whether others have abandoned or accepted Fodor's work, or the work of those working within the Fodorian paradigm of computational psychology, are of little *argumentative* worth. I shall do no more than suggest to Griffiths that there are numerous criticisms of Fodor's work, and the broader project of computational psychology and cognitive 'science' which are yet to be met.[21] However, and perhaps more importantly, it should be noted that while from one direction Fodor has become less committed to his (1983) claims regarding the extent of narrow content—which Griffiths (*WERA*: pp. 93–94) cites—with each subsequent publication[22] (see Button *et al.* 1995: p. 108, fn 10; Williams 1999c: p. 101), from the other direction, the very idea of narrow content has repeatedly come in for sustained (and varied) criticism (see Burge (1979), Putnam (1988) and Travis (2000), and Section 2.3).

I shall be satisfied here to draw attention to nothing more than the fact that Griffiths presents us with a contested philosophical view *as if it were* a progressive and dominant scientific research program that has furnished us with a set of scientific data. Cognitive science is not such a research program; cognitive science has as its foundations a computational view of the mind. Simply put this is one theory among others, vying for dominance in the philosophy of mind. It should be presented as such.

Griffiths' book contains so many *big* claims that it would be impossible to do them all justice in a chapter such as this, let alone do justice to those whose work Griffiths cites in support of his claims. I choose, therefore, to subject to close scrutiny his expressed philosophical foundations—his causal homeostatic theory of natural kind semantics. This theory of language is his original contribution (he tells us so on p. 14) to the claims of *What Emotions Really Are*; hence, it is upon this which I focus.

2. Natural kind semantics

As we have seen, Griffiths tells us a rough story about the evolution of philosophy (Griffiths' summarised version of this story is on pp. 4–6; it appears and/or is alluded to throughout his book, sometimes told at length, sometimes as asides). The story goes as follows: our subject emerged from the dark ages in the early 1970s, thanks to the work of Hilary Putnam and Saul Kripke on natural kind semantics. However, while this was a great leap forward, there was a problem: the essentialism and metaphysical realism which was, allegedly, at the heart of this 'first wave' of natural kind semantics was unsustainable. So, natural kind semantics needed overhauling, as it were, and this task was undertaken initially by Richard Boyd and Frank C. Keil, and latterly by Griffiths.

Alongside this story of progress and enlightenment in the philosophy of language and mind, there is another tale. This is a tale of woe. In this story there are a number of philosophers living in an 'odd backwater' (p. 172), engaged in a 30-year research program to explain the emotions. Unfortunately, while the rest of the 'philosophical community was shaken out of its complacency' (p. 172) by Kripke, Putnam, and those who followed them, these philosophers of the emotions have 'studiously ignored' (p. 1) the progress made in the philosophy of language and mind. Consequently, their accounts of the emotions are doomed to failure.

These two stories, taken together, frame Griffiths' book. They are myth. Indeed, I take these stories to be both substantively incorrect (i.e. misrepresentations), and based upon contentious or flawed assumptions (e.g. about the nature of language and of progress). In the remainder of this chapter, I shall make good these claims.

In Section 2.1 I begin by offering an account of Hilary Putnam's natural kind semantics, as advanced in 'The Meaning of "Meaning"'(1975d). I do this by way of a corrective to the story Griffiths tells. This will serve as a precursor to my discussion in Section 3 of Griffiths' own theory.

2.1. Cut the pie any way you like, 'meanings' just ain't in the head![23]

A natural kind term is such owing to real distinctions in nature.[24] Putnam expresses the role such distinctions play by engaging in a thought experiment (Putnam 1975d: pp. 223–227). This thought experiment might be summarised as follows.[25]

> Oscar lives on Earth. This is our Earth. He uses water in all the usual ways: he drinks it; heats it to use in the making of tea and coffee; he freezes it into cubes of ice to put in his 'g&t'; he swims in it when on holiday; pours it on to the soil around his plants; takes baths and showers in it; washes and cooks his rice in it; &c. Someone who is just like Oscar in every way, let's call him, following Putnam, Oscar$_2$, lives on Twin Earth. Twin Earth is like Earth in every way, bar one. Oscar's doppelganger on Twin Earth does all the things Oscar does with a liquid he calls water. When asked 'what do you use water for?' he lists those practices I listed above in which Oscar employs water. 'I drink it; heat it to use in the making of tea and coffee; I freeze it into cubes of ice . . . ;' &c. Now, while on Earth water has the chemical

composition H_2O, on Twin Earth water has the chemical composition XYZ. While Oscar and Oscar$_2$ use what they both call water, in the same way, for the same purposes, simultaneously on their almost identical Earths, they do so with different liquids. The referent (extension) of water on Earth and Twin Earth, for Oscar and Oscar$_2$, is different.

Putnam draws the conclusion that the content of Oscar's thoughts and the content of Oscar$_2$'s thoughts are different and this difference is only captured with reference to the extension of the natural kind. What is concluded from this is that the meaning of a natural kind term, such as water, is only fully captured by making reference to the extension of the term (and thus 'ain't in the head').

Putnam (ibid.: p. 269) breaks a natural kind term into four components: syntactic marker; semantic marker; stereotype; and extension. In the case of water the syntactic marker is 'mass noun', 'concrete'; semantic marker is 'natural kind', 'liquid'; stereotype is (something like) 'colourless, thirst-quenching, tasteless, transparent' etc.; the extension is the microstructural composition of water: 'H_2O'. Something is water, if and only if it has the microstructure H_2O. Whether something is water or not is, therefore, determined by a 'sameness relation' holding between the microstructure of a paradigm sample, discovered by empirical science, and the microstructure of the extension of the natural kind.

The usual way in which this is interpreted, and the way in which Griffiths understands Putnam's theory, is as metaphysical realist doctrine; such theories are frequently referred to in the literature as 'Kripke/Putnam essentialism' (Saul Kripke propounded an *almost* identical doctrine independently around the same time). Indeed, Griffiths refers to 'Kripke/Putnam essentialism' throughout *WERA*. This is a misnomer. Putnam's paper, *on his own account*, was an attempt to give an account of 'the division of linguistic labour' and it predates in composition his embracing of metaphysical realism. As Putnam (1992a) writes in his response to Gary Ebbs in *Philosophical Topics*,

> The general outlines of what came to be written up as 'The Meaning of "Meaning" ' became clear in my mind when I was teaching philosophy of language at Harvard in the academic year 1966–1967. I remember quite clearly that, when I worked out the account, I did not think of myself as presupposing metaphysical realism; I thought of myself as engaged in what I described to myself and others as 'a *mild* rational reconstruction' of the notion of meaning that is on the whole fairly

faithful to the ways we ordinarily speak of change of meaning, sameness and difference of meaning, etc. In short I saw myself as describing and, to a certain extent, reconstructing, the practices—e.g. the division of linguistic labour—that are presupposed by our ability to talk of meaning intertheoretically at all. (The only argument for realism in 'The Meaning of "Meaning"' is again, an appeal to our practices.)

(Putnam 1992a: p. 349; italics in the original)

Furthermore, and this is an aspect of the same point, Putnam was not seeking to advance an essentialist doctrine, at least not in the sense in which essence is understood as being separable from our current practices. Again, in his response to Garry Ebbs, Putnam bemoans this misreading of MoM, writing that the only person of whom he was aware as recognising the anti-essentialism in MoM, was Kripke, who, at a conference in Montreal, criticised Putnam for not arguing for a notion of the essence of a natural kind term in abstraction from scientific practice.

2.2. Putnam and his critics

So what was Putnam's argument in MoM? He has told us that his project was to effect a 'mild rational reconstruction of the notion of meaning' and that this entailed his advancing a 'meaning vector' theory. The components of the vector with which Putnam was particularly concerned in MoM were the stereotype and extension of a natural kind term,

(1) the *extension*—this is supposed to be described (as it is in actual dictionaries) **using any convenient description**, e.g. a Latin botanical term in the case of 'elm' or 'H_2O' in the case of water. And,
(2) the *stereotype*—a description of what a typical speaker thinks a paradigmatic 'elm', or whatever, is (or is conventionally assumed to be) like. In the case of 'elm', the stereotype is that elms are a common sort of deciduous tree.

(Putnam 1992a: p. 386; emboldened emphasis mine)

There are a number of ways in which one might question the account offered by Putnam. One way is to question any basis it might have in actual scientific classification. John Dupré (1981, 1983, 1993) has shown that to hold that natural kind semantics has a basis and/or finds support in the practices of biological taxonomy, or scientific classification in general, is simply mistaken. Indeed, Dupré shows that the converse is the case: the practices of biological taxonomy and scientific classification *counter* the claims made by Putnam in MoM.[26]

Another related set of criticisms are those advanced by Avrum Stroll (1998). Stroll suggests that there is an un-argued-for neglect of the phenomenological differences between natural kinds sharing the same microstructure but having a different phenomenology:[27] such as between water, steam, and ice; all have the same microstructure, but all are not sensically called water, and for good reason. The phenomenological differences are not only crucial to people in their day-to-day lives, but the understanding and harnessing of such differences has led to scientific advance such as steam power, to employ a somewhat dated though socially, historically, and scientifically significant example. The point to take from this criticism is that invocation of microstructure is not necessarily invocation of essence. Or put another way, what we take to be something's essence is itself pragmatically informed.

There is a further criticism advanced against Putnam, this time against his method in MoM. This addresses itself to the efficacy of the thought experiments he employs. Indeed, Putnam (1999: pp. 71–135) has employed arguments of this sort in critiquing the claims of Jaegwon Kim, in Part 2 of his *The Threefold Cord*. I shall not enter into the details of such a critique, but only indicate, with reference to the Twin-Earth thought experiment, what might be seen to count against the appropriateness of such a thought experiment. The point is as follows: we are asked at the outset to accept that Oscar and Oscar$_2$ are doppelgangers; however, given the large percentage of the human body that is water how can this be so? To make this point is *not* to attempt a factual refutation, but rather to show that we are asked to turn a blind eye to certain scientifically established facts, so that certain other new (intuitively established) 'facts' might be seen to be established as an outcome of the thought experiment. In effect the thought experiment is set up from the outset to yield the results Putnam claims are established by it.[28]

2.3. Content, kinds, and the functionalist's mind

Arguably the most telling criticism stems from John McDowell's (1992 [1998b]) paper 'Putnam on Mind and Meaning'. McDowell shows that Putnam's arguments, even as late as *Representation and Reality* in 1988, have a latent commitment to the assumption that the mind is an 'organ' located in the head. So when Putnam writes 'meanings ain't in the head' he takes himself to be meaning that they 'ain't in' *a person's* 'mind'; they are external. McDowell's point is that one does not *need* to see the mind in *this* way. For example, when Putnam critiques representationalist theories, such as Jerry Fodor's, he does so assuming that mental representing must always involve the existence of *representations* 'in the head' and thereby sets about critiquing *this* notion. Towards the end of his paper McDowell writes:

> My point in this paper is that the 'isolationist' conception of language that Putnam objects to is all of a piece with a similarly 'isolationist' conception of the mind—at least of the mind as it is in itself. And Putnam's attack on the 'isolationist' conception of language leaves the counterpart conception of mind unquestioned. Taking on the whole package would have yielded a deeper understanding of what underlies the 'isolationist' conception of language.
>
> (McDowell 1992: pp. 46–47)

Of course McDowell has argued on a number of occasions that there is no good reason to think of the mind in this—'isolationist'—way; i.e. one might rather think of the mind as a structured system of object-involving abilities. McDowell's deflationary critique is a powerful one; most importantly, however, Putnam has been persuaded, and now advocates McDowell's position on this issue. This indicates, and draws into question, one of the commitments often overlooked in discussions of Putnam's arguments for the meaning of natural kind terms; i.e. that the *structure* of the account of the meaning of natural kind terms, advanced by Putnam in his early writings, is inextricably linked with the theory of mind that he was advancing in the same period. It is not my purpose here to contribute to the huge number of papers on the merits or otherwise of functionalism (including the many (critical ones) by (later) Putnam); I merely seek to highlight why there might well be seen to be problems with Putnam's sustained attempt at defending the thesis of MoM, while having dispensed completely with functionalism and shed any remnants of an 'isolationist' picture of the mind.

Putnam was doing two—related—things in MoM:

a) making a strong case for externalism in the philosophy of mind—wide content (i.e. 'meanings ain't in the head'); and
b) attempting to show that the full meaning of a concept is a meaning vector made up of a number of components, one of which is the extension of the term.

The extension of a term is understood through current scientific practice; the practice is what Putnam was keen to emphasise in MoM, and to which Kripke took exception. It seems to me (though not to Putnam as yet) that McDowell's critique in being focused upon 'a'—i.e. deepening the critique of 'isolationism'—also brings down 'b'. As Putnam now accepts McDowell's suggestion that we see the mind as a structured system of object-involving abilities, then the notion of narrow (inner) content ultimately fades away, and thus no semantic theory is required to make the point about wide content. This Putnam not only accepts but argues for frequently. At the same time Putnam now argues further for the ubiquity of the normative (again in his reply to Ebbs):

> The problem that I have been becoming increasingly aware of since the early sixties, is that decisions as to rational acceptability, meaningfulness, sameness and change of meaning, etc., always have a normative aspect, and this normative aspect cannot be separated from the descriptive aspect **even notionally**; it is a 'fallacy of division' to think that these notions can be broken into a 'factual part' and a 'value part'. Describing and evaluating are **simply not independent** in that way. That this is the case was brilliantly argued by John McDowell in a famous series of papers[29], but it took me quite a few years to arrive at more or less the same point of view on my own.
>
> (Putnam 1992b: pp. 350–351; emboldened emphases mine)

The impact his acceptance of McDowell's suggested alternative picture of mind has on 'b', (meaning as comprised of a meaning *vector*) Putnam has yet to acknowledge, as far as I am aware. The impact is that it dissolves the distinctions between the two components of the meaning vector that Putnam sought to establish in MoM; that is between intension (stereotype) and extension. The distinction between intension and extension cannot be sustained because intension gained its purchase (i.e. its discrete identity) through being: (a) inside the head—or a representation in an 'isolated' mind; and (b) through having 'extension' as its contrast class. If intension is externalised, and extension is not essentialist, but the current results of scientific practice, and, furthermore, a term is not amenable to being drained of its normativity, then the distinction between extension and intension (stereotype) fades away.

To sum up, we might divide the criticisms into two categories. On the one hand the otherwise quite distinct substantive criticisms advanced by the likes of Dupré and Stroll. And on the other hand the deflationary immanent critiques advanced by McDowell and, implicitly, by Putnam himself. I suggest that these criticisms have drawn into question Griffiths' story of progress in the philosophy of language (and philosophy of mind). However, theories of natural kind semantics persist even in the face of these questionings, and it is to Griffiths' theory I now turn.

3. Natural kinds—The next generation: Griffiths and causal homeostasis

So where do we find natural kind semantics now? Griffiths maintains a theory of natural kinds is necessary to account for concept change over time and trans-theoretical stability of concepts. In place of the metaphysical realist account, putatively advanced by Putnam, Griffiths proposes a generalised version of Richard Boyd's (1991) account.

> [T]he theory of natural kinds not only gives a good account of certain elements of scientific practice, it captures an important aspect of the formation and use of concepts by humans in general. It is an important theoretical tool in the psychology of concepts. ... If the theory of natural kinds is part of the best scientific account of concept formation and use, then an ability to make sense of this becomes an adequacy condition of any account of how thought and language relate to the world.[30]
>
> (*WERA*: p. 175)

Here Griffiths makes two claims:

- First, he claims that in addition to the usefulness of natural kind terms in the sciences, as humans we form, revise, and employ concepts in a way in which is captured by a theory of natural kinds: this, I take it, is what ultimately warrants the employment of the predicate 'natural', given that the contemporary theorist of natural kinds has dispensed with the claim that the distinctions are real distinctions in nature: laws of nature.
- Second, Griffiths claims that if his first claim is correct then a theory of natural kinds can serve to bring together realists and 'all their rivals' (ibid.), offering the best account of the relationship between language and thought, on the one hand, and world, on the other.

Therefore, *much* rests upon Griffiths' account of concept formation.

3.1. The 'theory view' of concept formation
Griffiths draws upon Murphy's (1993) theory view of concept formation. Here we are told that in forming concepts people select certain relevant

features that will serve to form the exemplar of the category to which the concept corresponds. For example, when forming the concept of a particular animal such features as the animal's age and sex are discounted. Murphy's account, Griffiths tells us, is supported by research conducted by others; he cites a number of researchers who have conducted experiments with young children in order to ascertain if there is a shift from a definition in terms of the stereotype of a concept to a definition which is more theoretical, i.e. a move towards extension.

Keil (1989) conducted experiments designed to examine the development of children's identification of natural kind terms. The conclusion Griffiths draws from Keil's experiments is that children *develop* to recognise natural kinds as determined by their microstructure or 'inner essence' (*WERA*: p. 184). In contrast human artefacts, such as keys, are always defined according to their function. Griffiths writes: 'Keil has argued that children privilege the intended function of objects in grouping human artefacts. He has also argued that they assume that biological species have unseen properties that guarantee their identity and can survive the transformation of their measurable characteristics' (*WERA*: p. 186). Griffiths interprets Keil's results employing the developmental systems approach. Thus, children develop an implicit theory which guides them. This implicit theory is a pattern of reasoning that is domain-specific and is manifest in the actions and interpretations of the children studied. Griffiths suggests that this neural organisation is a consequence of interaction between many developmental resources that construct the psychological phenotype[31] (*WERA*: p. 187). Keil's experiments are said to show us that the theory implicit to the child's reasoning is an *evolved neural trait*.

3.2. Causal homeostasis and concept projectability

A category brings together a set of objects with correlated properties. The category has causal homeostasis if this set of properties has some underlying explanation that makes it projectable. A successful category captures what Keil calls a causal homeostatic mechanism—something which means that the correlations can be relied on to hold up in unobserved instances. The search for causal homeostatic mechanisms explains what has been called *psychological essentialism*. People do not simply note the existence of clusters of properties. They postulate a system of underlying causes of the clustering.

(*WERA*: p. 188)

Griffiths does not wish to claim that biological kinds, such as dogs, have intrinsic essences as would be demanded by—what he takes to be—'traditional' metaphysically realist natural kinds. Put another way, he is not arguing that biological natural kinds are determined by the microstructure of a paradigm sample standing in a sameness relation to the extension; as I noted, and Griffiths acknowledges, Dupré's work has put to rest the idea that this conception finds support in scientific practice (*WERA*: p. 191). However, for Griffiths, Keil's experiments demonstrate that in concept formation children develop a propensity to define biological kinds in virtue of an unobservable essence. Griffiths claims that the best explanation for this is to be found in the postulation of an underlying causal homeostatic mechanism (*WERA*: p. 189). So while dogs do not have an essence, as traditionally conceived, they act in a way which leads us to infer an essence. On the causal homeostatic theory of concepts an 'essence' can be any *theoretical* structure that accounts for the projectability of a category (*WERA*: p. 188). This breaks the link, which was put into place by equating the extension of a natural kind with the microstructural essence of the paradigm sample; and this approach is claimed to have good predictive capabilities as regards the change in intension *and* extension of a concept. Where the account in terms of microstructural essence was seen to fail in such fundamental areas as biological taxonomy (as I noted above, see Dupré 1981, 1983, 1993) the causal homeostatic theory of natural kinds succeeds. It, ostensibly, succeeds in that it groups taxa, which are projectable owing to their evolutionary descent from common ancestors.[32]

Griffiths, therefore, advances an account of concepts which identifies them as having at their core an 'explanation of causal homeostasis in the category corresponding to that concept' (*WERA*: p. 193). If a person wishes to employ a concept for inductive and explanatory purposes then they commit themselves to a *'project* of having a category with causal homeostasis' (ibid.). *The causal homeostasis of a category is what sanctions projecting properties of the category beyond the observed instances of that category.*

3.3. Different name, same game?

In Griffiths' reworking of natural kind semantics, 'causal homeostatic mechanisms' serve as substitutes for 'micro structural essences', and Keil's experiments serve as substitutes for Putnam's thought experiments. The former substitution, Griffiths assures us, puts to rest the possibility of Dupré's criticisms of Putnam's project being extended to his project (*WERA*: pp. 190–192). However, where causal homeostasis replaces microstructural properties, the substitution relies for its warrant upon the account of conceptual revision that replaces Putnam's Twin-Earth thought experiment. I will address whether this is a successful move a little later (Section 3.5). First, I shall raise an issue regarding the characterisation by Griffiths of his own project.

3.4. Metaphysics: rejected or thinly-veiled?

On Griffiths' account the concept is determined by its extension and the extension explains the causal homeostasis of the category to which the concept corresponds. I shall argue that this cashes out as little more than domain-specific pragmatism.[33] If we wish to explain phenomena in particular domains then we employ concepts in a way in which we believe will best facilitate that explanation. I say 'little more' than domain-specific pragmatism because the 'little' in this case makes a lot of difference. The only way in which the causal homeostatic theory of concepts differs from a pragmatic approach to concept formation and revision, in a particular scientific domain, is in the positing that the concept revision and formation will always be in terms of the theoretical postulation of an underlying causal mechanism. Hence, if Griffiths' account does more than say 'we categorise and form concepts in ways that serve useful purposes in different human practices', then it is still embedded in a metaphysical account of categories.

As we have seen, Griffiths argues that the theory of natural kinds 'gives a good account of **certain elements** of scientific practice' (*WERA*: p. 175; emphasis mine). What does this claim amount to? Well, really no more than 'where scientists are concerned to discover the causes of certain events they will do so by advancing conjectures as to the existence of causal laws;[34] then ascertaining through experimental practice whether the postulation of those causal laws is supported by the results of those experiments'. If this is indeed what Griffiths' 'theory' of natural kinds amounts to then is this not merely a restating of a very general and mundane point about the practice of some scientists? That is to say, that scientists advance conjectures and, when possible, conduct experiments to see if their conjectures might be supported thereby is not really going to surprise anyone. In this case the causal homeostatic theory of natural kinds does no more than give an account of what *some* (natural) scientists do. In that sense it is not a theory but a description of the practice of *some* scientists, and how they might proceed *most* of the time; though crucially bringing with it an implicit normative proposal that other scientists should do likewise.

That some scientists find it *useful* in certain contexts to group together objects in categories, which they take to be as such (i.e. categories) in virtue of the postulation of an underlying causal law, is not surprising. However, if scientists do postulate underlying causal laws, they will *only* be postulated so long as the evidence supports that postulation. If this is not the case in practice then science and dogma find themselves strange bedfellows. Of course to assume that scientists are, unlike most of us, immune to the occasional dogmatic tendency would be naïve. Nevertheless, Griffiths' championing of the causal homeostatic theory of concepts as *a priori* to induction and explanation is to make a positive move in the direction of such dogma.

We are likely to meet strong resistance at this point: 'the categories are revised in line with what we deem from induction, and thus the mechanism is not *a priori*', it will be argued. However, this response meets with difficulty. For the most telling problem with the positing of the notion of underlying mechanisms in scientific practice, whether invoked for pragmatic purposes or as unobservable entities, is that their ability to fulfil their purpose cannot be established to *our satisfaction*.[35] This is not to say that it is logically or conceptually impossible to invoke underlying causal mechanisms, only that in doing so we do not do what we had intended to do in positing them. For, while the theoretically postulated unobservable underlying mechanism is invoked to justify the grouping of objects (organisms or events) into categories, we can only ever be less certain about this underlying mechanism (its pragmatic worth or existence as an entity) than we can about the thing for which it is supposed to serve as justificatory grounds.[36] The invocation of underlying causal homeostatic mechanisms is an attempt to give grounds for the categorisation of objects. But as grounds, the underlying causal homeostatic mechanism can never be as certain as those things (concepts) that it is supposed to be grounds for. We group objects under a concept and then infer the grounds for that grouping. The grounds rely on our, prior, initial grouping.

Where we arrive is at the following: we can offer Griffiths a choice—if we wish to imbue the theoretically postulated unobservable underlying causal mechanism with the status whereby we accept it as serving as the grounds (ultimate justification) for our grouping of objects in categories, then we ascribe to that mechanism a status over and above the status of those things which are observable to us. This might not seem, at first glance, problematic; however, if we remind ourselves that it is 'what is observable to us' that has afforded our inference of the theoretically constructed underlying mechanism in the first place it ought to suggest to us a problem. The problem stems from using the theoretically constructed underlying mechanism as ultimate justification for the very thing that justified its own inference.

Therefore, the response that dogma is avoided owing to the fact that the causal homeostatic mechanism is revised in light of the evidence gleaned through induction merely gives rise to the question, namely, how does something that is unobservable, inferred from, *and* revised in line with our observations serve as grounds for our grouping together that which we have observed? For the unobservable underlying causal homeostatic mechanism to do the work demanded by its invocation, the scientist must ascribe to it a status (at least occasionally, when it is convenient for it to be) higher than the status of that from which its existence is inferred. In attributing to theoretically constructed unobservable underlying (or, for that matter, transcendental) mechanisms the ability to serve as ultimate justification for our observations, Griffiths' argument *is* metaphysical.

Let me clarify what I am *not* arguing here. I do not seek to draw into question functional relationships and explanations. My criticism of Griffiths does not rely on any substantive judgement as to the worth of functional explanation *per se*. I am concerned with the attribution of the role of ultimate justification to a necessarily unobservable 'entity', the existence of which is inferred from the observed side of the theoretically postulated functional relationship. My critique is not aimed at homeostatic functionalism, but at the theoretical construction of a homeostatic relationship in order to then claim that the—wholly theoretically constructed and articulated—causal mechanism serves as grounds (ultimate justification) for the observed part of the theoretically postulated relationship.

There is one place to which Griffiths might 'retreat'. He might retract his claim to have dispensed with metaphysics, but claim that his metaphysics is supported and legitimated by scientific experiments, or current scientific knowledge. He might cite Keil's experiments as showing that humans psychologically develop to group objects in nature into categories according to the unobservable underlying causal homeostatic mechanism. Let us take this imagined defence by Griffiths seriously and examine whether those experiments justify his metaphysics.

3.5. What do we learn from Keil's children?

Experiments were conducted on two groups of children: the first group was of kindergarten age; the second group was comprised of children between 8 and 10 years old. Both groups were presented with objects.

The first object was a biological kind; it had the outward appearance of a dog and behaved like a dog. The second object was a human artefact; it looked like a key and was shown to function as a key (*WERA*: p. 183). Both groups of children were then told that in the case of the biological kind scientists had discovered that the organism had the internal organs and blood of a cat. In addition the organism had been born of a cat and had itself given birth to a cat. Both groups were also told that scientists had found that the artefact had been found to be made out of melted-down pennies and that after its use it could be melted down and made back into pennies. In both cases, in each group, the children were asked what the object (organism and artefact respectively) *really* was. In the group of kindergarten children they said the organism was *really* a dog and that the human artefact was *really* a key.[37] In the group of 8- to 10-year-olds they said that the organism was *really* a cat and that the human artefact was *really* a key. We are told that supporting results were produced in similar natural kind/artefactual kind experiments.

According to Griffiths the results of the key/dog experiment, in addition to other similar experiments conducted by Keil, demonstrate that children develop to recognise natural kinds as determined by their microstructure or 'inner essence' (*WERA*: p. 184). Further writing 'Keil has argued that children privilege the intended function of objects in grouping human artefacts. He has also argued that they assume that biological species have unseen properties that guarantee their identity and can survive the transformation of their measurable characteristics' (*WERA*: p. 186). Furthermore this development, between the kindergarten children and the 8- to 10-year-olds, Griffiths argues, demonstrates the development of a psychological phenotype.

There are a number of ways in which one might be sceptical as to whether these 'experiments' demonstrate anything like what Griffiths claims. One might offer certain substantive arguments as to whether Keil's experiments provide the results that Keil takes them to provide. In this case we should scrutinise the way in which the experiment was structured, asking whether alternative reasons for the answers given were thoroughly explored, prior to being ruled out. One might also examine issues such as whether greater awareness of the role played by scientific knowledge in societies, the status of scientists, peer pressure, and the *way* in which children are taught, etc., might have been influential. But most importantly we might look at *what* those children are taught about animals between kindergarten and 8 to 10 years of age

These would be interesting lines of inquiry—inquiries, I suspect, which would provide enough reason to be very sceptical regarding Griffiths' claims—though I shall not pursue these here: Keil's experiments come to me second hand and this sort of substantive examination is one best conducted by ethnomethodologists. For now I will *assume* all is present and correct with the structure of the experiments. However, I still have difficulties with Griffiths' extrapolation from the results of those experiments.

First, there is no evidence for the development and existence of a phenotype. Griffiths merely infers from the results advanced by Keil, that a phenotype develops.[38] As with the postulation of a homeostatic mechanism (discussed above) the psychological phenotype is postulated as an underlying causal entity to serve as grounds for justifying something observable: the children's shift to essentialism regarding biological kinds and Griffiths' contention that it follows, therefore, that we should adopt a causal homeostatic theory of natural kinds. Again this not only commits Griffiths to an unnecessary—and on his own terms unwanted—metaphysics, but also to the prioritisation of the metaphysical over the observable from which the metaphysical 'entity' was initially inferred.[39] Griffiths might respond to this criticism by arguing that the invocation of the development of a phenotype was merely meant metaphorically and that the existence of an 'entity', metaphysical or otherwise, is not being invoked. But the response to this is to ask 'then why not instead just say that the children *learn*?' I suspect Griffiths' desire to talk of *development* and his desire to name *something* (a phenotype) as that which develops, rather than merely talk of *children learning*, stems from his desire to give weight to the thought that the distinctions picked out by natural kinds are distinctions in nature. I think it more than merely a point of passing note that Griffiths' writing of 'development of a phenotype' is, grammatically, a 'passive construction' rather than an 'active' construction, which writing of 'children learning' would be—i.e. that his is an attempt to abstract from human being.[40]

Second, even if we are to accept Griffiths' inference of the development of a psychological phenotype there is still a basic question of logic to be answered. It is an old but pertinent question of how one justifies moving from an *is* to an *ought*. Put another way, there is no argument, or acknowledgement that there needs to be an argument, in Griffiths' book for his extrapolation from a (purported) factual premise (Keil's experimental results) to a normative proposal (adopting a natural kind semantics on the causal homeostatic model for explanation of the human emotions).

It can seem like Griffiths merely takes-it-as-read that establishment of what *is* the case leads to a conclusion as to what *ought* to be the case. This is because the invocation of terms from evolutionary psychology (evolved neural traits and the development of psychological phenotypes) is done in an attempt to deny this logical 'gap' by denying there is any normative claim being made.[41] If there is no question to be answered here, it is because Griffiths understands that which has the appearance of a normative claim—*philosophers of the emotions ought to adopt a causal homeostatic theory of natural kinds*—as rather just a statement of fact—*we all, as members of the species, develop the psychological phenotype and thus all define **biological kinds** in terms of hidden essence.*[42] However, it pays one to note the absence of 'the emotions' in the translation of the latter of the two *italicised* sentences here. This absence makes perspicuous to us a leap in Griffiths' account. So, even were we—and this is, to coin a phrase, a '*big ask*'—to accept an evolutionary psychological account, and thus grant Griffiths that there is no normative claim as regards biological kinds, there is still a question about the status of the claim that philosophers who wish to explain emotions must adopt a causal homeostatic theory of natural kinds.

Griffiths' leap from what he writes about biological kinds to what that means for any attempt at explanation of emotions gives rise to the thought that there is a danger of him begging the question. The leap implicitly assumes the inaccuracy of the social constructivists' account of the emotions: for if social constructivists are correct, emotions have more in common with artefactual 'kinds' than with biological kinds, and thus might, on Griffiths own account of Keil's 'experiments', be defined in terms of their function.

4. Which way now? Notes towards a conclusion

In this final section I shall move towards conclusion by paying attention to Griffiths own use of language. I shall first (Section 4.1) give a little more attention to the terms we saw him employ in Section 3. Building on what I had to say there I offer some comments on his rhetoric: i.e. his propensity to substitute technical terms for ordinary terms to no explanatory gain. I do this by paying particular attention to his invocation of the development of a psychological phenotype. In Section 4.2, I show how Griffiths is insufficiently attuned to the different ways in which we express our concepts and the place those concepts have in our lives.

4.1. On trying to develop a psychological phenotype

The language Griffiths employs is intrinsic to his metaphysics. In order that we might be persuaded that our categories are supported by more than pragmatically informed norms, we are presented with an account which holds out the prospect of foundations and justifications for those categories. In order that these theoretically postulated foundations might strike us as firm enough to serve the purpose for which they are designed, we need to characterise them in a language which will persuade us of their stability and (human-)independent nature. Gone are the 'good old days' of boldly stated metaphysical realism; Griffiths closes this avenue off early on in his book (in the course of his misrepresentation of Putnam). The foundations must be the non-metaphysical results of scientific practice. This is the point of the talk of psychological phenotypes developing; of modules; of programs and computational states; of underlying causal homeostatic mechanisms; and of the non-arbitrary projectability of concepts. The terms on this list are all, ultimately, rhetorical in nature and purpose. If these rhetorical devices are surrendered then Griffiths' theory of natural kinds will be seen to be otiose.

In light of the foregoing list of terms, consider the following: people learning; people trying to learn something; people following and acting in accordance with rules and norms; people transgressing those rules and norms; people being corrected by other people and people establishing new rules and norms; people struggling to come to grips with what it means to feel real shame; people struggling to make sense of another person's fear; &c. People—enculturated human animals—do such things, and they do so while interacting with other people in a meaningful world. Do we not lose something if we translate such things—by way of abstraction—to passive statements about developing phenotypes &c.?[43]

Let us therefore pay attention to a phrase which was prominent in the discussion in the previous section: 'development of a psychological phenotype'. If anyone has doubts about my claims regarding the rhetorical nature of the employment of this term, try the following thought experiment: imaginatively become the author of *What Emotions Really Are*; now, answer the following two questions:

1. Is it possible to learn something without the development of a psychological phenotype?
2. Is it possible for a psychological phenotype to develop without anything taking place which we would ordinarily consider indicative of learning?

If your answer to both these questions is 'no', then one might want to ask what use the introduction of the concept of 'psychological phenotype' has for us; what purpose does it serve; what role can it possibly have in our lives? If you answer 'yes' to the first question, then you might ask what sort of evidence would count for you for the development and existence of such a psychological phenotype. If you answer 'yes' to the second question you might want to ask what the professed explanatory worth of the postulated psychological phenotype is: i.e. what is it intended to explain? And how does it achieve it?

If your imagination is serving you well, you should be well into the part by now. So let us try another brief thought experiment. You might rejoin, in defence of 'your' book, that 'learning' is no more than the development of a psychological phenotype, and as scientists this is how we should describe what 'folk' call 'learning'. Well, let us again ask some questions. What is it for me to try to learn something? Have I tried to develop a psychological phenotype; or has the psychological phenotype tried to develop? How are we to understand such development in terms of our trying—and maybe failing, maybe finding it difficult, maybe easy—to learn something? What if I try to learn something and fail; only half-learn it, so to speak? Does this mean I have a half-developed or an under-developed psychological phenotype? And how might this differ from the relative difference between the (respective) psychological phenotypes of two practitioners, one of whom is fully competent in the practice and one who is outstanding in the practice? For, consider the following illustrative thought: who of the following has the fully developed language phenotype—a competent adult user of the language, a Grammarian, or John Keats? If you answer the first of the three then do Keats and/or our grammarian have an extra phenotype? If you answer Keats, then do the other two have underdeveloped phenotypes; and do we accord Keats (the person) credit for his poetic skills?

Not only does the substitution of 'the development of a psychological phenotype' for 'children learning' play a rhetorical role, commitment to the substitution leads to an inability to make sense of everyday aspects of our lives such as trying to learn, holding a person responsible for their failure to learn, and giving credit to a person who has learned quickly and become exceptionally skilled.

This brings us full circle. Griffiths will always respond, in the final instance, by arguing that if we do not employ a theory of natural kinds then all we will do is merely recapitulate the current stereotype of the term in question. If the foregoing reflections (Sections 2 and 3) are seen to stand, then this is an empty charge. Indeed, this is why it is crucial to address Griffiths' challenge at the level of his theory of natural kinds; any other criticism will be dismissed as merely resisting science in defence of current stereotypical understanding. One needs to block this attack/response from Griffiths and those who share his predilections.

One can only do so by showing the terms of the attack/response to rest on prejudice regarding our lives with our language.[44] In the final section I shall try to uncover the sources of Griffiths' own antipathy towards those he considers as trading only in the stereotype of emotion terms, and the driving force behind his insistence on an explanation of the emotions being built upon a theory of natural kinds.

4.2. Whales, fear and the emotions

All conceptual analysis will reveal is the current stereotype of fear. To insist that all and only the things that fit this stereotype are examples of the kind is simply to stand in the way of clarifying the concept. It is exactly akin [sic] to insisting that whales are fish because people called them so. Current science, rather than conceptual analysis, must be used to fill in the schematic element of the meaning of 'fear.' If science can find no interesting kind corresponding to all the paradigm cases of fear, then we must either reclassify some of the paradigm cases or replace fear and its companions with some more adequate categories.

(*WERA*: p. 5)

In the following I shall move towards conclusion by using Griffiths' juxtaposition in the above quotation as a 'spring board' for reflection. We might first note that the juxtaposition trades on confusion. Griffiths juxtaposes the identification of the concept of 'fear' with its current use with the erroneous identification of the concept 'whale' as a member of the category captured by the concept 'fish'. This juxtaposition only has currency if one turns a blind eye to a number of significant factors.

So, we might ask, 'is examining the use of "fear" exactly akin [sic] to insisting that whales are fish because people once called them so?'[45] What of the utterance 'I am afraid'? *Must* it be a description?[46] It does share— for what it is worth—the syntax of a description. But if it is a description, one might ask of what? What might constitute a failure to describe one's fear? When I say 'I am afraid' *must* I do so in order to describe my 'state of fear' or the running of an 'affect program'? We are not *obliged* to see the employment of the concept of 'fear' as a description, nor are we *obliged* to see it as open to the same (formal) criteria for correct application as the substantive 'whale'. Griffiths' claim regarding stereotypical explanation relies on this very conflation, as do many other of his examples employed by way of showing how conceptual analysis fails to tell us more than the current stereotype of a word (see, in addition to *WERA*, p. 5, pp. 171, 191, 201, 247, also, 1999a: p. 56). In doing so, in making this assumption, Griffiths, once again, risks being guilty of begging the question, only this time in respect to those theorists he is keen to critique. In assuming that first-person present-tense fear statements are descriptions he merely assumes the structural truth of the James/Lange feeling theories, where emotional utterances are descriptions of sensations. While he is not committed to the descriptions being of sensations and discerned through introspection, he is committed to the basic structure; i.e. first-person present-tense emotional utterances are descriptions of states of affairs and not expressions, spontaneous declarations, or avowals. We do not need to reject this view wholesale to acknowledge that in invoking emotion utterances as descriptions, Griffiths merely assumes this structure without argument. This is precisely what cognitivists/propositional attitude theorists draw into question.

Needless to say, we are not *obliged* to take a substantive such as 'fear' and ascribe to it a role 'exactly akin' to the role played by the substantive 'whale'. Wittgenstein says something pertinent in this respect on the first page of *The Blue Book*,

> The questions 'What is length?' 'What is meaning?' 'What is the number one?' etc., produce in us a mental cramp. We feel that we can't point to anything in reply to them and yet ought to point to something. (We are up against one of the great sources of philosophical bewilderment: a substantive makes us look for a thing that corresponds to it.)
>
> (Wittgenstein 1969: p. 1)

To this list one might add some emotion terms. In the absence of a thing to point to, Griffiths offers us his theoretically constructed metaphysical 'entities'. I suggested that these cannot do the work demanded of them. Instead of searching for—or theoretically constructing—a 'thing' to which the substantive in question might correspond, Griffiths might be best served by engaging in some *genuine* clarification of our use of our words. One of Griffiths' declared motivations for his antipathy for conceptual analysis and his enthusiasm for his natural kind semantics is a desire to predict changes in our concepts; he assumes this is done by science 'getting underneath' the concepts, as it were, and seeing the nature of the categories to which the concepts correspond. As a prophylactic to such a thought one might offer Griffiths the following suggestion: ***concepts do not correspond to things or categories of things; people express concepts, by putting words to use, and sometimes they do so in order to refer to things or categories of things.***

Furthermore, Griffiths just does not seem to be alive to the thought that emotion terms might well have more in common with the terms employed when identifying moral virtues or character traits; that is to say, rather than with terms which refer to biological organisms or species. Griffiths states that issues such as this are merely matters of emphasis. In contrast I would like to suggest they are crucial. While he does acknowledge that concepts play all sorts of roles, and that some of those roles are non-epistemic (*WERA*: Section 7.7, pp. 196–207) he fails to either recognise or acknowledge that this raises problems for his project. That is to say, even if we are only interested in the concept when it plays an 'epistemic' role, this does not equate to there being a 'thing'—a non-normative 'given'—that corresponds to that concept, which we must then discover.

'Fear' is a paradigm case of an evaluative concept. As we saw, Putnam claimed (p. 24) that it is a 'fallacy of division' to think that one can simply separate out the normative aspects of concepts so as to leave ourselves with purely factual aspects; I quote the passage again here:

> The problem that I have been becoming increasingly aware of since the early sixties, is that decisions as to rational acceptability, meaningfulness, sameness and change of meaning, etc., always have a normative aspect, and this normative aspect cannot be separated from the descriptive aspect **even notionally**; it is a 'fallacy of division' to think that these notions can be broken into a 'factual part' and a 'value part'. Describing and evaluating are **simply not independent** in that way. That this is the case was brilliantly argued by John McDowell in a famous series of papers[47], but it took me quite a few years to arrive at more or less the same point of view on my own.
>
> (Putnam 1992b: pp. 350–351; emphases mine)

Now, Putnam might well be correct. Griffiths might disagree. However, let us here try think in terms of Griffiths' analogy between calling whales fish and identifying 'fear' with what people currently understand 'fear' to be. Putnam's thought, following McDowell, is that it makes little sense to think about rational acceptability, meaningfulness, sameness, and change of meaning, outside, as it were, the space of reasons—the realm of norms. While a philosopher such as Griffiths might baulk at such a claim regarding biological kinds—and in discussion of the criticisms of Putnam's natural kind semantics above, we saw that there was no reason to agree with Griffiths on this—in what might he base his resistance with respect to 'fear', or, indeed, other emotion terms? Even if the concept is expressed such that it plays a descriptive role, is it possible that it does so in abstraction from its evaluative aspects?

Consider what it *means* to say of oneself or of another that one is/they are 'afraid'. In describing ourselves/others as such we are acknowledging that a certain sort of behaviour is *merited*. It is internal to the meaning— it is an aspect of what it is to have grasped the concept—of fear that it *merits* a certain response, in certain conditions and given certain cultural facts regarding the (afraid) person. It is difficult (one is tempted to say impossible) to grasp the concept of fear in abstraction from such evaluative aspects.[48] So, let us for now—through generosity of spirit and *only* for *now*—grant Griffiths his causal homeostatic account of biological taxonomy; what is the warrant for the extension (no pun intended) of this theory to emotion terms?

While much of the force of Griffiths' argument for the existence of a causal homeostatic mechanism rested upon a contrast drawn between natural—biological—kinds and artefacts, he ignores a potentially-as-significant-a-difference between biological kinds and emotion terms. There is simply no reason to think of emotion terms on the model of species terms; while, as we have seen, there are a number of—reasonably straightforward and significant—reasons for holding them to be dis-analogous.

There is no need to stop here. We do not need to charge Griffiths with the fallacy of division in order to identify a problem with his account. Cora Diamond (1988) makes some relevant remarks in her paper 'Losing Your Concepts'. There she discusses contemporary ethics and the concept of 'human being'. She notes McDowell's remark regarding some evaluative concepts having no descriptive content discernible in abstraction from their evaluative content. She progresses to say that 'human being' is not such a concept; for we can imagine a non-evaluative, descriptive equivalent: *'member of the species Homo sapiens'*. She notes that what is of interest is not that these two concepts—*human being* and *member of the species Homo sapiens*—have the same referent (extension) only different senses, but rather what life with this concept rather than that is like. She writes:

> [G]rasping a concept (even one like that of a human being, which is a descriptive concept if any are) is not a matter of just knowing how to group things under that concept; it is being able to participate in life-with-the-concept. What kinds of descriptive concepts

there are is a matter of the different shapes life-with-a-concept can have. Life with the concept *human being* is very different to life with the concept *member of the species Homo sapiens*. To be able to use the concept 'human being' is to be able to think about human life and what happens in it; it is not [merely] to be able to pick human beings out from other things.

(Diamond 1988: p. 266)

So, let us—again, for now—grant Griffiths 'fear'-as-playing-an-epistemic-role; we can even—for now—grant him that it is not an evaluative concept that has no *separably graspable* descriptive content. Let us say then—for now—that 'fear' has descriptive content and that this can be separated from its evaluative content. Where does this leave us with regards to our knowing what *fear* really is? Well, we can still note, in a similar manner in which Diamond does with the concept of 'human being', that to reduce our knowledge of 'fear' to mere description of an affect program running is to seriously misrepresent our lives with this concept: for example, how one overcame fear, how my fear became dread, how I harnessed fear in order to overcome other obstacles in my life, how fear has dominated my life and the choices I have made, how fear of losing the one you love is part of what it is to love, how I recognise fear in the eyes of a stranger, &c. If telling us what emotions *really* are results in the eliding of the significance those emotions have for us, their place in the very fabric of our lives, then that would be, to say the least, a peculiar use of 'real'.

Finally, one more point, so as to avoid any charge that I am 'anti-science'. If we want to understand what philosophers and psychologists call 'the emotions' we ought to look at *people*, people expressing (say) shame or fear. And *looking* hereabouts does not mean merely looking at faces, or 'neural programs', much less theorising computational modules. Rather, *looking* means trying to understand how the expression of emotion makes sense to us and what role it plays for the person expressing it, in their lives and ours; why sometimes we fail to see another's fear; why sometimes I struggle against acknowledging my own fear; &c. I find little that is objectionable in Ekman's experiments; indeed, I find much that is interesting. I do find objectionable the all-too-quick extrapolation of unwarranted conclusions about programs, modules, and phenotypes, rather than the careful and detailed study and description of reactions to the photographs. After all the rhetoric, the talk of science, the talk of phenotypes and of underlying causal mechanisms, the talk of modules and of homeostasis, we leave Griffiths with no insight into the place of the emotions in the lives of people, what it is for them to have a life with emotion. This is, I submit, the most significant criticism. Like the microstructure of Twin Earth water, it seems *What Emotions **Really** Are* has no bearing on our practices and our lives.

2

To 'Make Our Voices Resonate' or 'To Be Silent'? Shame as Fundamental Ontology

After spending any degree of time immersed in recent work in the analytic philosophy of emotion, turning to a reading of discussions of people who have expressed shame in response to events can engender a degree of relief. For all his determination to, as it were, get to the bottom of things, I leave my reading of Paul Griffiths and many of those he recommends with little further appreciation of the place of the emotions in human lives.

It will doubtless strike some as strange to talk of feeling relief in this context. All I can say is that sometimes it is (feels) right to 'get back to the rough ground'. The feeling of relief may well be brought about by a concomitant feeling that in leaving behind the abstractions of philosophy one is returning to an engagement with *people*, a feeling all too often lost, at least to me, when 'doing philosophy'.

Of course it would be misleading to claim that the authors discussed in the previous chapter do not think of themselves, as in some way, contributing to the understanding of people and their emotional expressions: they clearly do think this. As I noted there, the discussion of 'the emotions' often takes the form of the study of a quasi-entity that exists independent from, though standing in causal relationship to, the person. Somewhere along the line, *people* are relegated to the back seat in the enquiries as the construction of theories is thrust into the driving seat. I have suggested that in the case of Paul Griffiths the problem can be traced to his underlying assumptions about language (and the world).

In moving from a prolonged engagement with scientistic philosophers' writings about emotions, to a reading of some of the testimonies of Rwandans following the 1994 genocide in that country, I, with a little trepidation, admit to feeling, among many other admittedly more powerful emotions, some relief. In addition to some of those books

I mentioned in the introduction, Jean Hatzfeld's *Into the Quick of Life* (2005a) is one book that brought me 'back to the rough ground'. Hatzfeld relays testimonies of survivors of the Rwandan genocide, some of whom express shame at having survived while others died. The sense of this expression of shame is, at least for me, easily grasped, with or without a philosophical theory of shame, and certainly without searching for the mythical 'Given' which will provide non-conceptual foundations for our emotional expressions. Reading Primo Levi's *If This is a Man* had a similar effect upon me. It is in this context that I came upon Giorgio Agamben's *Remnants of Auschwitz* ((1999) hereafter *RA*).

Agamben has recently achieved a degree of prominence within English-speaking academia, following the publication of a number of books; these books differ from those discussed in the previous chapter quite radically, and they do so in two ways.

First, Agamben's work is in the tradition of post-Heideggerian philosophy, complemented by his grounding in Classical scholarship—ancient rhetoric, grammar, and poetics—and Roman jurisprudence. Second, and more importantly regarding my comments above, when Agamben discusses shame he does so with reference to survivors of Auschwitz. In *RA* (1999) Agamben discusses Primo Levi, and Robert Antelme, also looking extensively at the phenomenon of the muselmänner, reported in survivor testimony. Nevertheless, despite this I do have significant misgivings as to Agamben's conclusions and these I shall explore below.

This chapter takes the following form:

- Section 1 provides a schematic overview of Agamben's project, so as to situate his discussion of shame. His discussion of shame can only be understood as part of his broader historico-political thesis—which has broad parallels in Michel Foucault's and Alasdair MacIntyre's work.[1] Agamben's thesis begins with a meditation on Greek ethics and politics and the way in which the concepts of 'life' and 'sovereignty' evolve and relate to one another. Agamben's reflection upon these concepts focuses upon how 'we moderns' have lost the Greek distinction between *zoē* and *bios*, and how sovereignty has the structure of potentiality.
- Section 2 provides a discussion of Agamben's metaphysical thesis, which underpins his politico-historical thesis. This begins by introducing Aristotle on potentiality and proceeds through to a discussion of how the structure of potentiality is mirrored in the structure of language and being. This section will do no more than introduce

these concepts; they will be engaged with in depth in the subsequent sections of the chapter.

- Section 3 provides a discussion of Agamben's account of shame. The section begins by discussing the 'lacuna' in Holocaust testimony; it progresses through an identification of the camp as the manifestation of (Foucauldian) biopower, to a discussion of the emotion of shame as discussed by Primo Levi, and later, Robert Antelme. The section continues to examine Agamben's engagement with Levinas, Kant, and Heidegger, and his locating of his account of shame in the metaphysical paradigm created by Heidegger (following (his) Kant).[2] In Heidegger's rendering of Kant, the category of time is the 'essential structure of subjectivity'; for Agamben the structure of shame is analogous to this. Identifying shame as the 'hidden structure of all subjectivity' is said to offer us a path between the poles of humanism and anti-humanism, and thus helps us to make sense of survivor shame, the lacuna of testimony, and the nature of human being.
- Section 4 critically engages Agamben's thesis by drawing attention to anomalies in his renditions of Levi and Antelme. These anomalies are traced back to Agamben's commitment to a particular theory of meaning.
- Section 5 focuses on Agamben's foundations in his post-structuralist linguistics. This section identifies the differences between Derrida's account and Agamben's, identifying the latter as failing to grasp the essence of Derrida's *deconstructive* project. However, the section concludes by identifying a problem with *both* accounts.
- Section 6 moves the chapter towards a conclusion, by drawing the moral from the engagement with Agamben.

1. Agamben's historico-political project

1.1. *Homo Sacer* and *Remnants of Auschwitz*

Agamben's account of shame takes its place in a larger project advanced in a trilogy of books; these, in turn, have theoretical antecedents in his earlier work on language, history, and poetics. The publication in English of two of these books, *Homo Sacer* ((1998) hereafter *HS*) and *RA*, marked a shift in focus *prima facie* unnoticeable in his hitherto available work. With these texts Agamben explicitly embarks on a project in political and moral theory, and his account of shame is at the heart of that theory. In *HS* he is concerned to effect a 'theoretical excavation of the biopolitical paradigm he sees as governing the West since the birth of the polis'

(Cohen 2001: p. 381). In *RA* Agamben seeks to complement his work in *HS* with a phenomenology of the same biopolitical paradigm.

1.2. *Zoē* and *bios*

Central to the project enunciated in both *HS* and *RA* is the Ancient Greek distinction between *zoē* and *bios* (*HS*: p. 1, *RA*: p. 156). The former term refers to the bare life common to all living things and the latter to the proper life of individuals or groups given their essential function or nature. A being that realises, or is in pursuit of the realisation of its essential nature, is a being that exists in a mode of life proper for that being: *bios*. A being that merely lives indifferent to the mode of living conveyed upon it by its nature is a being living a bare life *zoē*.

For Aristotle, the proper mode of living for a human being is a life lived in pursuit of the human *telos*, termed *eudaimonia*.[3] My life is *eudaimon* if I act in accordance with the virtues (*aretē*, also translated as 'excellence') incorporating them into my character: not only do I act in accordance with, say, the virtues of honesty, justice, care, and courage, but *I am* honest, just, caring, and courageous. To live life in accordance with the virtues, to be virtuous, is to live a *eudaimon* life. In this sense the clearest translation of *eudaimonia* is 'flourishing', though importantly it is *human* flourishing; for while plants and non-rational animals can flourish, they cannot live a *eudaimon* life for the term, as employed by Aristotle, requires the prior capacity for practical reason (wisdom).

Incorporating the virtues into my character, through a process of learning and training, within a community—*polis*—and living a life employing those virtues—having a virtuous character and living a virtuous life—in pursuit of the human *telos*, is to live a *eudaimon* life. Here a further term is introduced; for Aristotle, in order that I am able to live a virtuous life, I must be able to reason correctly in practical matters. In order to do so I must have *phronesis*: translated as 'practical reason' or 'wisdom'. In the absence of *phronesis*, I would not be able to distinguish between situations in which to φ[4] would be (say) courageous and situations in which to φ would be foolhardy, reckless, or even cowardly. In this sense the virtues are occasion-sensitive, and *phronesis* is the capacity to appreciate this sensitivity. Therefore, *eudaimonia* is most clearly translated as 'to flourish as a human *qua* rational animal'.[5]

The final piece of the Aristotelian jigsaw is that which enables, in the first instance, the human capacity for *phronesis*, that is to say, that which Aristotle claims enables human rationality. Aristotle claims that it is the human animal's capacity for speech that primarily distinguishes it from non-human, non-rational animals. The ability to 'speak of' rather than merely 'give voice to' affords the human animal the distinctions which Aristotle depicts as the 'sense' enabling associations such as the family and the state. Agamben (*HS*: pp. 7–8) cites the following passage from Aristotle's *Politics* in which the link is manifest.

Now, that man is more of a political animal than bees or any other gregarious animals is evident. Nature, as we often say, makes nothing in vain, and man is the only animal who has the gift of speech. And whereas **mere voice** is but an indication of **mere** pleasure and pain, and is therefore found in other animals (for their nature attains to the perception of pleasure and pain and the intimation of them to one another, and no further), the **power of speech** is intended to set forth the expedient and inexpedient, and therefore likewise the just and the unjust. And it is characteristic of man that **he alone** has any sense of good and evil, of just and unjust, and the like, and the association of living beings who have this sense makes a family and a state.

(Aristotle *Politics*: 1253^a pp. 10–18, my emphasis)[6]

A human in a state of *zoē* is a human who does not have recourse to those things that facilitate an *eudaimon* life. For Aristotle, this would be a human who was without *phronesis*, or who was in persistent state of *akrasia*—weakness of the will—and thus unable to incorporate the virtues into their character. However, a human in a state of *zoē* might also be a person who is excluded from the *polis*, unable to gain access to the necessary training and conditions for pursuit of their human potential, thus becoming virtuous and living an *eudaimon* life. Such a being would live a life no different to that lived by a non-rational animal.

Whereas *zoē* and *bios* are two terms that correspond to the English word 'life', for the Greeks '*zoē politikē*' would not have made sense, while '*bios politikē*' did make sense. This picture changes in modern democracy, now the 'vindication and liberation of *zoē*' (*HS*: p. 10) are declared goals; the goal is to find *bios* in *zoē*. What was, in Ancient Greek political thought to be excluded from, though presupposed by, political life (*zoē*) is now in modern democracies brought to the centre of political life. Put another way, that which in Greek political thought was designed to transform and supplant *zoē* (bare life) in the polis is now sought *in* bare life. In modernity the distinction between *zoē* and *bios* is collapsed.

1.3. Critics of modernity: Foucault, MacIntyre, Agamben

Up to this point Agamben's historico-political narrative will be resonant to those who are familiar with Alasdair MacIntyre's (1985, 1988) diagnosis of modern moral philosophy or Michel Foucault's (1978) diagnosis of modern politics. Agamben sees the modern state's championing of 'the rights of man' as a conflation of *zoē* and *bios*, and this conflation corresponds to the conflation of the ethical and the juridical (*RA*: p. 18). Similarly, in *After Virtue* (1985) MacIntyre argues that the modern move from the Classical teleological ethical framework, which was found in Aristotle (and later in Aquinas), to a modern framework, where moral principles are now derived from a conception of human nature, is a good reason to see the modern project of rationally justifying morality as 'having to fail' (MacIntyre 1985: pp. 51–61). The problem MacIntyre identifies is that in the classical framework the moral principles served to transform humans from their untutored natural state (*zoē*, bare life) into rational beings living an *eudaimon* life (*bios*). In contrast, in the modern moral framework the untutored state (*zoē*, bare life) is taken as the axiom (the conception of human nature) from which rational moral principles are deduced. Given that we (moderns) are working with the same moral concepts as our classical ancestors, our project, according to MacIntyre, is doomed to failure; for, where moral principles for Aristotle were expressly designed to transform us from life lived in a state of *zoē* to one lived in a state of *bios*—true to our purpose as human animals—in the modern moral framework, the distinction between *zoē* and *bios* has been dispensed with in favour of a minimal conception of 'the human' characterised by the possession of a set of legally inscribed rights. Modern moral philosophy[7] then attempts to justify morality by deducing a set of moral principles or procedures from this minimal conception of 'the human'.[8] Thus, not only is *zoē* now taken as an axiom for moral reasoning, as opposed to that which needs to be transformed by morality, but the same moral concepts that were designed to transform *zoē* are now seeking justification in *zoē*.

MacIntyre's purpose in *After Virtue* and *Whose Justice? Which Rationality?* was to demonstrate that modern moral philosophy's project of rationally justifying morality *had* to fail owing to the contradictions brought about by attempting to derive moral principles from that which in Greek ethics and politics they were expressly designed to transform. Similarly, Foucault's genealogical enquiries in the *History of Sexuality* were intended to show how with the onset of modernity came the onset of biopolitics. On Foucault's account, in dispensing with the notion of a human *telos* and thus a notion of the good life, the politics of modernity concerns itself only with bare life.

> For millennia, man remained what he was for Aristotle: a living animal with the additional capacity for a political existence; modern man is an animal whose politics places his existence as a living being in question.
>
> (Foucault 1984: p. 265)

The subject of power is now bare life. The similarity between Agamben and MacIntyre is then striking, but it stops here. The relationship between Agamben and Foucault is closer and explicit, though it differs in important respects.

Agamben seeks to interrogate the link between bare life and politics. Such an interrogation, he claims, 'will be able to bring the political out of its concealment and, at the same time, return thought to its practical calling' (*HS*: p. 5). According to Agamben, this continues and improves upon Foucault's investigations of power. In the *History of Sexuality*, Foucault had dispensed with traditional frameworks of analysis where these had investigated power on juridical models ('what legitimates power?') or on institutional models ('what is the state?'). Foucault had sought to execute an 'unprejudiced analysis of the concrete ways in which power penetrates subjects' very bodies and forms of life' (*HS*: p. 5). Agamben sees a shortcoming in Foucault's approach in its neglect of objective power; he writes, '[c]onfronted with phenomena such as the power of the society of the spectacle that is everywhere transforming the political realm today, is it legitimate or even possible to hold subjective technologies [Foucault's favoured area of power analysis] and political techniques [traditional areas of power analysis] apart?' (*HS*: p. 6).

Agamben seeks to interrogate the intersection between the traditional juridico-institutional and Foucauldian biopolitical models of power. This gives sense to Agamben's discussion of *zoē* and *bios*, because the modern incorporation of *zoē* in the political sphere 'constitutes the original—if concealed—nucleus of sovereign power. *It can even be said that the production of the biopolitical body is the original activity of sovereign power*' (*HR*: p. 6, italics in original). Agamben then asserts, *pace* Foucault, that rather than biopolitics—the tie between power and bare life—being a peculiarly modern phenomenon, it has been central to Western politics from inception and is merely made manifest in modernity.

Agamben, in contrast to Foucault and MacIntyre, seeks to emphasise that the antecedents of the politics of modernity are to be found in Aristotelian political thought; biopolitics (Foucault), and failure of the 'Enlightenment project of rationally justifying morality' (MacIntyre), are not radical, and doomed,[9] modern departures from Aristotelian politics and ethics, but are outcomes of it. The actual manifestation of the distinction between *zoē* and *bios* in Aristotelian thought can be captured by seeing *zoē's* exclusion from the *polis* made manifest in the exclusion of women, slaves, and foreigners from political life.[10] At the same time, *zoē* is essential to the life of the *polis* not only because women, slaves, and foreigners serve an essential purpose enabling the continued existence of the *polis*, even if denied the opportunity to participate in political life, but also because each citizen was born into a life of *zoē* before learning language, and developing *phronesis*.

1.4. The collapsing of zoe and bios: the ethical becomes the juridical

The move to modernity is better characterised not as the bringing of *zoē* into the political but rather the slow movement towards a collapsing of the distinction between *zoē* and *bios*, and the resultant elevation of *zoē* as the (bare) form of life with which the political is concerned. The outcome of Agamben's recasting of the Foucault/MacIntyre analyses[11] is that what must be analysed is the relationship between sovereign power and bare life (*zoē*). For, throughout the history of Western political thought bare life has not only been the subject of sovereign exception, through inclusive exclusion from the *polis*, but shares with the sovereign this inclusive exclusion. What Agamben means by inclusive exclusion is (as I noted above) the fact that while *zoē* is excluded from political life it is necessary to it, in that political life presupposes bare life. Agamben follows Carl Schmitt in claiming that sovereignty also shares this paradoxical structure, in that the sovereign is both inside and outside the law.

To sum up Agamben's claims so far, the history of Western political thought is to be understood within the Foucauldian paradigm of biopolitics. However, *pace* Foucault, Agamben understands the biopolitical paradigm as not merely confined to modernity. In again following but also amending Foucault, Agamben's study of biopolitics is undertaken by analysis of the 'zone of indistinction' between sovereign power and bare life. The zone of indistinction is the sovereign ban, also termed the state of exception, where bare life is found in the form of homo sacer. The sovereign ban, which brings about the state of exception, reaches its historical zenith in the concentration camps of the twentieth century, where law is suspended and bare life is produced in the extreme.

1.5. Outside law; outside modern ethics: homo sacer and sovereign

Homo sacer is a term originally found in Roman law and means a 'man who can be killed and yet who cannot be sacrificed'. Historians have commented upon this ambivalence in the pre-modern conception of sacredness for centuries; however, Agamben is keen to focus upon the 'double exclusion into which he (homo sacer) is taken and the violence to which he finds himself exposed' (*HS*: p. 82) that springs from the ambivalence. Homo sacer's killing is recognised as neither sacrifice nor murder (homicide); thus, homo sacer lives in a state of exception, outside the law: law in this instance being both human and divine law. Agamben's thesis is that 'the sacred' and 'the sovereign' are inextricably linked through the sovereign ban, which brings about the state of exception.

> *The Sovereign sphere is the sphere in which it is permitted to kill without committing homicide and without celebrating sacrifice, and sacred life—that is, life that may be killed but not sacrificed—is the life that has been captured in this sphere.*
>
> (*HS*: p. 83, italics in original)

In modernity the sacredness of life inscribed in universal declarations of rights as a defence against the tyranny of sovereign power, in the first instance, merely signifies life's irreparable exposure in the relation of abandonment and life's subjection to power over death (*HS*: p. 83).

2. Metaphysical foundations of the historico-political thesis

2.1. Aristotle on potentiality

The link between sovereign power and bare life finds its ontological locus in Agamben's reading of Aristotle on potentiality. Agamben cites Aristotle's remarks on potentiality in book *theta* of *The Metaphysics* and in *De Anima*:

> To suffer is not a simple term, but is in one sense a certain destruction through the opposite principle and, in another sense, the preservation [*sōtēria*, salvation] of what is in potentiality by what is in actuality and what is similar to it.... For he who possesses science [in potentiality] becomes someone who contemplates in actuality, and either this is

not an alteration—since here there is the gift of the self to itself and to actuality [*epidosis eis eauto*]—or this is an alteration of a different kind.

(Aristotle *De Anima*: 417^b 2–16, cited in Agamben 2000: p. 184 and *HS*: p. 46)

Agamben claims that in this passage Aristotle 'bequeathed the paradigm of sovereignty to the west' (*HS*: p. 46). He does so, according to Agamben, because the structure of the sovereign ban corresponds to the (Aristotelian) structure of potentiality. Sovereignty has the structure whereby it applies to the exception—the camp—in not applying. Similarly, potentiality 'maintains itself in relation to actuality precisely through its ability not to be' (*HS*: p. 46). Agamben formulates the relationship between potentiality and sovereignty as follows:

> Potentiality (in its double relationship as potentiality to and potentiality not to) is that through which Being founds itself *sovereignly*, which is to say, without anything preceding or determining it (*superium non recognoscens*) other than its own ability not to be. And an act is sovereign when it realizes itself by simply taking away its own potentiality not to be, letting itself be, giving itself to itself.
>
> (*HS*: p. 46)

Sovereignty is the original mode in which Being founds itself prior to anything other than Being's own ability to be. An act can be called sovereign when its potentiality not to be is removed, and the act is 'given to itself'. The originary activity of sovereignty, the production of bare life, is none other than the (metaphysical) function of sovereignty: sovereign's letting itself be.

2.2. Language, potentiality, and being

As Josh Cohen (2001: p. 380) has noted, Agamben's historico-political narrative in *HS* is a culmination of his earlier enquiries into language. The relationship between Agamben's enquiries into language and his enquiries in *HS* and, as I shall outline below, in *RA* is to be found in his reading of Aristotle's depiction of potentiality. 'Language itself', as opposed to events of language, or enunciation, which must *logically* presuppose it, shares potentiality's structure. If we, as does Agamben, accept Aristotle's account (depicted above) of man as a political animal owing to his also being a linguistic animal, then the political significance is amplified. Because 'language itself' is what must be presupposed by all enunciation, 'language itself' is identified *as* potentiality. Potentiality, as outlined above, is potential to be impotential; that is to say, actuality is potentiality holding itself in suspension, or put yet another way, actuality is the suspension of the ability *not* to be. If the potentiality of language is the potentiality to signify, then it is also the potentiality to stay silent, not signify, and in actually referring to something in the event of language we are suspending the potential *not* to refer.

In referring to Plato's 'Seventh Letter', Agamben finds Being in the potentiality of language. As Agamben's English translator and author of the Introduction to *Potentialities*, Heller-Roazen, puts it, 'Being itself, in its very actuality, appears as essentially and irreducibly potential' (2000: p. 18). The study of language is therefore the study of potentiality, and thus of Being. I shall leave this discussion here and return to it later in more detail. These enquiries feed into the conclusions Agamben draws in *RA*, and his account of shame with which I am particularly interested. I turn to this next.

3. The state of exception, Auschwitz, and shame

3.1. Witness: *testis* and *superstes*

> I must repeat—we, the survivors, are not the true witnesses. This is an uncomfortable notion, of which I have become conscious little by little, reading the memoirs of others and mine at a distance of years. We survivors are not only an exiguous but also anomalous minority: we are those who by their prevarications or abilities or good luck did not touch bottom. Those who did so, those who saw the Gorgon, have not returned to tell about it or have returned mute, but they are the 'Muslims', the submerged, the complete witnesses, the ones whose deposition would have a general significance. They are the rule, we are the exception.
>
> (Levi 1989: pp. 63–64)

The above quote is taken from Primo Levi's late reflections on Auschwitz and the literature of the Holocaust: *The Drowned and the Saved*. In the passage Levi is referring to what Agamben, following Levi,[12] terms a 'lacuna' at the heart of testimony. The word witness has two words that correspond to it in Latin: *'testis'* and *'superstes'* (*RA*: p. 17). The first word, *testis*, signifies a person who is a third party and who in disputes between two parties can offer another perspective; this approximates to the use of 'witness' in contemporary Western law. The second word, *superstes*, signifies a person who has 'experienced an event from beginning to end and can therefore bear witness to it' (ibid.).[13] Where the first word, *testis*, invokes impartiality and authority through neutrality, the second does not. To this effect, Levi says in an interview 'I never appear as judge'; 'I do not have the authority to grant pardon.... I am without authority' (Levi, cited in *RA*: p. 17). Levi does not think that one should not pass judgement, only that he is without authority to do so owing to his lack of impartiality. If the facts are that someone committed a crime then they should pay: 'If I had had Eichmann before me, I would have condemned him to death' and further, 'if they have committed a crime, then they must pay' (Levi, cited in *RA*: p. 17).

Agamben explains our propensity to see Levi's remarks as contradictory as a confusion of ethical and juridical categories. While Levi is committed to fulfilling the demand that he make an ethical judgement, he sees himself as unable to make a legal judgement. Thus Agamben takes Levi to have made a discovery in his writing on Auschwitz. The discovery is what Levi calls 'the grey zone' (Levi 1989: pp. 22–51) where the distinctions between executioner and victim, good and evil become blurred. Of Levi's conception of the grey zone, Agamben writes,

> What is at issue here, therefore, is a zone of irresponsibility and *'impotentia judicandi'* (Levi 1989: 43) that is situated not *beyond* good and evil but rather, so to speak, *before* them. With a gesture that is symmetrically opposed to Nietzsche, Levi places ethics before the area in which we are accustomed to consider it. And, without our being able to say why, we sense that this 'before' is more important than any 'beyond' – that the 'underman' must matter more than the 'overman'.
> (*RA*: p. 21)[14]

Levi serves to remind us of the distinction between the law and morality. Prior to our being in a position to be responsible and to ascribe responsibility to others, to be guilty and ascribe guilt, prior, that is to say, to the juridical is the ethical. Guilt (*culpa*) being related to responsibility is also a legal concept: '[r]esponsibility and guilt thus express simply two aspects of legal imputability; only later, in modernity, were they interiorized and moved outside the law' (*RA*: p. 22) to become ethical categories. The conclusion is that there is no paradox in Levi's assertion that he is not in a position to pass impartial judgement—to impute guilt and responsibility—but is in a position to morally condemn: Auschwitz is prior to responsibility and guilt, prior to law. It is this very zone of indistinction, prior to law, that testimony interrogates.

3.2. Auschwitz as manifestation of biopower

It is here then that we can see the relationship of *RA* to *HS*. Auschwitz is the most brutal and pure manifestation of biopower. The inmates of Auschwitz are subject to the sovereign ban, being placed outside the law and transformed into bare life. The starkest manifestation of bare life is the muselmänner. These are those inmates who were barely alive; they moved very slowly, did not speak, were incontinent, fluid sacs often hung from their eyelids, and they showed no emotion, nor recognisably-human expression. They were the walking dead.[15] Testimony contains a lacuna owing to the sort of witness Levi and other writers must have been; it also contains the further lacuna, on the other side as it were, in that neither were writers such as Levi the true *superstes*. So when we differentiate the *testis* from the *superstes*, the juridical from the ethical, the phenomenon of camp testimony still contains the lacuna identified by Levi. The author of testimony is not the true witness in either sense of the word. It will serve to dwell on the camp phenomenon of the muselmänner for a while.

A contemporary of Primo Levi's and another survivor of Auschwitz, Jean Améry, writes of the muselmänner in the context of his discussion of the experience of an intellectual at Auschwitz:

> It is clear that the entire question of the effectiveness of the intellect can no longer be raised where the subject, faced directly with death through hunger and exhaustion, is not only de-intellectualized, but in the actual sense of the word dehumanised. The so-called Mussulmann, as the camp language termed the prisoner who was giving up and was given up by his comrades, no longer had room in his consciousness for the contrasts good or bad, noble or base, intellectual or unintellectual. He was a staggering corpse, a bundle of physical functions in its last convulsions. As hard as it may be for us to do so we must exclude him from our considerations.
>
> (Améry [1980] 1999: p. 9, also partially cited in *RA*: p. 41)[16]

Furthermore, as quoted above, Primo Levi identifies the muselmänner as that which gives rise to the lacuna of testimony. The quote is worth repeating here:

We survivors are not only an exiguous but also anomalous minority: we are those who by their prevarications or abilities or good luck did not touch bottom. Those who did so, those who saw the Gorgon, have not returned to tell about it or have returned mute, but they are the 'Muslims', the submerged, the complete witnesses, the ones whose deposition would have a general significance. They are the rule, we are the exception.

(Levi 1989: pp. 63–64)

The lacuna found in testimony stems from the true witnesses (*superstes*) being those who died or who are unable to speak for themselves in survival. It is here that Agamben draws parallels with his vision of language. Where in post-structuralist linguistics the trace is inscribed by past uses (events) of language, in the case of testimony it is inscribed by the true witness, the one who cannot bear witness owing to their demise, or their muteness. The figure occupying this role in the camp is the muselmänner.

Agamben has sought to furnish us with a way of understanding the philosophical significance of the lacuna in camp testimony. This he does by first identifying the camp as being the embodiment of a zone of indistinction, subject to the sovereign ban, where law is suspended and bare life produced. Here it makes no sense to employ juridical categories such as guilt and responsibility in the 'ethical' sense in which they have come to be employed in modern moral philosophy,[17] for the camp is outside the law. Ethical reflection upon Auschwitz must employ non-juridical terms if it is to capture the ethical reality of Auschwitz.[18] The witness is not, as in law, an impartial observer: *testis*; rather, the witness is the inmate who has been subjected to the complete brutality of Auschwitz: *superstes*. Here *zoē* and *superstes* are one. While the authors of testimonies, such as Primo Levi and Jean Améry, were Auschwitz inmates, they feel themselves not to be the true witnesses of Auschwitz. This feeling manifests itself in different ways in Levi's and Améry's writings. Améry chooses to offer a 'phenomenological' study of the life of the intellectual in Auschwitz, thus bypassing that which gives rise to the lacuna. Améry avoids the lacuna through his choice not to write, strictly speaking, a testimony. In Levi the lacuna itself becomes the topic of discussion, with Levi remarking that he is 'not the true witness because he did not touch bottom' and that the submerged are the complete witnesses (*superstes*). Levi faces the lacuna and acknowledges the implications, and his reflections become increasingly occupied with those implications.

3.3. Primo Levi: shame and subjectivity

In Primo Levi's work there seem to be two characterisations of shame. An instance of the first is to be found at the beginning of *The Truce* and is seen by Levi in the faces of the liberating Russian soldiers. It is the passage that opens *The Truce*; the SS (*Schutzstaffel*) have departed Auschwitz ten days earlier, taking with them all inmates who were 'fit for work'. Prior to the departure of the SS, Levi had become ill and was confined to the camp infirmary; thus, he was one of those left behind in the camp. As the liberating Russian soldiers approach the camp on horseback, Levi and a fellow inmate are carrying a corpse from the infirmary to an overflowing common grave, piled high with snow-covered corpses. Levi writes,

> They were four young soldiers on horseback who advanced along the road that marked the limits of the camp, cautiously holding their sten-guns. When they reached the barbed wire, they stopped to look, exchanging a few timid words, and throwing strangely embarrassed glances at the sprawling bodies, at the battered huts and at us few still alive. [...]
>
> They did not greet us, nor did they smile; they seemed oppressed not only by compassion but by confused restraint, which sealed their lips and bound their eyes to the funeral scene. It was that shame we knew so well, the shame that drowned us after the selections, and every time we had to watch, or submit to, some outrage: the shame the Germans did not know, that the just man experiences at another man's crime; the feeling of guilt that such a crime should exist, that it should have been introduced irrevocably into the world of things that exist, and that this will for good should have proved too weak or null, and should not have availed in defence.
>
> (Levi 2000: pp. 187–188, also cited in Agamben *RA*: pp. 87–88)

Earlier in *If This is a Man*, Levi had discussed what he obliquely refers to in the above quotation as 'the shame that drowned us after selections, and every time we had to watch, or submit to, some outrage'. The passage comes at the end of the penultimate chapter of *If This is a Man*, a chapter titled 'The Last One'. The chapter tells the story of the hanging of an Auschwitz inmate who had connections with a group of prisoners who had blown up one of the crematoria at Birkenau and who was said to be in the process of plotting something similar at Auschwitz. Along with the other Auschwitz inmates, Levi and his friend Alberto were forced to watch the hanging. As the trapdoor upon which the condemned man stands is to open, he shouts *'Kamaraden, ich bin der letz!'* ('Comrades I am the last one!'). Following the hanging, the inmates are forced to file past the 'quivering body' of the hanged man. Levi writes,

> At the foot of the gallows, the SS watch us pass with indifferent eyes: their work is finished, and well finished. The Russians can come now: there are no longer any strong men among us, the last one is now hanging above our heads, and as for the others a few halters had been enough. The Russians can come now: they will only find us, the slaves, the worn-out, worthy of the unarmed death which awaits us.[...]
>
> Alberto and I went back to the hut, and we could not look each other in the face. That man must have been tough, he must have been made of another metal than us if this condition of ours, which has broken us, could not bend him.
>
> Because we also are broken, conquered: even if we know how to adapt ourselves, even if we have finally learnt how to find our food and to resist the fatigue and cold, even if we return home.
>
> We lifted the *menaschka* on to the bunk and divided it, we satisfied the daily ragings of hunger, and now we are oppressed by shame.
>
> (Levi 2000: pp. 155–156)

In *If This is a Man* and *The Truce*, Levi provides us with two episodes of shame and identifies them—that felt by Alberto and himself and that shown on the faces of the liberating Russian soldiers—with each other. When Levi returns to discuss shame in *The Drowned and the Saved* (1989), written more than 30 years later, he does so in a context in which shame has become an emotion closely associated with Holocaust survivors. The shame talked about by Levi in his later work, and also talked about by Wiesel (1996), Bettelheim (1979), and many others, is often used synonymously with 'survivor guilt'.

3.3.1. *Levi's backsliding*

For Agamben (*RA*: p. 88) Levi's later reflections conflate shame with guilt; thus they retreat from the ethical insight of his earlier work, and of an earlier chapter of *The Drowned and The Saved*: 'The Grey Zone'. Agamben cites passages from Levi's later reflections such as: 'many (including me) experienced 'shame', that is, a feeling of guilt' (cited in *RA*: p. 88). There does, at first glance, appear to be a tension in Levi's (later) work. When he begins to ask the question 'what is shame?', rather than merely documenting his own episodes of shame, he does *appear*, at first glance, to contradict some of his earlier remarks. In the later reflections, shame, it seems, is experienced by the survivor as a feeling of guilt, only lacking the outward criteria that we might usually associate with guilt. Shame, or survivor guilt, has the form of 'guilt minus culpability'. In a poem (after the 'Rime of the Ancient Mariner'), we find Levi addressing this seeming contradiction.

> Since then, at an uncertain hour, that punishment comes back. And if it doesn't find someone who will listen to it, it burns his heart in his chest. Once again he sees the faces of the other inmates, blueish in the light of dawn, grey with cement dust, shrouded in mist, painted with death in their restless sleep. At night their jaws grind away, in the absence of dreams, chewing on a stone that isn't there. 'Get away from here, drowned people, go away. I didn't usurp anyone's place. I didn't steal anyone's. No one died in my stead. No one. Go back to your mist. It isn't my fault if I live and breathe, eat and drink and sleep and wear clothes'.
>
> (Levi 1988: p. 581, cited in Agamben *RA*: p. 90)

Agamben clearly sees Levi's later writing on shame as 'backsliding' on earlier insights; thus he focuses his attention elsewhere in the search for an account of shame, which might help us understand the peculiar experience of the camp inmate: homo sacer, existing in the zone of indistinction.

I am unsure as to whether Levi is indeed backsliding here. When he says he experiences 'shame, that is a feeling of guilt', it seems clear, to me at least, that in the context of this passage he is not using guilt in the legal sense but rather he is using guilt in the sense of 'survivor guilt'. When the term 'survivor guilt' is used it is by way of distinguishing it from guilt, as employed in the more usual (legal) sense of being found to be responsible for a particular action, an action judged by a further authority to be unjust. Put another way, 'survivor guilt' is a *feeling* of guilt that one might have when one is not *actually* guilty.

Agamben fails to entertain the distinction between guilt used as *'guilt'* and guilt used as *'survivor guilt'*; the result is that he is left unsatisfied with Levi's account of shame owing to its (perceived) conflation with (legal) guilt. This leads Agamben to move on to examine other accounts.

3.4. Robert Antelme: *L'Espèce Humaine*

The first of these accounts is claimed to be found in Robert Antelme's *The Human Race*. Antelme was a member of the French resistance arrested in the summer of 1944; he was taken first to Buchenwald, then moved to Gandersheim as part of a forced labour kommando. Finally, Antelme was one of a number of prisoners marched to Dachau by SS officers, who were by this time fleeing the advancing allied forces. Antelme's only published work, *L'Espèce Humaine*—translated as *The Human Race*—tells of his time at Gandersheim, the march to Dachau, and the liberation of Dachau. Agamben's interest in Antelme is unsurprising, his testimony is among the most profound (alongside Levi's, and a small number of others). However, I find Agamben's discussion of an episode of shame, which he claims to find in Antelme's book, somewhat obscure.

Antelme, we are told, clearly bears witness to the fact that shame is *not* a feeling of guilt or shame for having survived another but, rather, has a different, darker and more difficult cause. Agamben cites a passage from the section of Antelme's book titled 'The Road'; in this section Antelme tells of the forced march to Dachau and the arbitrary killings meted out by the increasingly anxious and agitated SS soldiers. The agitation and anxiety stems from the closeness of the oncoming allied forces and the fact that the SS have been ordered to bring Antelme's kommando to Dachau. The weakened prisoners inevitably slow down the SS, the result being more arbitrary killings than was usual. The passage that Agamben quotes is the following:

> The SS continues. *'Du, Komm her!'*
>
> Another Italian steps out of the column, a student from Bologna. I know him. I look at him. His face has turned pink. I look at him closely. I still have that pink before my eyes. He stands there at the side of the road he doesn't know what to do with his hands either. He seems embarrassed. We pass in front of him. No one has a hand on him, he hasn't been handcuffed. He's alone at the side of the road, close to the ditch, and he doesn't move. He's waiting for Fritz, he will give himself up to Fritz.
>
> (Antelme 1992: p. 231, partially cited in *RA*: p. 103)

While the above passage is quoted by Agamben, it is only partially so. Agamben's citation stops with the sentence 'He stands there at the side of the road he doesn't know what to do with his hands either', and then continues with a passage from the following page. The omission might strike us as a significant one because the omitted sentence shows that Antelme *explicitly* predicates of the student 'embarrassment', and *not* shame. I will not pursue this further (here); Agamben might well want to align the emotions of shame and embarrassment, or might just think Antelme's own choice of word injudicious.

Having omitted Antelme's explicit predication of embarrassment, Agamben then quotes Antelme's further remarks regarding the student from Bologna from the following page:

He turned pink after the SS man said to him, '*Du komm her!*' He must have glanced around him before he flushed; but yes, it was he who had been picked, and when he doubted it no longer, he turned pink. The SS who was looking for a man, any man, to kill, had found him. And having found him, he looked no further. He didn't ask himself: Why him, instead of someone else? And the Italian, having understood it was really him, accepted this chance selection. He didn't wonder: Why me, instead of someone else?

(Antelme 1992: p. 232, cited in *RA*: p. 103)

What is of interest to Agamben is that, accepting the case of the student from Bologna as an instance of shame, it is an instance of shame that explicitly eschews the standard depiction of shame as brought about by having survived another.[19] The student from Bologna, if ashamed, is so for having to die, not for surviving in another's stead. Thus Agamben writes, '[i]n any case, the student is not ashamed for having survived. On the contrary, what survives him is shame' (*RA*: p. 104).

One question I would like to pose is, whether Agamben, in his determination to sustain the distinction between the ethical and juridical, and thus to differentiate between shame and guilt, has conflated shame and embarrassment? (It would, I think, be a mistake to linger too much on this seeming infelicity here, though I will return to it towards the end of the chapter.) Agamben draws parallels between Antelme's story of the student of Bologna and Kafka's description of Josef K. at the end of *The Trial*; he might therefore just recast Antelme's story within his account, as an example of a flawed account (as he does with Levi's later reflections of shame), and continue with the Kafka example as exemplar. In *The Trial*, when K. is at the point of death, when the executioner's knife is twisted twice in his heart, the narrator says 'it was as if his shame were to outlive him' (Kafka 1994: p. 177, cited in *RA*: p. 104).

Agamben's selective reading of Antelme then is not crucial to his position, but rather crucial to his finding support for his position in Antelme's writing.

Agamben's discussion (with or without support from Antelme) takes a radically different route to that of Levi and conventional discussions; rather than shame being the result of having survived while another dies, or resulting from 'consciousness of an imperfection or lack in our being from which we take distance' (*RA*: p. 104), shame is the very inability to distance ourselves from our being. Shame survives us. This understanding then brings Agamben close to Levinas's account of shame.

3.5. Shame as attachment to, and awareness of, oneself: Levinas and shame

For Levinas, shame springs from the 'fact of being chained to oneself, the radical impossibility of fleeing oneself to hide oneself from oneself, the intolerable presence of the self to itself.... What shame discovers is the being that *discovers* itself' (Levinas 1982: p. 87, cited in *RA*: p. 105). Shame is the awareness of our own being—Agamben writes, formulating a provisional definition: shame 'is the fundamental sentiment of being *a subject*, in the two apparently opposed senses of this phrase: to be subjected and to be sovereign. Shame is what is produced in the absolute concomitance of subjectification and desubjectification, self-loss and self-possession, servitude and sovereignty' (*RA*: p. 107). When Josef K. is dying, with the two twists of the knife in his heart; when, with fading sight he is looking into the face of his executioner, his shame will 'outlive him', because it is at the point at which his subjectivity is slipping away in death that 'being's inability to break from itself' is made manifest.

In the passages preceding the final sentence of Kafka's text, the narrator tells us that K. is aware that he is expected to 'seize the knife... and drive it into himself' (Kafka 1994: p. 177). He does not do so. Similarly, Antelme writes of the student from Bologna that 'no one has a hand on him, he hasn't been handcuffed'; we might assume that he could at least try to avoid the seemingly inevitable. He does not do so. It is in these moments when shame becomes present; when all other courses of action have been closed off, or, more precisely, accepted as closed off by the subject, then subjectivication and desubjectivication meet. Shame, the concept, survives K. and (if we suspend my misgivings outlined above for the moment) the student from Bologna in the outward signs of the conflation of subjectification and desubjectification, and their reporting in Kafka's narrative and Antelme's testimony, respectively.

3.6. Kant and Heidegger on auto-affection

Agamben's discussion of Antelme's reporting of the flush of the student from Bologna and Kafka's narration of the final moments of Josef K. are taken to support his embracing of Levinas's account of shame. By way of further deepening the account, Agamben draws an analogy between his account of shame, Kant's discussion of auto-affection, and Heidegger's discussion and development of Kant's thought. For Kant auto-affection is the basic structure of subjectivity, arguing in the *Critique of Pure Reason* (hereafter *CPR*) that time is a 'pure form of sensible intuition' and that, therefore, propositions that predicate certain qualities of time, such as 'different times cannot be simultaneous', are not analytic but synthetic (Kant 1929: p. 75 [A 32]). Thus, the truth of the proposition is not founded in the meaning of its constituent words, or the meaning of the sentence which the proposition comprises: it 'cannot have its origin in concepts alone' (ibid.).[20] The proposition has its origin, Kant claims, in the intuition and representation of time. Therefore, for Kant, time does not exist in and of itself, in abstraction from 'all subjective conditions of its intuition' (ibid.: p. 76 [A 33]). This is so, because if it were able to exist in abstraction, it would at one and the same time be both an actual and a non-actual object. On the other hand, were it to be a quality inherent in objects, then it would not be able to serve as a pre-existing condition for those objects and intuited *a priori* by synthetic propositions, and Kant deduces that time *can* be intuited *a priori* by synthetic propositions: 'if time is nothing but the subjective condition under which alone intuition can take place in us. ... [T]his form of inner intuition can be represented prior to the objects, and therefore *a priori*' (ibid.). Time then is synthetic *a priori*, a *subjective* condition of possibility. Time is, on Kant's account, 'nothing but the form of inner sense, that is, of the intuition of ourselves and of our inner state. It cannot be a determination of outer appearances; it has to do neither with shape nor position, but with the relation of representations in our inner state' (ibid.: p. 77 [B 50]). Space is the formal *a priori* condition of outward appearances only (ibid. [A 34]). Time, in contrast, is the formal *a priori* condition of inner intuition, and thus of *all representations*, whether of outer or inner things. Representations belong as 'determinations of the mind' (ibid.); therefore time is the 'formal *a priori* condition of all appearances ... all objects of the senses, are in time, and necessarily stand in time-relations' (ibid. [B 51]).

Once Kant has established the foregoing through his transcendental deduction, it remains to explicitly introduce the notion of auto-affection:

> If, then, as regards [determinations of outer sense], we admit that we know objects only in so far as we are externally affected, we must also recognise, as regards inner sense, that by means of it we intuit ourselves only as we are inwardly affected by ourselves; in other words, that, so far as inner intuition is concerned, we know our own subject only as appearance, not as it is in itself.
>
> (Ibid.: p. 168 [B 156])

Auto-affection is, following Kant, the condition under which we intuit ourselves: 'as we are inwardly affected by ourselves'. Auto-affection is a condition of our *knowledge* of our own subjectivity, our knowledge of ourselves: where knowledge of ourselves is to be distinguished from consciousness of ourselves.

> Just as for knowledge of an object distinct from me I require, besides the thought of an object in general (in the category), an intuition by which I determine that general concept, so for knowledge of myself I require, besides the consciousness, that is besides the thought of myself, an intuition of the manifold in me.
>
> (Ibid.: p. 169 [B 158])

In *Kant and the Problem of Metaphysics* (Heidegger 1997 [5th edn]), Heidegger gives close attention to the passages from Kant's first critique, just summarised. Originally intended as part of *Being and Time*, this work was part of Heidegger's 'Destruktion' of Western metaphysics. Heidegger claims that in editions subsequent to the first edition of *CPR* Kant played down the centrality of time as the basis of metaphysics. In those subsequent editions, Kant gives more weight to rational-cognitive subjectivity. Heidegger claims to have 'found Kant out', arguing that not only is rational-cognitive subjectivity unnecessary as a foundation for metaphysics, but that Kant recognised this himself in the first edition of *CPR* before recoiling to the, now accepted, 'Kantian' position of the last edition. Heidegger writes,

> Time is not an active affection that strikes an already existing subject. As pure auto-affection, it forms the very essence of what can be defined as seeing oneself in general. . . . But the self itself that, as such, can

be seen by something is, in essence, the finite subject. Insofar as it is pure auto-affection, time forms the essential structure of subjectivity. Only on the basis of this selfhood can finite Being be what it must be: delivered over to receiving.

(Heidegger 1990: pp. 132–131, modified translation as cited in *RA*: p. 110)[21]

Heidegger's point is that the self that can be seen by something is the finite subject, not the transcendental 'I'. Heidegger's stated task in *Kant and the Problem of Metaphysics* is not to critique Kant, only correct him by bringing him back to his original insight: 'what Kant had wanted to say' (Heidegger 1997: p. 141). The understanding is not 'the manifold in me' (the universal in the finite being) that I intuit, but my looking back at my history and my looking forward: my potentiality. Hence, a little further on Heidegger writes,

The idea of pure self-affection, which as we have seen determines the inner most essence of transcendence, was thus not introduced by Kant for the first time in the second edition. In that edition it was simply formulated more explicitly and indeed, it appears characteristically [at the beginning] in the Transcendental Aesthetic. [. . .] Sense means finite intuition. The form of sense is pure taking-in-stride. Inner sense does not receive 'from without', but rather from the self. In pure taking-in-stride, the inner affection must come forth from out of the pure self; i.e., it must be formed in the essence of selfhood as such, and therefore it must constitute this self in the first place. Pure self-affection provides the transcendental, primal structure of the finite self as such. Thus it is *absolutely not the case* that a mind exists among others which, for it, are also something related to it, and that it practices self positing. Rather, this 'from-out-of-itself-toward . . . and back-to-itself' first constitutes the mental character of the mind as a finite self.

(Heidegger 1997: pp. 133–134, emphasis added)[22]

3.6.1. *The analogy between auto-affection and shame*

In the passages quoted from Kant, from the later editions of *CPR*, the category of time (as auto-affection) is the condition of possibility for knowledge, including knowledge of oneself; in Heidegger's rendering of Kant it is the 'essential structure of subjectivity' (ibid.). The claim has transformed from an epistemological one in the later editions of Kant's *CPR* to a stage in the preparatory work for a phenomenological ontology in Heidegger's work. It is in Heidegger's 'correction' of Kant that shame, as discerned by Agamben, shame a manifestation of auto-affection, is found. In discussing the passage from Heidegger, just quoted, Agamben writes,

> Here [in the modified quotation of Heidegger (above) *PH*] what is revealed is the analogy with shame, defined as being consigned to a passivity that cannot be assumed. Shame, indeed, then appears as the most proper emotive tonality[23] of subjectivity. For there is certainly nothing shameful in a human being who suffers on account of sexual violence; but if he takes pleasure in his suffering violence, if he is moved by his passivity—if, that is, auto-affection is produced—only then can one speak of shame. [...] The *self* is what is produced as a remainder in the double movement—active and passive—of auto-affection. This is why subjectivity constitutively has the form of subjectification and desubjectification; this is why it is, at bottom, shame. Flush is the remainder that, in every subjectification, betrays a desubjectification and that, in every desubjectification, bears witness to a subject.
>
> (*RA*: pp. 110–112)

Referring back to Levi's remarks about the writers of testimony not being the 'true witnesses', Agamben situates Levi's remarks in the framework just outlined: if the muselmänner is the true witness, 'the one who has seen the Gorgon', and the testimony of the survivor speaks for, and on behalf of, the true witness, then *the true witness is the inhuman* (or the *dehumanised*). Hence, the true witness to the human is (that which has been made) inhuman (*RA*: p. 120).

To speak, to bear witness, is thus to enter into a vertiginous movement in which something sinks to the bottom, wholly desubjectified and silenced, and something subjectified speaks without truly having anything to say of its own ('I tell of things ... that I did not actually experience'). Testimony takes place where the speechless one makes the speaking one speak and where the one who speaks bears the impossibility of speaking in his own speech, such that the silent and the speaking, the inhuman and the human enter into a zone of indistinction in which it is impossible to establish the position of the subject, to identify the 'imagined substance' of the 'I' and, along with it, the true witness. . . . *the subject of testimony is the one who bears witness to a desubjectification.*

(*RA*: pp. 120–121, italics in original)[24]

3.7. Between humanism and anti-humanism

Agamben claims that reflections on the moral significance of Auschwitz have often been conducted from two opposed vantage points: humanists who wish to emphasise that all human beings (members of the human species or human race)[25] are human, and anti-humanists who claim that being human is something over and above mere membership of the species. The reflection on testimony, subjectivity, and shame conducted by Agamben gives a different account to both of the above: ' "human beings are human insofar as they are not human" or, more precisely, "human beings are human insofar as they bear witness to the inhuman" ' (*RA*: p. 121).

It is the human's consciousness of his inhumanity (in both senses: the capacity of his species to be savage and brutal with regard to its own (and we might ask, why not being so to other animals too?) and the capacity to live beyond the human, as bare life) that makes him human; shame is the manifestation of this consciousness. Shame is the 'hidden structure of all subjectivity and consciousness' (*RA*: p. 128). The outward signs discerned by (Agamben's) Antelme on the face of the student from Bologna testify to the student's consciousness of his own inhumanity (and the inhumanity of the species). The shame of survivors can be recast in Agamben's framework. Survivors feel shame *not* for having survived while others died (we might call this quasi-guilt), not because they feel tainted by the crimes of others (we might call this associative shame), but because they have become conscious of their own subjectivity.

The structure of camp testimony, having at its centre a lacuna, is one manifestation of the zone of indistinction that is the Nazi death camp. The camp is a zone of indistinction so complete that it leaves those who survive it with a sense of shame borne of their consciousness of their subjectivity, consciousness of the inhumanity that is an essential part of their humanity. The inability of the author of testimony to claim the status of witness (either *testis* or *superstes*) and the inability of the true witness (muselmänner) to testify are testimony to the structure of human subjectivity. In a move that builds upon Derrida's vision of language, and attempts to give it an ethical import hitherto absent, Agamben writes,

Testimony takes place in the non-place of articulation. In the non-place of the Voice stands not writing, but the witness. And it is precisely because the relation (or, rather, non-relation) between living being and the speaking being has the form of shame, of being reciprocally confined to something that cannot be assumed by a subject, that the *ethos* of this disjunction can only be testimony – that is, something that cannot be assigned to a subject but that nevertheless constitutes the subject's only dwelling place, its only possible consistency.

(*RA*: p. 130)

3.8. To be a human being

What does this all mean? Well, the existence of the muselmänner testifies to the fact that the human animal can survive the human being.[26] Secondly, the existence of the survivor testifies to the fact that the human can survive the non-human. The two are brought together in the sense that the truly human is the one whose humanity has been destroyed, 'truly' in that they are the only true witnesses to the human (recall Levi's words quoted above). For Agamben, the human is never fully destroyed. There is always a remainder: '[t]he witness is this remnant' (*RA*: p. 134). The essence of the human is continuously deferred; the human being is to be found in the being's *potential* to be human.

The human being is thus always beyond or before the human, the central threshold through which pass currents of the human and the inhuman, subjectification and desubjectification, the living being's becoming speaking and logos' becoming living. These currents are coextensive, but not coincident; their non-coincidence, the subtle ridge that divides them, is the place of testimony.

(*RA*: p. 135)

4. The distorting power of theory and the ethics of exegesis

4.1. Levi and Antelme revisited

Agamben's analysis gives us much on which to muse. I find it at turns intriguing and obscure. It is intriguing in that it situates an analysis of shame in a wider historico-political framework; something which is undoubtedly required if we are to understand shame, particularly shame as experienced by survivors of extreme trauma. This serves as a much-needed prophylactic to the sort of abstracting tendencies of scientism that we encountered in Chapter 1. In situating his analysis of shame in, broadly-speaking, Heideggerian terms, Agamben provides us with a way of making sense of shame-as-involving-our-self-understanding and self-awareness, which, of course, can only be conceptually mediated, and experienced as being-in-the-world, not that is, as an abstract, transcendental, 'I'. So much, so much for the better. Unfortunately, the insights gained tend to drift towards theoretical excess. In what follows I diagnose the source of this excess; in doing so I hope to distil that which is of genuine value in Agamben's account of shame, and from which I can learn as I progress to Chapter 3.

The engagement with Agamben's remarks in *RA* which I undertook in Section 3 has, in addition to elucidating Agamben's argumentative moves, served to highlight certain anomalies in those moves. Two of these are particularly prominent. First, he depicts Levi's insights in the chapter on shame from *The Drowned and the Saved* as indicating a 'backsliding' on earlier insights. The second anomaly was Agamben's employment of Antelme's recounting of the story of the student from Bologna as an instance of shame. It is instructive to examine these two cases in more detail.

4.1.1. Levi's regress?

In respect of Agamben's treatment of Levi, I noted that the accusation of backsliding rested on Agamben's own failure to pay attention to the different context and purpose of Levi's later writing, thus conflating two different contexts of discussion. Levi's first-person testimony of an episode of shame, which follows the forced viewing of the hanging of the fellow inmate, and Levi's testimony of his third-person ascription of shame to the liberating Russian soldiers are made in the context of testimony and for the purpose of bearing witness to the event. The second context is Levi's reflection on shame as an emotion that has, over time, become associated with the peculiar post-War experience of survivors of the Holocaust. Agamben conflates these. It would be misleading to claim that Levi makes the distinction I am drawing here wholly explicit; his own lack of clarity on the issue must then contribute to Agamben's misinterpretation. But not being wholly explicit about what one is doing in one's writing is not the same thing as not doing something. Indeed, others have commented on Levi's lack of clarity in this area while also discerning that Levi is talking of two different 'things' in his early *documenting* of episodes of shame in *If This is a Man* and *The Truce*, and the much later *meditation* on the phenomenon of shame in *The Drowned and the Saved* (for example, see Cicioni *Primo Levi:*

Bridges of Knowledge 1995: p. 162). I would want to add that I would not wish to make too much of the different context, only it should be taken into account; this Agamben fails to do. Instead, Agamben sees Levi as having a good *theory* of shame in his early writing, which he then fails to fully realise in his later writing and thus backslides on his 'insights'.

What continuity is there then between the passages from *If This is a Man* and *The Truce* together with the chapter 'The Grey Zone' on the one hand and the chapter 'Shame' on the other? My answer is that the chapter on shame still bears the hallmarks of Levi's style of writing testimony; that is to say, it is still testimony, but that it is so has much to do with Levi's distinct approach to testimony. The chapter entitled 'Shame' in *The Drowned and the Saved* comes to us as testimony, in the sense that it is testimony to Levi's 'grappling' with the emergence of survivor shame—i.e. 'shame' used as a synonym for 'survivor guilt'—and his own, earlier documented episodes of shame recounted in the earlier texts. Levi is grappling because of his honesty, and because of the seeming confusion bestowed by one word being used to denote seemingly distinct phenomena. Levi's honesty denies him the comfort of a quick dismissal of his guilt (however minute and 'irrational' we might judge any such acceptance of guilt on his part to be); he wants to explore whether when he feels shame, when he says 'now we are oppressed by shame' he is doing so owing to his being culpable. He responds, following deliberation, with a resounding 'no'. Crucially the *deliberation* is what constitutes the text that leads, ultimately, to Levi's rejection of his guilt. Levi wishes to show us the anguish to which the survivor is subject, constantly playing over and over the possibility that they have some degree of responsibility for the crimes perpetrated against them and against those who did not survive. True, it turns out that any accusation of guilt would be crass, but in a sense part of what constitutes the crime is that survivors are left feeling shame . . . that is a feeling of guilt—does this not seem appropriate to you here? It does to me, and saying that Levi cannot, or ought not, to say this strikes me as a demonstration of one's failure to grasp what is important in Levi's text.

It is, then, shame's (conceptual/phenomenological[27]) closeness to guilt that serves to continue the effects of the moral crime,[28] long after liberation, and long after the demise of the Third Reich. The closeness of shame and guilt means that those survivors are left to persistently question themselves; to replay events in their minds; and to try to find some reassurance that they were not in someway partially responsible for the existence of those moral crimes. When one feels shame it does seem to make one question whether one is, in fact, culpable; that this is part of—the grammar[29]/phenomenology of—shame can be deemed through looking at documented expressions of shame.

In support of the foregoing recall that one of the passages Agamben quotes as evidence of Levi's backsliding contains the following: 'many (including me) experienced 'shame', that is, a feeling of guilt' (Levi 1989: p. 73, cited in *RA*: p. 88). Agamben cites this sentence as evidence of Levi's backsliding; there is no reason to see it as such. I have yet to find someone who would deny that to *feel* shame is *akin to feeling* guilt, only without being actually guilty of something. That is to say, Levi does not say he *is* guilty (of some legally proscribed act or even of a moral 'crime'), only that the shame he and other survivors experience is a *feeling* of guilt. It is not too difficult to understand this, even if one has never experienced shame (if that is possible): i.e. they might feel similar in the way that touching something extremely cold and touching something extremely hot can feel similar (though easily distinguished from each other by feeling the temperature emanating from them from (say) a metre away).

There is another reason not to accept this 'late' quotation from Levi as an instance of backsliding, and this is something Agamben ought to have commented upon, particularly having read Levi in the original Italian. Stuart Woolf's English translation, found in the UK and US editions of *If This is a Man/The Truce*, renders the passage that refers to the shame on the faces of the Russian soldiers that opens *The Truce*, as the following:

> It was that shame we knew so well, the shame that drowned us after the selections, and every time we had to watch, or submit to, some outrage: the shame the Germans did not know, that the just man experiences at another man's crime; the **feeling of guilt** that such a crime should exist, that it should have been introduced irrevocably into the world of things that exist.
>
> (Levi 2000: p. 188, my emphasis)

Levi quotes the same passage in his chapter on shame in *The Drowned and the Saved*; Raymond Rosenthal, the English translator of that text renders the passage as follows:

the shame that the Germans never knew, the shame which the just man experiences when confronted by a crime committed by another, and he **feels remorse** because of its having been irrevocably introduced into the world of existing things.

(Levi 1989: p. 54, my emphasis)

The problem of how to translate the key part of this passage stems from the difficulty of translating the Italian '*rimorde*', which has no literal counterpart in English. Agamben's translator is careful not to reproduce the Woolf translation (though citing it in amended form rather than citing the Rosenthal or merely quoting from the Italian and providing his own translation) and renders the crucial part as follows:

the shame the Germans did not know, that the just man experiences at another man's crime, at the fact that such a crime should exist, that it should have been introduced irrevocably into the world of things that exist.

(Levi, cited in *RA*: pp. 87–88)[30]

Here the problem of translating *rimorde* is overcome by merely omitting the problematic clause from the sentence which contains it: *e gli rimorde che esista* (and in doing so, I find, making the passage difficult to follow). The Woolf translation is not, strictly speaking, correct but I think captures Levi's meaning. Agamben's omission in his translation is, however, problematic. Rosenthal's is the all together most satisfactory of the translations. To me, however, Levi is clearly saying here that he feels *remorse* at being part of a world in which these crimes took place.[31]

So the problem for Agamben is not that Levi explicitly equates shame and guilt, but that he equates his shame with a feeling of remorse. Leading one to ask what has he to feel remorse *about*. There are, I would like to suggest, two related consequences for Agamben: first it means that Levi, at this stage (in his early writing), does not offer an account of shame that conforms to Agamben's theory of shame (as the hidden structure of all subjectivity), and second, Levi explicitly ties feeling shame to a feeling of remorse, a concept as closely related to guilt as it is to shame. This leaves the claim of Agamben's, that Levi resolutely differentiated between ethical and juridical categories in his early work, looking somewhat empty. Levi, I venture, like most, would see such a *clear* division as a fantasy.

That modern moral philosophy has become saturated with juridical reflection is not in question; that one might criticise it for being so is, at the least, possible. Indeed, this is a form of criticism for which I have much sympathy. What is in question, however, is that there can be any clear line drawn between the two 'categories'—the ethical and the juridical—at the conceptual level, as Agamben claims, and champions the early Levi as discovering.[32] As will transpire I think Agamben's remarks here are determined by his theory of language.

Agamben mistakes Levi's honesty in his writing about shame for an indication of his backsliding from one theoretical position to another—less insightful—one, where guilt and shame are identified with each other. For Agamben this is to imply the modern conflation of the juridical and the ethical, and thus fail to think outside the conceptual constraints of biopolitics. Agamben is thus committed to the concept of guilt as never having played any role outside a juridical realm, and to the concomitant thought that to employ the concept in ethical and political thought is to be committed to modern biopolitics. This strikes me as a somewhat rigid and over generalised/simplified depiction of our lives with our language. Etymology might well show us that the concept of guilt originates in jurisprudence, maybe even Roman jurisprudence, in the case of the Latin *culpa*; but the etymology of a term is not the meaning of a term. Etymological and genealogical investigation do not show us what words mean, rather they are useful for disrupting other settled (ensconced) views of meaning (such as those that appeal to the intentions of the author, or the properties of concepts for example). The reading of Levi advanced in *RA* is, in the main, simply based on Agamben's own theoretical agenda.

In contrast to Agamben's depiction of Levi, Levi's genius is, to a large extent, reflected in his ability to reflect with wisdom and dignity on complex moral issues with a linguistic simplicity and clarity, and authorial honesty, that eschews easy invocation of (and the often obfuscatory language of some philosophical) theories (cf. Chapter1). Not only does Levi advocate the ordinary virtues[33] (cf. Robert S. C. Gordon 2001) but he also manifests them in his own practice as a writer. His unrelenting quest for testimonial honesty is often unsettling for the reader, at least it is for this reader, and one might only surmise how it must have affected the writer. But, however difficult, Levi refused to rest with comforting explanations and continued the public process of reflection. Indeed, those contemporaries of Levi's, former inmates such as Bettelheim and Améry,[34] who do advance theoretical claims in their writings on the camps are often the subjects of Levi's distaste in his later writing.

4.1.2. Antelme, Agamben, and embarrassment

Similarly, and as I noted above, in his discussion of a passage from Robert Antelme's *The Human Race*, Agamben took liberties with his quotation of an episode involving a student from Bologna. Here Agamben omitted a sentence from the quoted paragraph, a sentence in which Antelme explicitly predicated of the student from Bologna embarrassment and not shame.

> His face turned pink. I look at him closely. I still have that pink before my eyes. He stands there at the side of the road. He does not know what to do with his hands. He seems embarrassed [*embarassé*].
>
> (Antelme 1998: p. 231)

When the passage is quoted in *RA*, we are given no hint that the translation has been modified over and above the use of the ellipsis in the quote. The sentence which is problematic for Agamben—'he seems embarrassed'—is simply omitted; an ellipsis takes its place and leads us directly on to a passage from the following page—a jump of 34 lines or3 paragraphs.

With Levi, Agamben employs him for as long as his writings *superficially* appear to lend support, rejecting his writings at the point at which Levi's refusal to rest (stop wrestling with problems and seek security in theory) leads to disagreement with Agamben's thesis. In order to give the impression that Antelme's writing supports his thesis, Agamben ignores, and omits from quotation, what is explicitly said in the text. This is important because what is also clear from Antelme's reporting of the incident of the student from Bologna is that the predication of embarrassment went hand in hand with a reporting of the flush— i.e. the blushing, the pinkness—on the student's face as he was selected for execution by the SS officer. While embarrassment and shame are closely related emotions, a flush or blushing is *usually* associated with embarrassment: it is one of the most 'to-hand' instances of the outward criteria of embarrassment. I do not of course say this by way of claiming one *cannot* be ashamed and blush, or by way of advancing any positive account of *what shame is*. Nor do I want to claim that one cannot be embarrassed without blushing; obviously one can be so. I do not advance any claim as to blushing being either a necessary or a sufficient condition for embarrassment. I only *suggest* that even taking Antelme's passage as presented by Agamben, with the omission of the explicit reference to embarrassment, one would likely, on reading the description of the student, predicate of him embarrassment, just as does Antelme. It is not merely the omitted sentence but the whole passage that might lead one, with Antelme, to predicate of the student embarrassment—Antelme wrote: 'he does not know what to do...'; if he were ashamed surely he would be concerned with *being*, not *doing*.

Of course, as with shame and guilt one might find it difficult to discern a distinction in some cases but Agamben presents us with no hint that there might be something that needs to be addressed here. It is, as will become clear, of more than a little interest that Agamben seems to find clear conceptual distinctions even in areas where, if there were such clear distinctions at all, they would be difficult to sustain and be context-dependent. Embarrassment-shame-guilt is just one of those areas. Levi recognises this and faces it both as a writer and as a survivor. Agamben overlooks it owing to his own theoretical predilections.

4.2. The tyranny of theory

What I want to emphasise then is while the chapter on shame in *RA* gives the impression of a study of shame in testimony, and the philosophical (phenomenological/metaphysical) insight we can glean from such a study, it transpires to be no more than a masquerade for a theoretical agenda already conceived. From the outset Agamben is seeking to outline and advance his post-Heideggerian theory of shame, as the hidden structure of all subjectivity and consciousness. When Levi's persistent quest for testimonial honesty leads him to reflect on the overlap (actual or seeming) between shame and guilt, his writings fail to lend phenomenological support for Agamben's theory, and thus he is dismissed—the 'later' Levi—or selectively represented—the 'early' Levi. When Antelme's text explicitly predicates of the student embarrassment, and not shame, Agamben simply omits the sentence from the quotation in order that Antelme's text can be harnessed as phenomenological support for his theory. This might well not be a surprise to those familiar with Agamben's oeuvre; his early, overtly theoretical, writing on language and poetics have proceeded to writings on political philosophy and ethics. Unfortunately, this has not meant a tempering of theoretical excess in the light of a reading of testimony. Agamben's writings on language dictate what is said in the writings on political philosophy and ethics.[35] In the next section I will seek to examine Agamben's theory of language.

5. Derrida (plus a little?): Agamben on potentiality

5.1. Derrida and the (structural) logic of writing

In the process of discussing *HS*, I quoted Agamben's citing of Aristotle on both language and on potentiality; these are crucial for understanding Agamben's theoretical foundations, being citations that appear in a number of his essays and monographs. Importantly, the understanding of language which informs Agamben's championing of Aristotle's depiction of man as *zōon logon echōn*, that is the living being who has language, is a very particular view of language. The view is a moderately modified version of that propounded by Jacques Derrida, though crucially, I will show, with more emphasis given to the notion of *trace*, and thus to the import of etymological investigation. The shift in emphasis from Derrida's account of language to Agamben's version of it stems from Agamben's discussion of Aristotle's conception of potentiality. Where Derrida talks of what remains in the absence of presence ('presence' being the 'I', 'intention', 'context of production', 'producer', 'receiver', etc.) being the *trace* of previous events of language and events of language being enabled by the iterability of marks ('marks' include such things as a wink, as well as written words of a natural language such as the English word 'France'), Agamben talks of potentiality. I shall briefly reflect on the key points of Derrida's account.

For Derrida, the event of language structurally presupposes the iterability of signs; that is to say, a sign can be used over and over again. Writing, for it to be such, must structurally allow for the absence of the author and of the intended recipient of the text. Writing *must* be able, in order to function—i.e. must be able to allow for in its functioning—the absence of such things as the presence of intention, the context of production, a determinable author, a destined reader, etc., Derrida writes,

> I repeat, therefore, since it can never be repeated too often: if one admits that writing (and the mark in general) *must be able* to function in the absence of the sender, the receiver, the context of production, etc., that implies that this power, this *being able*, this *possibility* is *always* inscribed, hence *necessarily* inscribed *as possibility* in the functioning or the functional structure of the mark. Once the mark *is able* to function, once it is possible for it to function, once it is possible for it to function in case of an absence, etc., it follows that this possibility is a necessary part of its structure, that the latter must *necessarily be such that* this functioning is possible.
>
> (Derrida 1988: p. 48)

In the above passage, Derrida is responding to the criticisms advanced by John Searle; in doing so he emphasises the 'necessity' of 'possibility' in the functioning of the mark so that the mark can communicate in the absence of (determined) author, (destined) recipient, and context of production; this is what I called, following Derrida, iterability of the mark, and what Agamben is calling potentiality. It is important not to make Searle's mistake, and take Derrida's claims about structure (which might also be termed 'logic') and take them as (quasi-) empirical claims. For example, Searle provides, by way of proposed refutation of Derrida, a scenario that is as follows: Searle and his friend are sat in an auditorium during a performance and one of them passes a note to the other, the note is read and understood in the presence of both author/sender and destined recipient, as well as in the context of production. One can only surmise as to what Searle expects this example to demonstrate, and further what he must have thought Derrida's argument was for this to stand as a refutation of it. I presume Searle assumed that Derrida was making an empirical statement about writing which could be refuted by the production of a counterexample, showing that things do not have to be thus and so. Searle's objection has no bearing whatsoever on Derrida's theory in this respect.[36] Derrida is making a structural (logical) point about writing (marks), i.e. that meaning cannot be *reduced to* presence (intentions of the author (speaker), context of production, etc.). Simon Glendinning sums this up as follows:

> Any written message is such, is what it is, only to the extent that a reader could read what a (determinable) sender could write in the radical absence of that sender: *writing can and must be able to do without the presence of the (determinable) sender.* Equally, any message is readable only to the extent that the reader could read whatever the sender could write in the radical absence of a (determinable or destined) receiver's presence: *writing can and must be able to do without the presence of the (destined) receiver.*
>
> (Glendinning 1998: p. 119)

The point is that it is part of the logic of writing, part of what it is to be writing, that it must be able to operate in a condition of 'radical absence' (the death of the author). If a mark cannot operate in a condition of 'radical absence', then it serves *no purpose*;[37] it must be able to operate whether in the absence or not of the sender, receiver, and context of production. One might surmise whether Derrida would commit himself to either saying, as he seems to be implying, that it is analytic to the concept of writing that it can operate under conditions of radical absence or whether it is part of the grammar of 'writing'. Much hinges upon which way he might go here. This is an important question to ask as it strikes at the heart of what it is to be 'writing', in Derrida's sense. Derrida provides us with an answer, which Glendinning cites,

> The structure of iteration ... implies *both* identity *and* difference. Iteration in its 'purest form' – and it is always impure – contains *in itself* the discrepancy of difference that constitutes it as iteration. The iterability of an element divides its own identity *a priori*, even without taking into account that this identity can only *determine* or delimit itself through differential relations to other elements and hence that it bears the mark of this difference. It is because this iterability is differential, within each individual 'element' as well as between 'elements' ... that the remainder, although indispensable, is never that of a full or fulfilling presence: it is a differential structure escaping the logic of presence.
>
> (Derrida 1988: p. 53, cited in Glendinning 1998: pp. 110–111)

Iterability of the element is *a priori*; it is therefore analytic to the concept of 'writing'; and writing is generalised to include any events of communication, which can operate in the absence of the writer. 'Writing' in Derrida's sense then is generalised beyond its usual use[38] and includes all communicable 'elements'; it is analytic to this (generalised) concept of writing (as it is to 'writing' in the usual sense) that the communicable elements are iterable, *a priori*. To this end Glendinning writes,

> A 'singular event' that can 'communicate' (e.g. an event of speech) is possible only on condition of a necessary or structural relation to an iteration that is *another such* 'singular event' which is *not present* at the time of its production or reception. That is, an occasion other than this one which, as a singular event, cannot be conceived as being 'writing' without reference to *another such* event, an occasion other than this one which, as a singular event, cannot be conceived as being 'writing' without reference to *another such* event ... Numbers are not accumulating here. The limit is only that it is *not once*. This is the differentiality 'within each individual 'element'' which is 'the positive condition of the emergence of the mark'. This is what Derrida is insisting upon when he states that the 'unity of the signifying form' that is 'required to permit its recognition' 'only constitutes itself by virtue of its iterability'. The point is that something which could not function in the

absence of the current presence of the empirically determinable user *could not be* 'writing' – *no matter of what kind.*

(Glendinning 1998: pp. 119–120)[39]

The point to take from Derrida (and Glendinning's rendition of him) is that our relationship to 'writing' is a relationship to something which of necessity—i.e. in virtue of its structure—can survive our radical absence. The concept of 'writing' is generalised to include all communicable marks and this results in our relation to events of communication being a relationship to something that always has within itself the possibility to recur in our absence. This is where Agamben's invocation of potentiality becomes pertinent.

5.2. Reading Derrida within the 'Aristotelian' framework of potentiality

If we recall Agamben read Aristotle on potentiality as holding the following: potentiality is the potential to be impotential, hence actuality is potentiality holding itself in suspension; i.e. actuality is the suspension of the ability *not* to be. Drawing on his reading of Plato's 'Seventh Letter' Agamben finds Being *in* the potentiality of language. As Agamben's English translator and author of the 'Introduction' to *Potentialities*, Daniel Heller-Roazen puts it, 'Being itself, in its very actuality, appears as essentially and irreducibly potential' (2000: p. 18). The study of language is therefore the study of potentiality and thus of Being. Being is found in the potentiality of language because while an event of communication is capable of recurring without our presence, what an event presupposes is iterability i.e. the potential to communicate. Iterability, and thus the potential to communicate, is thus a necessary condition for an event of communication.

Our relation to other beings cannot be reduced to our actual interactions with others who are present in the present, our behavioural interactions presuppose that which remains—in the sense of 'goes beyond'—presence: that which remains the event. That is to say, our behavioural interactions with others presuppose a structural logic, such that my reactions to your actions in the present, in being seen as reactions (having meaning for you as such), must be iterable and thus are constituted by a logic which means they must be able to be seen as reactions in my absence.

It is important to recall where we began in Section 5.1; I said there that Searle's attempt at a refutation of Derrida's thesis missed the point, and quite fundamentally so. Therefore, one must guard against offering the same criticism of Agamben here. However, I showed, towards the end of Section 4, that Agamben's own theoretical predilections led him to misrepresent both Primo Levi and Robert Antelme. If Agamben's theory of 'language',[40] which leads him to the conclusions I identified him arriving at in Section 4, is a sound theory, then he might just dispense with Antelme and Levi as providers of phenomenological support for his theory of shame and just construct the theory on the ontological foundations deemed from his account of potentiality and language.[41] I shall show that it is not a sound theory.

5.3. Challenging Agamben: the purpose of deconstruction

In the opening paragraph of Section 5.1, I mentioned the Derridean conception of 'trace'; this finds its place in his framework in that 'trace' is inscribed in events of communication through their relationship to past events of communication—through the logic of the iterability of marks. Conducting a genealogical or an etymological investigation into a concept can serve to make the trace manifest. The purpose of such an investigation is to disrupt the 'philosophy of presence', whereby meaning is determined by attempting to discover the intentions of the author, the linguistic context in which a text was formed, etc. Such attempts at discovery endorse the logic of presence in that in attempting to recover the meaning of a text they attempt to reconstruct the presence of the author, the 'I' (intentions), the context of writing, etc.; in doing so they deny the trace. Thus such theories are reductionist and in being so are misleading through their suppression of the trace. A genealogical or an etymological investigation moves in the other direction, as it were, not even attempting to reconstruct presence (in any form: context, intentions, etc.) it rather attempts to make manifest the 'trace' of previous events.

Where genealogy and etymology differ is in the weighting they give to the form of historical investigation of a concept. Genealogy lays emphasis on examination of the stream of events of communication, highlighting the tributaries that flow into the stream and their effects on its course (the meaning of the concept). Etymology favours searching for the source of the stream—the origins of the concept, the originary event of communication involving that mark—taking that to have significance for the course of that stream further downstream—for the meaning of current events of communication.[42]

Both genealogical and etymological investigations are employed so as to disrupt pictures of an event of communication that deem the meaning of the event to be reducible to 'presence'. The purpose of Derrida's formulation is to unsettle the philosophy of presence from its hegemony as a metaphysical picture of meaning (and here 'meaning' should be taken in the broad sense of 'what we mean to each other', 'what I mean when I say *x*', 'what *x* means', and 'what it means to be human', etc.). This he began in his early engagement with Husserl.[43] The original step in the critique was the establishment of the theory; this is done by identification of the structural logic of the mark, i.e. the iterability of communicable marks. The next step is to deconstruct the philosophy of presence by giving voice to the trace. As Derrida puts it towards the end of his early essay on Husserl's theory of signs, 'it remains, then, for us to *speak*, to make our voices *resonate* throughout the corridors in order to make up for the break-up of presence' (Derrida 1973: p. 104).

How we make our voices resonate, and in what context, is important. I suggest that the Derridean 'method', on its own terms, should be to engage in a genealogy of a concept and thus to give voice to the *other* (the *other* non-present—non-contextual, non-intentional, etc.—aspect of meaning). This serves to give voice to that marginalised by conventional approaches; it serves to bring to our attention both the contingent nature of current meanings and the contingency of the changes which have led us to our current meanings, as rendered by the various philosophies of presence, i.e. change is not always the result of the progress of reason. It serves, therefore, to give voice to that suppressed by the philosophy of presence. Agamben, however, favours etymology. Etymological investigation can serve to bring awareness to the contingent nature of the current meanings of terms. However, *HS* and *RA* are littered with references to the origins of concepts and Agamben does not examine such origins merely to bring about awareness of the contingency of the current meanings of terms, nor simply to disrupt those meanings as rendered by the various philosophies of presence. His strict division between ethical and juridical categories that is at the heart of both texts, and to which much of Levi's writing is said to lend support, is deemed in the first instance from etymological investigations of 'guilt' (*culpa*) and 'witness' (*superstes* and *testis*), and their origins in Roman jurisprudence. The discussion in *HS* of the ambiguity inherent to the concept 'sacred' is deemed from its early Latin origins. The point of making the trace manifest is, as I have noted, to disrupt the philosophy of presence. However, Agamben's etymological investigations are not designed to merely serve this purpose. They frequently go beyond giving voice to the trace, rather being proposed as alternative *accounts*, the true account, of the meaning of the term under investigation. This is then to exchange one philosophy of presence for another.[44]

To illustrate, think of the philosophy of presence in the guise of a prominent current picture of meaning, such as meaning being conveyed by presence of the intentions of the author (speaker) of a text. Take this as one side of a coin. Given Derrida's critique of such a theory of presence, and his remarks about the structural logic of communicable marks, i.e. their iterability, we take the picture of meaning offered by the 'intentions-of-the-author account' to suppress the role of the trace of previous events of communication in the meaning of communicable marks. We therefore give voice to the trace, to the other, through a genealogical investigation of the concept. Take this as the other side of the coin. For Derrida, the point, on his own account of deconstruction, *should be* to keep the coin spinning. To let one side show and not the other is to give into the philosophy of presence. In other words, presence might be intentions of the author, it might be the context of production (see quotes from Derrida cited above) *and*, and this is sometimes missed—indeed, is so by Agamben—it might be the etymologically arrived at determination of the concept. Exchanging intentions of the author for a meaning deemed through an etymological investigation is to exchange one philosophy of presence for another.

Agamben's take on Derrida misinterprets Derrida as offering another theory of meaning that stands in opposition to, and corrects, those that require the presence of a (determinate) author and a (destined) recipient, or the context of production. Derrida claims to offer no theory of meaning, only a theory of deconstruction, which disrupts all attempts at a fully determinate theory of meaning. Agamben's choice of etymology rather than genealogy is indicative of his mistake. It also leads him to draw unwarranted structural parallels with his view of language, structural parallels which lead him to his misrepresentations of Levi and Antelme.

Some who have been persuaded by Agamben's writing, and have seen him as aligned with Derrida, might have misgivings as to my claims here. They might also object to my depiction of what Derrida is doing. However, there is one more point, a point which if it does not serve to show a gulf between Agamben and Derrida, then it draws both of their accounts into question—I take it to achieve the latter. The point pertains to the role accorded to the concept of iterability. If iterability is to serve as a key to and/or theory of meaning, i.e. warrant our determining meaning through etymological investigation of concepts as Agamben's practice implies, then it must be able to serve alone as something that can convey meaning. It cannot, and it is part of my argument here that

Derrida holds that it cannot. I'll use the passage from Antelme regarding the student from Bologna and his blush as an example.

5.4. Between the logic of iterability and the meaning conveying properties of trace: a Wittgensteinian challenge to deconstruction—Derridean and Agambendian

On Derrida's account a blush would be taken to be an iterable mark. It can be reproduced as a different blush on different occasions yet we recognise it as a blush on each of those occasions. Now, imagine the following: the student is called by the SS officer, as he steps forward he glances around, he looks at Antelme and in a broken voice says 'help me'. These words are iterable marks. The point is this, if iterability can capture meaning, if we let the coin stop spinning and drop on one side, if we let our gaze fix on iterability in our quest to deconstruct the philosophy of presence, then we lose the ability to distinguish between the nature of the blush and the nature of the request for help.

Why should we want to distinguish between the two? Well, if, constrained by our theory of meaning, we are unable to distinguish between iterable marks such as a 'blush' and those such as a 'verbal request for help', then we lose a basic distinction between passivity and activity. To blush is to be passively subject to a physiological reaction, albeit one borne of our seeing something, a situation, as having a certain—say, embarrassment-conveying—meaning for us.[45] To make a verbal request is to act with intent. The flight from the philosophy of presence can result in recoil to a position whereby one elides the distinction between intentional and non-intentional 'marks'. This would be a significant loss.

The concept of intention plays a role, it has a place in our lives, and in the example I have given, it allows us to distinguish a physiological reaction from a verbal request—an intentional act. Both are iterable marks, both can mean something, in that they have a place in the lives of people, and in that their meaningful content might elicit responses from others. It is unclear as to whether Derrida would/does forego the concept of intention in favour of iterability being the only key to meaning. Deconstruction does not demand it of him. However, his emphasis on the structure (logic) of writing does seem to become, at least on occasion, an essentialist thesis.[46] In making this structure—the iterability of signs—essential to meaning, Derrida relegates intentions to the status of mere contingencies. This is the point of deconstruction, to displace the philosophy of presence, by showing that those things hitherto taken to be determinate of meaning are mere contingencies, while that which we have down-played, the trace, is what is essential to meaning-ful communicative events. But in the case of differentiating between the 'blush' and the 'request', intentions are far from contingent. How might this be?

There are two problems in play here, I suggest: the first is the very fact of having a theory of meaning; of trying to say anything meaningful about 'meaning', treated in such an abstract generalised sense. Wittgenstein remarked in the *Blue Book* (1969: pp. 43–44) that 'meaning is an odd-job word', and we might do well to take this as a prophylactic to generalised accounts of meaning, such as Derrida's. For even those who pay attention to the context- and occasion-sensitivity of meaning, often progress to assume that one can discuss 'meaning' in a manner which abstracts *it*, the word 'meaning', from contexts and occasions of use. Second, there is a confusion of identification of the 'conditions for meaning' and 'content of meaning'. The two problems are intrinsically related.

Consider the following example: one of the opening scenes of Werner Herzog's (stunning) film *The Enigma of Kaspar Hauser* consists of a linger-ing, static, shot of wheat blowing back and forth in a field; over the scene Johann Pachelbel's *Kanon D-dur* is played, and the wheat's move-ment in the breeze is seemingly in time with the music. In the context of the opening of the film, this movement of the wheat has meaning; as a piece of film, or even purely as moving grass, one might also char-acterise it as an iterable mark. Does it, therefore, follow that this is what we should take meaning to be? To think about the meaning of this scene from Herzog's film, and to think of the meaning of a blush, and then to think of the meaning of a request for help, and then again to think of an order to help, to think of a *look of* abject despair . . . and we might con-tinue; to think of these things and how they come to mean something by focussing upon the structural conditions for them meaning something (iterability) is to mistake the meaning of 'meaning' in contexts, for the logical conditions for a mark being able to 'mean'.

To further illustrate, consider the following: it is a condition of my being the person here now, in the British Library reading room, enga-ging in certain acts, that certain facts hold true of some actions taking place at some time in the past (such as my parents meeting, etc.); what does this tell you about my actions here and now? It might tell you something, but you are not *driven by logic* to conclude that it can tell you anything about what I am doing here and now. Analogously, if we agree with Derrida that it must be a condition of meaning that marks are iterable, what does this tell us about the meaning of any particular mark employed on any particular occasion in any particular context?

Well, not *necessarily* anything. It is important, therefore, not to conflate 'conditions for meaning' with 'content of meaning'.

It is apparent then that there is a leap taking place, from acknowledgement of the logic of iterability to the claim that the trace of previous events of communication can convey meaning. It is important to be clear here. Of course in using an iterable mark, its past use might—we could even say, 'probably', or 'is very likely to'—impact upon the meaning of the current event of communication; however, we are not *logically compelled* to accept it as having to do so, for the logic of iterability is about conditions for, not about content of.

One might be tempted to mount a defence of Derrida here. One might argue that Derrida would not have been averse to what I say about intention having a role in the conveying of meaning of some events of communication. This might be so. However, it is not borne out by paying attention to his writings. I submit that Derrida and his followers overplay the meaning-disrupting effects of trace. They ultimately suggest an account which is sceptical about our chances of ever meaning, in a determinate sense, anything; because meaning *is* always disrupted by the trace of previous iterations of the same marks. So, in identifying the conditions of meaning with the iterability of marks, Derrida progresses to the conclusion that any attempt to determine the meaning of any event of language (writing) will be disrupted by the trace of previous iterations, and then further to the claim that, therefore, a communicative event's meaning can never be determinate. This is, to repeat, to conflate 'logical conditions for meaning' with 'content of a meaningful communicative event'. I suggest that Derrida and Agamben are led to such a conflation owing to a propensity to think of 'meaning' in too abstract a manner *and* to search for its essence. We can, therefore, respond and suggest to them that 'meaning' is a word that is used in different ways, in different language-games, on different occasions. It is a word that might not have something common, something essential, to all uses; at least nothing that is both essential and significant. Sure we can grant that iterability might well be part of the structural logic of the mark and thus be common to all meaning-conveying marks, but it does not follow from this that it is something that, of necessity, has *significance* for the meaningful content of those marks. To put it in more conventional terms, we can grant that iterability is a necessary condition for a mark being a meaning-conveying mark, but holding that to be the case does not entail that it is a sufficient condition for that same mark conveying meaning.

The recoil from intention is also, I suggest, based on a particular assumption about what intention must be: e.g. a mental process. We do not *need* to think of intention in this way, as something having queer properties which bestow meaning through some sort of mental act. In any case, we can stay agnostic on the nature of intention when differentiating between the intentional employment of marks and a non-intentional, though meaningful, instance of a mark. In this case we can merely identify the former, for procedural purposes, in a far more mundane way. Here we might merely note that the relevant distinction for distinguishing an intentional employment of a mark from a non-intentional one is that we *learn* to wield the former; that is to say, we learn to master the intentional expression of concepts as part of our lives with words, and with others; learning such ways of employing concepts involves not merely learning criteria for their expression, but also learning to see the significance they have for us and others. We learn what it is to—to coin a phrase of Cora Diamond's—have a life with concepts. In contrast we do not need to learn how to blush, in order to blush; to blush is to physiologically *react to* a way of seeing a (meaningful) state of affairs—as opposed to intentionally act. Indeed, it is central to the meaning a blush has for us that it is not something which is employed with intent to communicate something by the person who is blushing.

Derrida and (even more so) Agamben forego this distinction and their investigations thus become one-sided. It is this one-sided nature which leads Agamben, at great cost, to try to force Levi and Antelme into moulds in which they just will not fit. This collapsing of intentional (normative) marks (actions) and non-intentional marks (movements, physiological reactions) through a neglect of the place of learning in human life is even more surprising given Agamben's approving references to Aristotle.

6. Towards conclusion

What can be learned from the engagement with Agamben is that in thinking about emotions, we think about people in the world, meaningfully engaged with the world and with others. Unfortunately, while Agamben makes this initial step beyond (say) Griffiths, he swiftly takes a step backwards, for he allows himself to become constrained by a view of how things must be, and this is forced onto him by his theory of meaning. What I shall take into the next chapter is the sense in which philosophical enquiries into emotion should be conducted by engaging with the expressions of those experiencing emotion.

I wish to finish with a note that will make the title clear (I hope). To make our voices resonate and to make up for the break up of presence might well be, philosophically, a worthwhile endeavour; we can even grant—for now—that it may even be necessary. That is, we might well be willing to grant that it is a good thing for philosophers to engage in so that they might seek to reset the balance after the domination of the philosophy of presence—to begin the coin spinning after a history of showing just one side, as it were. A genealogical investigation, in making manifest the trace, might serve an important purpose *in this respect.* But when one engages in etymology and brings this to bear on testimony one misses the point on two counts. First, as I have argued, one exchanges one philosophy of presence for another. Second, one brings philosophical reflection upon the logical structure of our lives with our words to bear in an area in which it has no business. Testimony is not philosophy's playground; the philosopher has no *right* to speak, no *right* to impose his theoretical agenda, when reading testimony. In doing such the philosopher *renders* the meaning of the words of testimony, where one should rather be *identifying* the meaning of those words. Whereof one cannot speak, as a philosopher, one must be silent.[47]

3
Emotion, Cognition, and World

At the beginning of Chapter 1, I said that the dominant research program in the philosophy of the emotions for over 30 years has been what is variously called cognitivism, propositional attitude theory, or (quasi-)judgementalism. The number of terms is apt to confuse; so to begin I shall try to settle on one and then sort through the main differences. As we saw, Paul Griffiths refers to this—somewhat disparate—group as propositional attitude theorists. This is misleading. Griffiths claims that theorists from Anthony Kenny (1963) and Robert Solomon (1976) to Robert Nash (1989), Michael Stocker (1987), and Robert C. Roberts (1988) hold that to have an emotion is to have a specific type of propositional attitude. This misrepresents quite a number of those Griffiths intends as his targets; even a 'pure cognitivist' such as Solomon does not hold the emotions to necessarily have propositional content (see Solomon 2004: p. 77). In this respect Griffiths runs the risk of electing as his nemesis no more than a straw man. Similarly judgementalism[1] is too narrow; if we broaden it to quasi-judgementalism,[2] we will have included many of those philosophers who have studied the emotions over the past 30 years. However, the term is still too narrow as it implies that the thoughts that constitute the emotion are judgements (or quasi-judgements/evaluative beliefs) and this is simply false as regards those theorists such as Anthony Kenny (1963) who take the cognitive and explanatory elements of emotions to be (plain, non-evaluative) beliefs, and those such as Robert C. Roberts (1988, 2003) who take them to be construals. We could work with the term employed by many cognitive psychologists, and that which Jesse Prinz (2004a) employs to denote the non- or counter-Jamesian theories of emotions: 'appraisal theory'. However, here we might risk running into confusion, for both

Prinz and Jenifer Robinson also talk of non- or pre-cognitive 'apprais-als' from a computational or a neuroscience perspective, respectively. Despite some problems, the term that seems best suited, therefore, is cognitivism.[3]

The emergence of cognitivism in the philosophy of emotions owes much to Anthony Kenny's work, which was in turn influenced by Gilbert Ryle's *Concept of Mind* and Elizabeth Anscombe's *Intention*, in addition to Kenny's grounding in ancient and medieval philosophy. Kenny's was the first work in the analytic tradition to try to think in terms of emotions as constituted and explained by 'thoughts'. Similarly, but with a different set of influences—chiefly Sartre and Nietzsche—Robert Solomon's work in the early 1970s advanced an account of the emotions which sought to explain them in terms of the judgements of the agent. The signific-ance of this 'turn to "thoughts"' is that hitherto it had been broadly assumed that emotions were feelings, irrupting within the individual as irrational disturbances in an otherwise rational life.[4] The main impetus behind 'feeling theories' of emotion in the twentieth century was what has come to be referred to as the James-Lange theory. William James (1884) and Carl Lange (1885) independently advanced the theory that the emotions were responses to patterned changes in the body (sensa-tions). In advancing theories of the emotions which took them to be constituted by 'thoughts', Kenny and Solomon, and the many that have followed since, see emotions as rational responses to, or perceptions of, our environment.

The name 'cognitivism' in the philosophy of emotions, therefore, denotes an account which explains emotions in terms of the thoughts which constitute them (or are, at least, necessary to their intelligibility). This is only part of the story. Of course 'thought' is a somewhat imprecise term; by this I mean merely that when one invokes 'thoughts' the invoc-ation often merits the response: 'what sort of thoughts precisely?' And this has served to fuel much of the debate within cognitivism. What is the nature of these thoughts? Are they beliefs? Are they evaluative beliefs? Are they judgements? Are they combinations of distinct beliefs and desires? Are they perceptions? Or are they combinations of some of these plus a little affect, a little context, a little feeling, or a little narrative? In what follows, I shall explore some answers to these questions by way of leading us to a way in which I think it fruitful to think about emotion.

I ended Chapter 1 by hinting at a role for—a form of—'conceptual analysis'. This chapter will take the hint and try to implement it. We saw that Griffiths was apt to mislead us into thinking, with him, that noth-ing could be learned about what the emotions *really* are by engaging in any form of conceptual analysis. We also saw that Griffiths' alternative, an approach rooted in a reconstructed natural kind semantics, faced insurmountable problems. So, while we began Chapter 1 by being informed by Griffiths that conceptual analysis had been the cause of all our problems, needing replacement with his natural kind semantics, we ended the chapter by returning to 'conceptual analysis' as a provider of hope in our further understanding. What I hope will transpire in the course of this chapter is that what we take to be conceptual analysis—i.e. what form of analysis is suited to understanding our concepts—is crucially important.

Although it is the term I shall work with, 'cognitivism' is far from informative; while it captures something in general—at a minimum, that emotions are responses to the world and are not 'non-cognitive', as that term is used in metaethics[5]—it does not really serve to denote a coherent group of theorists, much less a 'research program'. In order that we can work our way through, I shall divide cognitivists into three categories; I shall call these categories syllogistic cognitivism, reason-giving cognitivism, and world-taking cognitivism. These should be treated as three 'ideal types'. For, although it is still commonplace to talk of the philosophy of emotions as a new discipline, one should not infer from this that it is a minor one. It is simply beyond the scope of a single chapter to deal in depth with all the cognitivist theories of emotion, hence the ideal types.[6]

This chapter takes the following form.

- Section 1 will critically engage the reflex/affect distinction. I do this because the existence of affective emotional episodes, often depicted as the existence of affective emotions, are seen by many as posing a problem for cognitive accounts. The thought seems to be that one can have an emotion which is necessarily closed to cognition; the latent thought seems to be that one can have an emotion which is purely *non-conceptual*;[7] some, such as Jenefer Robinson (1995), even go so far as to recommend this as what is essential to all emotions, what emotions really are, as it were. I show that there is little reason to hold this view. Indeed, to hold this view is to merely make manifest one's prejudice in such matters.
- Section 2 provides an outline of what I present here as three 'ideal types' of cognitivism: syllogistic, reason-giving, and world-taking. I recommend one of these as a framework for understanding emotion: world-taking cognitivism.

- Section 3 discusses a reason-giving cognitivist account of shame, offered by Gabriele Taylor, and identifies some problems this account faces. The major problem facing reason-giving cognitivist accounts of the emotions is the problem of recalcitrant emotion: e.g. where one (say) fears something even though one believes the object of one's fear to be harmless/safe, i.e. not warranting fear. I explore the notion of recalcitrant emotion with particular focus upon shame. I suggest that world-taking cognitivism need not see the 'problem' of recalcitrant emotion as a problem, in that it need not accept the depiction of such phenomena as recalcitrant at all. I do this with reference to Primo Levi's writings on shame.
- Section 4 compares world-taking cognitivism (as I present it[8]) with a recent theory of emotions as 'embodied appraisals' (Prinz 2003a, b, 2004a, b). Prinz's theory is also an attempt to incorporate the insights afforded by cognitivism while also responding to the problem posed by (so called) recalcitrant emotion.[9]

The chapter, *as a work of criticism*, operates something of a pincer movement: I begin by showing that acknowledgement of affective emotions—and, indeed, reflex actions—as being seemingly devoid of cognitive content on their taking place, *does not* necessitate the conclusion that they are, in principle, cognitively closed, non-conceptual or hard-wired. The other arm of the pincers closes in (as it were) later in the chapter. Here I attempt to persuade the reader that shame—as an emotion generally understood to be a paradigm of a higher cognitive emotion—can be purely felt; i.e. shame can be felt in the absence of a stable set of propositional beliefs about one's shame.[10] What purpose does such an acknowledgement serve? Well, most importantly it gives us a better grasp of human emotional experience. One might be forgiven for thinking this a point of marginal significance; however, it has been an unfortunate consequence of cognitivist accounts of the higher cognitive emotions that they have often been explained (or been judged by critics to have been so) in abstraction from feeling—leading to what Michael Stocker (1987: pp. xv–xvi, 235) and Peter Goldie (2000: p. 50) have (independently and for different purposes) referred to as 'Mr Spock theories of the emotions'.[11,12] The other purpose that the acknowledgement of purely-felt-shame serves is that it provides the context in which I can discuss the problem of recalcitrant emotions and offer my dissolution of the problem, without the recourse to a modular theory of mind.

There is one issue, which in different guises recurs throughout this chapter: how to make sense of perception and/or cognition, when neither seems present, yet the person acts in a manner (has emotional responses) which suggests some such has taken place? This appears in Section 1 in the course of my discussion of Jenefer Robinson's claim that 'skin "knew" ' (when the person did not); in Section 2 it reappears when I discuss Peter Goldie's suggestion that we have 'feelings directed at objects' (in contradistinction to, and in the absence of, thoughts, beliefs, and judgements being so); in Section 3 it appears in the course of my discussion of reason-giving cognitivist responses to the problem of recalcitrance; and in Section 4 it appears in the course of the discussion of that which Jesse Prinz identifies as the 'Emotion Problem', and his 'solution' to the problem by invoking sub-personal modules with psychosemantic content.

Providing an adequate understanding of emotional experience would seem to require an adequate understanding of the phenomenon of cognition in the absence of cognition (as it were). The task is, as I take it here, to provide an understanding which does not rely upon the mere—unsupported—accordance of mysterious powers to biological or psychological mechanisms (or modules).

1. Reflex, affect, and closure to cognition

1.1. Exploring the distinction between reflex and affect

There are a number of reasons why reflex and affect are often taken to present a problem for cognitive accounts. The main reason is that affective emotional episodes are taken to be cognitively closed, in principle; that is to say, not only they 'run'[13] without any need for manifest cognition, but cognition can have no role in that running. This is usually taken to imply a number of related points: first, such episodes are taken to be paradigmatic cases of all emotions (e.g. Robinson 1995) or of a class or kind of emotions (e.g. Griffiths 1997); second, their content is non- or pre-conceptual; third, they are pan-cultural and 'hard-wired'; and fourth, their proper study should be undertaken by cognitive neuroscientists and evolutionary psychologists, not philosophers preoccupied with meanings.[14]

In Chapter 1 we saw that the conflict Griffiths identified between the cognitivist (propositional attitude theory/conceptual analysis) approach to emotion and what he took to be the scientific approach rested upon conceptual confusion. It is pertinent then to reiterate what I said there. Griffiths' conceptual confusion and the (subsequent) collapse of his theory of natural kind semantics do not necessarily obviate scientific study of the emotions, along the lines of Ekman *et al.*[15] What it does rule out is the putative conflict between the 'scientific' approach (championed by Griffiths) and the philosophical approach, pursued by those philosophers falling under the broad heading of cognitivism. The identifying of the emotions along (broadly speaking) cognitivist lines does not *necessitate* detracting from the affective qualities of many emotions.[16] (Nor does it necessitate a denial that biological (evolved) mechanisms are involved.) Indeed, where many, even most, episodes of fear and disgust are concerned, it seems no more than a trivial truth to assert that they are often primarily affective in nature, while only secondarily cognitive. The converse seems to be, equally obviously, the case for an emotion such as shame.[17] However, this, again, is to assert little more than a truism. What is of importance is the *nature* of the classification: are the affective emotions cognitively closed and thus something we might want to claim are of a different (non-intersecting) class of emotions to the higher cognitive emotions?[18] Or cognitively closed and supervened upon by cognition, where the latter exists?[19]

The affective–cognitive distinction is not as clear as one might at first take it to be.[20] The distinction fails to genuinely apprehend such things as habit, enculturation into a second nature (*Bildung*), and learning and becoming proficient in a complex practice,[21] and this is without mentioning our ability to 'deprogram' our habits, *Bildung*, and learning. For every empirical study that claims to demonstrate the disgust response in (pre-cognitive/pre-linguistic) human infants, one can find another which counters it; indeed, this would be enough in itself to sow seeds of doubt, without our noting the problems one faces in deciding what such infants should/should not be disgusted at.

However, let us say—for now—that the matter is settled to our satisfaction; we are shown that disgust is not learnt, but is rather an affective state: e.g. young babies not yet old enough to be habituated, encultured, or taught anything can be shown to act with disgust towards certain objects; thus disgust (towards this object) is non-conceptual, is pan-cultural, is hard-wired, and should be studied by cognitive neuroscientists. But then we are presented with some further questions. How do our scientists differentiate this affective state from a reflex (such as the choking or gagging reflex)? Well, usually some distinction is made whereby the *immediate* nature of reflex is cited in contradistinction to the *persistent* nature of the affective emotion. *Emotions are persistent states, they occur over time, while reflexes are immediate.* But this merely leads one to another set of questions: *how* immediate does something have to be to be said to be immediate? And *how* persistent does something have to be to be said to be persistent? Well of course the answer to these questions can rest on nothing other than a matter of judgement, or even *fiat*; this might then suggest some question-begging is taking place, hereabouts.

Nevertheless, even without our raising of such questions, we are thrown back in the direction of cognition; for if (affective) emotions are persistent (and let us just be satisfied here to read 'persistent' as meaning 'not a reflex') then there seems, at least intuitively, an opportunity for their having some cognitive content. Let us explore this from a number of directions.

The first direction then we might call 'grammatical'. Here we look at the limits of the application of 'reflex'; we do not stipulate such limits through our linguistic intuitions, or our (professed) knowledge of 'logical grammar', and nor do we do so based upon our observance of previous uses of the term.[22] Such methods are little better than the invoking of intuitions as a philosophical argument. What we want to understand is what those for whom the affect–reflex distinction is operative understand by the distinction. It is *their grammar*, the grammatical rules implicit in their use of language, of which we seek to avail ourselves. Well, affect programs for Ekman *et al.* are not reflexes because they persist, and because Ekman and his various co-authors *believe* that the psychological mechanisms underlying them are different from those underlying reflexes; as Griffiths writes, 'Ekman excludes startle from the category of affect programs because he **believes** that the psychological mechanisms are not of the same kind as those underlying the affect program' (*What Emotions Really Are*: p. 246; emphasis mine).[23] What we have is an affect program defined as a persistent psychological event, in contradistinction to a reflex which, though having a degree of phenomenological similarity, is characteristically an immediate psychological event. In drawing the distinction thus, our theorists have said nothing which excludes-of-necessity a role for cognition in the latter. Indeed, Ekman (1984: p. 329) readily acknowledges that we can cognitively overcome the affect program emotions. So, both the distinction itself and Ekman's explicit remarks about the affect program emotions would seem to *suggest the possibility* of affect being *at least* open to cognition, rather than closed in principle to the same.[24] Or, put another way, there is nothing intrinsic to their characterisation of affective emotions which suggests that they are *in principle* cognitively closed.

1.2. Who, what, where, knows?

There are, however, some attempts to buttress the anti-cognitivist claim through the *extrapolation from* experimental results.[25] For example, in a paper arguing for an understanding of affective emotions as non-cognitive, non-conceptual, and primary[26]—i.e. all emotions, correctly called so, supervene upon these basic affective emotions— Jenefer Robinson (1995) discusses some experiments which in turn were discussed by the psychologist Robert Zajonc (1984); Robinson writes:

> In the subception experiments, subjects are presented with ten nonsense syllables, five of which are associated with electric shocks. Eventually, the subject gets a galvanic skin response before the shock occurs. Then the stimuli are presented very fast and the subjects are asked to guess what they are. Even when the subjects guess wrong, the level of galvanic skin response is higher for the stimuli that were associated with the electric shocks: the subjects' skin 'knew' which ones were associated with shock, although the subjects did not!
>
> (Robinson 1995: pp. 59–60)[27]

Before a philosopher suggests to us that skin 'knew', even with a scare-quote qualifier, one would hope that they might first explore other possible ways of understanding the results; Robinson seems not to have done so. Here is one possibility: maybe in guessing wrongly the subjects were aware that there was a good chance that they might well have done so (guessed wrongly) and thus prepared themselves for the possibility of a shock. To be aware that one is *guessing* is to know that there is a decent chance of having guessed incorrectly. It is a feature of the literature that such philosophers tend to make the following moves:

1. Cognition is absent, i.e. it is not manifest to the person—sometimes the stronger claim is made that in certain situations it can't *possibly* be present (Robinson);[28]
2. While cognition is (or must be) absent, experiments show that certain physiological reactions take place with a regularity and congruence with events that suggests something akin to cognition is taking place;
3. The conclusion is drawn that some sub-personal systems/ mechanisms—unbeknownst to the person, i.e. of which there is no awareness at the personal level—are doing something akin to perceiving and cognising: 'Bob's skin knew, but Bob didn't!'.

What we need to be clear about then is what licenses the conclusion? It is certainly not the premises taken alone. What licenses the conclusion is, I venture, distinctly opaque. Furthermore, think of what it is to say that 'skin knew', in any meaningful sense. Has Bob's skin grasped the concepts of 'electricity' and 'pain', and also the (internal) relationship between these concepts as regards human beings? What would it be for Bob and his skin to seriously disagree on this matter? If kept alive artificially, could a piece of skin, literally detached from the person, 'know'? Could the skin of a corpse 'know'? It is vitally important to be clear here, Robinson is *not* talking about physiological reactions to stimuli, nor of biological mechanisms processing structured data; she is talking about 'skin **"knowing"** ' that *it is about to get an electric shock*, and preparing itself for such. To mount a defence through drawing attention to the scare-quote qualifier that she puts around 'knew' doesn't help Robinson; she is still attributing cognitive abilities to something sub-personal (something not Bob).[29] Robinson, therefore, is illustrative because of her initially bold (and somewhat eccentric) claim. Why this makes her so illustrative is that this claim of hers helps make us alive to the thought that there is something to be *prima facie* sceptical about in all appeals to sub-personal cognition as a solution to the seeming absence of manifest cognition at the personal level.

1.3. Reflex, affect, and cognitive overcoming

To return to reflex, affect, and cognition, let us approach the matter from another perspective. Fear is often taken to be a paradigm of an affective emotion. Now, it is beyond contest that one can train oneself to overcome (affective) fear.[30] I do not merely mean to suggest here the ability to master one's fear, but, rather, to actually *absent* the fear in comparable fear scenarios: future situations where in the past one would have always been fearful—in an affect-type way—one is so no longer. All that I seek to suggest here then, in line with Ekman, and in contrast to Robinson, is that affective emotions are not *necessarily* cognitively closed; we can cognitively overcome them. What seems to define them therefore—in contradistinction to the higher cognitive emotions—is *not* cognitive closure, but rather the *relative* lack of *manifest* cognition; it is on this, that it is important to be clear.

Let us not be satisfied and stop here. So far I have sought to exploit the affect program theorist's own distinction between affective emotions and reflexes and in the process support their case against Robinson. But what of those reflexes? Again, let us take a paradigm case of a reflex response mechanism: the gagging/choking mechanism. Can we not find examples of cognitively overcoming—absenting—such reflexes? Well, yes. It is difficult, to say the least, to understand the ability to undertake and increase 'proficiency' in a number of widespread—and some less-widespread— human practices without acknowledging that one can cognitively overcome reflex responses. I list a number here: smoking cigars and cigarettes, performing an act of fellatio, sword swallowing, undergoing a gastroscopy (gagging/choking); wearing contact lenses, participating in combat sports—boxing, some martial arts, etc. (blinking/flinching); trekking in the Amazonian rain forests, regular watching of horror— 'slasher'—films, having a partner and child that find it amusing to jump out on one when one is least expecting it, working on a firing range, firing a submachine gun[31] (startle). I'm sure the list could continue.

The defence might be offered that each of these examples is not an example of the cognitive overcoming of a reflex, but rather, the cognitive overcoming of an affective emotion which is a close relative of the reflex. On this account, when we manage to stop ourselves gagging in order to enjoy a cigarette or perform an act of sword swallowing, we are overcoming our fear of suffocation which led us to react *as if to* gag. When we overcome our propensity to flinch as one way of attempting to last more than a few seconds upright in the boxing ring, we do so by overcoming our fear of the punch which led to our reacting *as if to* flinch. These responses to my challenge, however, do no more than embroil our theorists in a circular definition of a reflex: a genuine reflex will be, then, anything for which we have yet to provide an example of cognitive overcoming of the reflex. To take such reasoning as one's starting point in understanding emotions is to take an *a posteriori* claim and treat it as *a priori* to any subsequent investigation. In addition, what these potential attempts at defence also do is suggest how one can embed reflexes in wider cognitive schema, which give them sense. It is an interesting question to muse—and I merely suggest it here without following up and musing—to ask why we take gagging to be a reflex action and discrete with respect to the fear of choking or suffocating, while we do not take blushing to be a reflex action and discrete with respect to embarrassment.

What I hope to have shown here—in addition to my suggestions in Chapter 1—is that attempts, *at any level*, to deny a *potential* role for cognition in emotion rest on prejudice. Moreover, the thought that reflex/affect and cognition are discrete categories—i.e. something is either affective or cognitive but never (possessing the potential to be) both—is to commit the fallacy of division.[32] Henceforth, therefore, my use of the terms 'affective emotion' and 'higher cognitive emotions' merely indexes the phenomenological (and mundane and trivial) sense in which some emotional episodes are more affective and others more cognitive; I'll take a paradigm case of the former to be (affective) 'fear', and of the latter to be 'shame'; both can, and often do, appear in converse guise.

2. Three ideal types of cognitive accounts of emotion

As I noted above, I divide cognitive accounts into three ideal types: syllogistic, reason-giving, and world-taking.

2.1. Syllogistic cognitivism

Syllogistic cognitivism defines the emotion in terms of constitutive beliefs (judgements or thoughts can be employed here). These beliefs take syllogistic form, thus providing a rational explanation of the emotional state. So my pride[33] in my large house can be rationally explained by placing the beliefs that constitute that pride into syllogistic form. This is what Gabriele Taylor has called objective cognitivism, and she identifies Donald Davidson's (1976) account as an exemplar of such a position.

> Firstly, one (or more) of the beliefs makes the emotional experience what it is, it identifies it as, for example, anger, and so differentiates it from other states, such as envy or jealousy. But secondly, there will also be further beliefs because of which the person experiencing the emotion will hold the identificatory belief(s). These are constitutive of the emotion in that they are causally responsible for it being what it is: I hold the first, identificatory belief only because I hold this second(s).
>
> (Taylor 1985: p. 2)

Davidson structures his account of 'propositional emotion' in syllogistic form, and Taylor gives an example of a (Davidsonian) syllogistic explanation of pride:[34]

Premise 1: 'I have purchased a large house';
Premise 2: 'the ownership of large houses is praiseworthy'—this serves as the universal premise.[35]
Conclusion: 'I am praiseworthy'—this follows from the two premises.

The person's pride is explained through the invocation of and conclusion drawn from the universal belief, 'the ownership of large houses is praiseworthy'.

This is syllogistic cognitivism: any theory where the explanation of the emotion can be rendered in syllogistic form and in which a universal belief forms one of the premises, thus playing an explanatory role. Such a theory is endorsed by Davidson and (according to Davidson) by

David Hume. It is not a view held by many of those who are identified as philosophers of the emotions.

2.2. Reason-giving cognitivism

Reason-giving cognitivism differs in that there is no requirement for a universal belief. In her 1985 book *Pride, Shame and Guilt*, Gabriele Taylor, while still seeking to provide a rational explanation of our emotions, rejects the necessary invocation—necessary for explanatory purposes—of a universal belief. Taylor takes issue with the primary explanatory role of the universal belief that Davidson demands. In short, on Davidson's account, if we—that is we, the enquirers searching for beliefs that will explain the emotional state—dig deep enough we will find a belief that is universal in form, and thus enabling us to construct the syllogism. What Taylor denies is that this universal belief will necessarily serve such an explanatory role,thus being relevant to the emotional state in the way in which Davidson thinks it will.

So, both Taylor and Davidson seek rational intelligibility; however, for Taylor the word 'rational' means no more than 'supported by reasons offered by the agent of the emotional state'. Taylor writes,

[i]f rational intelligibility implies the kind of deductive reasoning Davidson suggests, then I am now speaking of a different or an additional, kind of intelligibility. It is still rational, in that the explanation is in terms of the agent's reasons for his identificatory belief, and these beliefs in turn are open to rational assessment.

(ibid.: p. 14)

Taylor's replacement for the explanatory universal belief of Davidson's that she has dismissed is rather to look at the agent's wider history. An examination of other beliefs held by the agent, she claims, helps to make those beliefs that constitute the agent's emotional state intelligible; she sums this up by saying,

At this point the constraints on what is explanatory are not provided by what must be the case in all rationality. The appeal is no longer to the wholly rational being; it is to the admittedly far less neat and precise notion of what it would be human and natural for a person to feel under certain circumstances, given that person's relevant other beliefs and attitudes.

(ibid.)

What is important to note here, and Taylor does so, is that what the relevant framework is will change depending on the object of the emotional state. That is to say, it depends on the nature of the beliefs as to where we should look for those further beliefs that will render the emotional state intelligible to us.

This is reason-giving cognitivism: here what is significant for explanatory purposes are the reasons *we can find* for someone feeling the way they do,[36] given certain other beliefs and attitudes they might hold. These reasons are only required to make the emotional state of this person rationally intelligible to us; and they need fulfil no further criteria.[37]

This is what one might call the paradigm case of philosophical cognitivism in the philosophy of the emotions; with small changes in emphasis and/or terminology, one might find echoes of other prominent cognitivist theories of the emotions in Taylor's account. For example, one need only replace 'evaluative beliefs' with 'judgements' and one will find that one has something very close to Robert Solomon's (1976, 2003c) account. One can replace the 'evaluative beliefs' with 'evaluative thoughts held in mind by intentional states of comfort or discomfort' and one has Patricia Greenspan's (1992) version. Furthermore, when Taylor writes, 'The appeal is no longer to the wholly rational being [as in Davidson]; it is to the admittedly far less neat and precise notion of what it would be **human and natural for a person to feel under certain circumstances, given that person's relevant other beliefs and attitudes'** (1985: p. 14; emphasis mine), one might replace 'relevant other beliefs and attitudes' with an explicit appeal to/invocation of a person's narrative and a concomitant modification of what the person 'feel[s]' by claiming that the feelings are intentional; then one would find oneself with something very close to Peter Goldie's (2000) account. Moving from early cognitivist accounts such as found in Taylor and Solomon, through to later accounts advanced by (say) Greenspan and Goldie, what one finds is increasing sensitivity, further attempts, to adequately characterise the phenomenology while retaining the early cognitivist insights. To take emotions in terms of evaluative beliefs or judgements just seems too cold and detached with respect to the experience of an emotional episode. It also—as I shall detail below (this chapter, Section 3)—gives rise to problems in accounting for recalcitrant emotions. However, Taylor or Goldie, Solomon or Greenspan, the structure is almost the same. What all these versions of reason-giving cognitivism share is the commitment to the thought that emotions can be type-individuated by their cognitive constituents, which in turn serve as reasons for being in the emotional state.

2.2.1. *Goldie and 'Feeling Towards': to be, or not to be, cognition?*

I mentioned Peter Goldie as one of those to whom I am referring as reason-giving cognitivists. Goldie (2000, ch. 3, 2004) presents an interesting test case. I (very strongly) suspect he would offer resistance to this characterisation of him as a reason-giving cognitivist. However, I think the characterisation sticks. In short, Goldie is responding to a similar qualm to that to which we saw Robinson respond, above: how to make sense of cognition taking place when there is no evidence of cognition taking place? Goldie's response is to give explanatory priority to the 'intentional feelings', that is 'feelings directed at objects in the world', in contrast to/instead of perceptions of (which can give rise to beliefs about and/or judgements on) those objects. However, Goldie's tactics have a structural similarity to those employed by Robinson; while he doesn't make any claim quite so bizarre as that 'skin knows' (even acknowledging the scare-quote qualifier), he does make an analogous move in merely identifying the locus of cognition to be something that has hitherto been assumed to be *pre* or *non* or *a* cognitive: feeling.[38] Goldie's strategy can be broken down as follows:

1. Cognition is absent, i.e. it is not manifest to the person: the person is not perceiving, in the sense of believing or judging something in the world. Put another way, the person is not taking a propositional stance towards anything. The person is not directing his/her thoughts onto things in the world (at least not the things which would count as objects of the emotion).
2. (While cognition is absent, and the person is not directing his/her thoughts onto things in the world), the person is in an emotional state and this suggests that something *akin* to cognition is taking place, i.e. something akin to the perception and evaluation of an object.
3. The conclusion is drawn that something else, other than thoughts, must be playing a role akin to that usually referred to as cognition; *something* must be intentional, must be directed onto things in the world. Since cognition is not present but feelings are, it must be feelings that are directed onto things in the world.

For the simple reason that his claim is bolstered by the general phenomenology of much emotional experience, Goldie is clearly better off than was Robinson (this chapter, Section 1.1); but is he enough-so for his account to avoid difficulty? I think not, as things stand. Not only does it strike one as a little too convenient, more problematically, it leaves hanging in the air how we are best to make sense of such 'intentional feelings' without invoking standard perception-terms. It can seem too convenient because, as we saw with Robinson, all that has been done in order to circumvent the problem is to attribute certain powers that are standardly associated with a person to something sub-personal. Goldie might respond and say that he merely means that sometimes we feel something about a thing in the world without perceiving that thing (holding a propositional belief *that*), thus 'feeling about' must be invoked. But think this through; can one feel something about a thing without perceiving (in the broad sense) the thing? It is opaque as to what such 'feeling about' could be like if it does not involve perception of the thing. And, of course, Goldie then readily acknowledges perception's role in this notion of feeling towards; so feeling towards is then akin to non-propositional perception (with 'felt quality'). But what is doing the (non-propositional) 'perceiving' here? How is it done? Well Goldie tells us such feeling towards *is* a sort of perception. This starts to sound like the invocation of something akin to intuitions about the things in the world. Might it not rather be that we can perceive non-propositionally (as do, for example, dogs) and this gives rise to the feelings?

Goldie might go one of two ways: one way would be to go the route of attributing some queer quasi-perceptual (and quasi-conceptual) powers to a theoretically postulated sub-personal feeling system; this is the modular way, similar to that recently advanced by Jesse Prinz (2003a, b, 2004a, b). If Goldie doesn't follow Prinz (and I think he would be unwise to do so; see Section 4), then I think he needs to rethink the terms of his theory, for the solution he proposes is forced upon him by assuming that standard perception must be propositional. This is what leads him to conclude that if emotions are not propositional and they are often, characteristically, felt, then it is feeling which (non-propositionally) perceives. Goldie responds to a familiar question levelled at reason-giving cognitivists by saying 'well, feelings can be about things too'. And this is to be a reason-giving cognitivist: sometimes the reasons will be object-directed thoughts, sometimes object-directed feelings. Whether thoughts or feelings, their structure is the same; only their content and phenomenology are different.[39] If you doubt my claims here, consider the following: Solomon readily admits non-propositional, non-manifest, content to his judgementalist emotional schema; does Goldie give us any advance—in anything other than a nominal sense—on Solomon? Thus are we better off than when we began by acknowledging that sometimes cognition seems to take place (we *have a* stance towards the world) when there is no evidence of cognition taking place (no evidence of *having taken* or of *taking* the stance)? Goldie has told us that that which gives warrant to the 'seems' (a feeling) is what is doing the taking of the stance, while not telling us how that might be done.

Goldie's route is tempting. Most of the time, talk of *people* perceiving is both acceptable to us and sufficient for our purposes. Sometimes such talk seems to be unavailable to us because the person simply does not appear (to themselves or to us) to have *done* any perceiving (there just seems to be little that affords awareness of having done so). On other occasions the person might well be in a state that, to all intents and purposes, relies on his having perceived, while at the same time we happily acknowledge him not to have *done* so, in the standard sense of a person perceiving. This is what is brought out by the experiments that Robinson discussed, and by an analysis of emotion. It is easy to lose sight of the fact that what we are dealing with is the *unconscious*. The temptation then is to merely attribute perceptive capacities sub-personally. In the cases of Robinson and Goldie, I've suggested some reasons as to why this might not be the solution they assume it to be. If I can show them that there is an alternative way of dissolving the problem to which they address their theories, we will have done even more to guard against the temptation to which they, to different degrees, succumb. On this note I progress to world-taking cognitivism. This, I suggest, could provide Goldie with a non-modular lifeline.

2.3. World-taking 'cognitivism'

World-taking cognitivism dispenses with the *need* for beliefs (thoughts or judgements). Here what is significant in our making sense of the emotion is how the person 'takes the world'. The notion of 'seeing as' looms in the background—moving to the fore (in various ways) in William Lyons' (1980), Cheshire Calhoun's (1984), and Robert C. Roberts' (1988, 2003) (respective) accounts.[40] In outlining a world-taking cognitivist account below, I will present my own, rather than that of Calhoun or Roberts; in doing so I hope to overcome the standard charge, that such ways of describing a person having an emotion are too metaphorical[41] and to provide a framework for understanding emotional experience and expression which eschews theorising the emotions.[42]

The classic example of seeing as (or aspect seeing) is the duck-rabbit, as discussed by Wittgenstein in *PI* and suggested to him by Gestalt psychology.[43] So, for example, when someone comes to see that we might see the below picture as a rabbit, as well as a duck—of which they had hitherto assumed it was exclusively a picture—a new aspect has dawned

for them. In world-taking cognitivism the emotional state *is* a way of see-ing (taking) the world: being alive to an aspect of the world. My sadness at the pictures of suffering and violence in Darfur, and my colleague's indifference, can be understood through my being alive to that aspect of those pictures, my seeing those pictures as meriting (taking them to merit) sadness, and he not being so. I can try to make him *see* that the pictures merit sadness, I can try to bring him to a position where he might take the pictures in that way—meriting this response—but it is *he* that must come to take them this way.

The 'world', of which we are speaking here, is, therefore, not the disen-chanted or 'pre'-conceptualised (Given) 'world' of the natural sciences, but rather the conceptualised world: the world as we inhabit it, within the 'space of reasons', as Wilfred Sellars (1956) and John McDowell (1994) have termed it.[44] As McDowell has argued on a number of occasions (see, for example McDowell 1994 and 2000a, b), there is no slip towards ideal-ism when talking this way. In talking of the 'conceptualised world', we are not talking of the world as constituted by conceptually structured acts of thinking but of a thinkable world. Thoughts about the world, takings of the world, are thoughts with thinkable contents (see *Mind and World*: p. 28). In turn, the concepts through which we take this/our world have normative properties inseparable from their descriptive properties. It is in perceiving, grasping, and acknowledging[45] such properties that our emotional responses to the world are elicited.

For example, when one sees an event as (say) shameful, one has perceived an *internal relation* between one's way of taking (see-ing) that event—i.e. one's conceptual characterisation of it[46]—and one's conception of shame. Or, put another way, what the event of one walking-on-by-on-witnessing-an-unprovoked-and-violent-attack-on-an-innocent-individual (call this 'walking*')[47] *means* for one (the way one sees or takes such an event) is internally related to the way one sees or takes the concept of a shameful act (call this 'shame*'). Internal relations are invoked to merely make the point that what we take walk-ing* to mean invokes or carries with it (for this person under the right conditions) what we take shame* to mean. That is to say, shame* is part of the normative content of walking* (as well as might be fear-of-intervening: fear*). Such internal relations can come to be formed through the forming of both our human and second nature (*Bildung*). Furthermore, where we are not alive to such aspects at time t1, we can come to be so at time t2, by means of the dawning of an aspect, i.e. perceive a new (to us) internal relation: for example, at a reasonably late stage in my life, when one would usually consider one's *Bildung* to be reasonably well formed, my reading of Mark Curtis's *Web of Deceit* might facilitate in me an aspect shift, whereby I now perceive an internal relation between recent-British-foreign-policy-and-my-complicity-in-such[48] (call this UK-complicity*) and shame-at-being-British (call this UK-shame*). It is part of what it means—for me here, in this context, as this person, with this history, these hopes, this self-image—then to take the events as UK-complicity* to also experience UK-shame*. What should be clear then is that one can either experience the dawning: e.g. 'wow, I actually feel a real sense of shame at being British and having hitherto devoted no time and effort to trying to stop this or distance myself from it; I'd not considered this before my reading of Curtis's book'. Or just experience the aspect: I *feel* ashamed.[49]

The benefits of the world-taking framework is that it can facilitate intelligibility of the emotional experience in the absence of the manifest beliefs, judgements, and the like without invoking the metaphysical and explanatorily dubious speculative baggage of modules.[50] We can *feel* shame without having the attendant beliefs or judgements in a similar way in which we can employ words in new contexts without making a manifest judgement regarding the appropriateness and meaningfulness of that use, or in the way in which we can *grasp* the meaning of a word in a new context without that grasping being an *interpretation*. Yes, one *can* take up a sceptical stance and judge whether one's shame is appropriate, as one can take up a sceptical stance and question whether one has succeeded in meaning anything by one's employment of a word on an occasion and in a particular (new) context; but such scepticism is no more *typical* of our normal life with shame than it is *typical* of our life with words.[51]

This is one of the ways in which world-taking cognitivism is an advance over its reason-giving sibling. Reason-giving cognitivism treats the 'coming-to-be-in-an-emotional-state' on the model of *interpretation* of a rule for the appropriate having of the emotion.[52] When reason-giving cognitivists say in their defence that they do not imply that the beliefs must be manifest, or with Goldie say that sometimes it is our feelings about objects, not necessarily beliefs, this doesn't, ultimately, help them avoid the criticisms to which they have been subject. It doesn't help them because they are still working with the interpretivist model: i.e. there is a brute, given world and there is us and our beliefs (and intentional feelings) about that world; *it is down to us to interpret that world*. Another way of putting this is the following: where reason-giving cognitivists admit non-manifest believing/judging to be taking place they do so, at *best*, on the model of the notion of secondary quality perception; that is to say on the model of what they understand to be taking place when cognition is manifest. I think this model (as an analogy) fine as regards instances of (manifestly) *judging* something to be thus and so (so long as we remember we are talking of both mind and world as within the space of reasons here), but not in *taking* something to be thus and so; in the latter case there is no 'mixing' taking place, the way the *world is taken to be is simply forced upon us by the way the world is*—and remember this is the conceptualised world located, as are we, within the space of reasons. World-taking cognitivism treats 'coming-to-be-in-an-emotional-state' on the model of a *grasping* of a rule for the appropriate having of the emotion: i.e. because of one's perception of the internal relations, one sees the world as meriting the emotional response, and what this means is simply that for you, you *have* the emotional response. So, it is important, for heuristic purposes, to keep this distinction between *grasping* and *interpreting* in mind—and the concomitant distinctions between *taking* and *judging*; and between *seeing as* and *perception of secondary (or tertiary) qualities*; and between *having the emotion* and *believing, judging, or (intentionally) feeling that one has the emotion*.

Now, I shall readily concede that while scepticism towards the appropriateness of our shame is not *typical* of our life with shame it is *relatively* (relative in comparison to scepticism about the meaning of words on new occasions of use) *common* to it, and this is one of the reasons—I suggest—that allows for the depiction of shame as a higher cognitive emotion,[53] in contradistinction to those emotions usually thought of as paradigmatically affective, such as fear. I wish to suggest that affective emotional episodes predominantly occur in the absence of a sceptical stance towards their appropriateness, in a similar way in which our taking a sceptical stance to our own employment of words on a reasonably regular basis is both uncommon and would 'get in the way' somewhat.

Why is this so? One reason is that shame's objects are more slippery than are fear's;[54] the internal relations one perceives that bring one to shame* are brought into place at a higher level of cultural specificity—one needs more enculturation, more intimate knowledge of people, their hopes, their desires, and their non-affective fears regarding those hopes, desires, etc.—than are those which merit affective fear. Put another way, it is more difficult to arrive at a stage whereby one can merely unreflectively grasp a shame rule—follow it blindly—as it were; one can, but it requires more cultural capital.[55] We, as individual human beings, our lives, our hopes, our desires, etc. are more interwoven with shame, where the individual (as opposed to the generic) human being (the person) is less central in the affective emotions.[56] The world-taker experiencing shame is therefore *first and foremost* you, the individual human being with a history, and hopes for the future: a *person*, a culturally-encumbered individual living with others in a conceptualised world of shared norms (and what other sort of *person* in what other world could there possibly be?). The world-taker (person) experiencing (affective) fear is therefore *first and foremost* you, a human being with the sorts of human frailties characteristic of the species: a *person*; though now the emphasis is upon how they are encumbered by awareness of their flesh and blood existence. This is—*emphatically*—not an attempt at categorisation, nor at definition in terms of essential characteristics of each emotion; this is merely a purpose-relative sorting, a way of giving sense to the characteristic differences between two paradigm cases of affective emotion and higher cognitive emotion. As should be abundantly apparent (see Section 1; above) the *'first and foremost'* clauses in the above sorting need to be given much emphasis. Other factors can, and frequently do, override. Fear can often emerge in a characteristically higher cognitive sense: such as my fear of engaging my philosophical hero in debate. And shame can often appear in a characteristically affective sense. (One might even take this to be *one* purpose for our having the concept of embarrassment: a *sort* of affective shame.)

The notion of scepticism is central to the account I am essaying here. There is a tendency to aim for sceptic-proof theories in philosophy, whether it be of knowledge, of meaning, or of emotion. However, I eschew such a tendency. It is a part of our lives with our emotions that we can on occasion take up a sceptical stance to their appropriateness; as it is a part of our lives with words that we can take up, on reflection, a sceptical stance to a word's applicability (and thus sense) in a new context and on a new occasion.

2.3.1. Being in denial: Diogenes' shamelessness and acknowledgement

I have commented that one needs to be alive to the internal relations between concepts; this requirement should not be contrasted with denying, or resisting, the force of those internal relations, through an act of 'turning away from'; that is to say, that one can be alive to those internal relations while having trained oneself to deny their significance for one. Put another way, seeing the internal relations, being alive to them, should be contrasted with not seeing, not being alive to them. The question of acknowledging their significance (once seen), accepting their claim on one, is secondary. In turning away from, in refusing to acknowledge those internal relations, one can achieve shamelessness.[57] Raymond Geuss discusses Diogenes of Sinope in this regard;[58] he writes,

> Diogenes of Sinope, who lived in the fourth century B.C., was in the habit of masturbating in the middle of the Athenian marketplace. He was not pathologically unaware of his surroundings, psychotic, or simple-minded. Nor was he living in a society that stood at the very beginning of what Elias calls 'the process of civilization'; that is, he was not living in a society fairly low on the scale of what we take to be our cultural evolution, one in which such forms of behaviour were not yet subject to systematic disapproval and socially regulated. Rather, we know that the Athenians objected to his mode of life in general and to this form of behaviour in particular. They clearly considered him a public nuisance and made their disapproval known to him. We know this because the doxographic tradition specifically records Diogenes' response to a criticism of his masturbating in public. He is said to have replied that he wished only that it were as easy to satisfy hunger by just rubbing one's belly.
>
> (Geuss 2001: pp. 12–13)

On one reading, Diogenes' public masturbation is thought to have been a statement to the effect that he wished to highlight the arbitrariness of certain rules (cultural norms) regarding the satisfaction of bodily needs. For, while eating satisfies hunger, and is, broadly speaking, an acceptable act in which to publicly engage,[59] masturbation, which can satisfy one's sexual desire, is not similarly publicly acceptable. Diogenes' masturbation was a deliberate turning away from the internal relations that would normally give rise to one's shame at being viewed masturbating in the Athenian marketplace; his act is undertaken with a refusal to acknowledge the internal relation between the disgust of others directed at his action and his own disgustingness and lack of dignity; that is to say, Diogenes refuses to acknowledge his act, and its viewing and judging by others, as diminishing his dignity. In refusing to acknowledge such, shame cannot gain a foothold. Diogenes denies shame.[60] Shame relies on acceding to a number of sophisticated relations between concepts; in refusing to acknowledge the applicability of one of those concepts, he achieves, here, shamelessness.

It is important to recognise what is taking place here. Diogenes *sees* the relations but *denies* certain of them; he refuses to admit, to *acknowledge*, them. This, in itself, takes a degree of training. Diogenes must teach himself that *to elicit disgust* in others is *not to be disgusting* or *devoid of dignity*; such a relation is generally *grasped*, and not in need of *interpretation*; to deny it, therefore, takes work; it is not merely a matter of judging differently. It might be possible that one, if acting as did Diogenes, might deny the relationship between being disgusting and devoid of dignity, on the one hand, and being worthy of shame, on the other. If this is indeed possible, without denying shame *per se*, it is not, as I read the story of Diogenes of Synope, what he is doing. Diogenes is not refusing to acknowledge that the concepts of disgustingness and lack of dignity are internally related to the concept of shame; but rather, he is refusing to admit, refusing to acknowledge, that he is disgusting and devoid of dignity by virtue of his actions eliciting disgust in others. Diogenes' shamelessness, then, involves an active 'turning away from', a denial of, that second nature (*Bildung*) which invokes, which *activates*, relations between the meaning of disgust, dignity, and shame; such 'a turning away', such a denial, a refusal to acknowledge, needs to be, if successful, the product of training, a process whereby the place those concepts have in one's life, the significance they have for one, becomes fundamentally altered. In this sense Diogenes can be seen to be aligning himself with those in the philosophical tradition who would see second nature as something negative, a pseudo-version or a perversion of our primary nature, such as Augustine and Rousseau. Not as something positive, as do Hegel and McDowell. Diogenes sees his second nature, his *Bildung*, in the shame it bequeaths him as tyrannical, as restricting his natural (in first nature sense) freedom.

3. Shame, cognitivism, and recalcitrance

3.1. Sartre and Taylor: Two reason-giving cognitivist accounts of shame

Gabriele Taylor's understanding of the basic structure of shame incorporates both the *thought* that as the agent of shame I have been seen by another and the acknowledgement of the value of the judgement embodied in that thought. In order to make Taylor's cognitive account clearer, I shall discuss it in the light of Sartre's account and her comments on this. In *Being and Nothingness*, Sartre provides the following example of an episode of shame.

> I have just made an awkward or vulgar gesture. This gesture clings to me; I neither judge it nor blame it. I simply live it. I realise it in the mode of for itself. But now suddenly I raise my head. Somebody was there and has seen me. Suddenly I realise the vulgarity of my gesture, and I am ashamed. It is certain that my shame is not reflective, for the presence of another in my consciousness, even as a catalyst is incompatible with the reflective attitude; in the field of my reflection I can never meet with anything but the consciousness which is mine. But the Other is the indispensable mediator between myself and me. I am ashamed of myself as *I appear* to the Other.
>
> (Sartre 1957: pp. 221–222)

In Sartre's case, the person feels shame because he sees his action, the vulgar gesture, from another perspective. This aspect switch is, on Sartre's view, initiated in the person by the awareness of an audience to his action. There are two issues I will raise prompted by Sartre's example. First, for Sartre (according to Taylor), an actual audience is required for an aspect switch on the part of the agent. Second, on seeing his own action from the perspective of the observer—the 'Other' in Sartre's example—the agent must give credence to the observer perspective. In short, for Sartre, the person must, when seeing the gesture from the observer's perspective, come to recognise it as vulgar. It follows that this requires the agent to recognise and subscribe to the same norms as he perceives the observer to; that is to say, at least he must do so as far as the vulgarity of this gesture, on this occasion and in this context, is concerned. This would suggest the existence of a tacit honour group, which the thought that eyes are upon one makes manifest to the agent. The person's perception that he has failed to 'live up to' the standards of the honour group gains expression as a feeling of shame.

In relation to the first issue raised by Sartre's depiction, Sartre invokes the existence of an actual audience implying that it is required for the aspect switch to take place. Gabriele Taylor writes that,

> it is plainly untrue that all cases of feeling shame are cases of public exposure, untrue that is, that an actual observer is required for shame to be felt. Nor is it true even that the agent must believe, rightly or wrongly, that he is being observed by some other person.
>
> (Taylor 1985: p. 58)

The *actual* audience in Sartre's 'example' serves only to *prompt* the aspect switch. However, the audience that brings about the feeling of shame is the agent and *not* the third party. It is the agent's seeing of the gesture from a different perspective, a perspective that affords him the recognition of the gesture as vulgar that brings about his shame. Once we have conceded this point, we can concede that an actual audience is not required. For an aspect switch does not require the presence of the Other.[61]

Taylor argues that we can dispense with the necessity for an *actual* audience while retaining the notion that one can switch perspectives and become an audience to one's own actions, thus becoming aware of another perspective that sees the gesture as vulgar. Taylor's argument, contra her reading of Sartre, seems persuasive; one can take a different perspective on one's own actions without either an actual observer or even the *thought* that there is an observer to those actions. The thought, or actual existence, of an audience may help facilitate our taking up another perspective but is not a requirement for it.

In establishing that there is no requirement for an actual or imagined audience, Taylor addresses what she sees as a further problem,

> It seems that we now have a dilemma: 'shame requires an audience' is either given too much or too little content; it is given too much if we insist on at least the imagined presence of another [as she takes Sartre to do]. But if all it requires is that one should occupy an observer's position *vis-à-vis* oneself then the metaphors of eyes being upon one or being revealed to an audience seem to be rather heavy machinery for making just this point. The problem therefore is to give adequate content to the notion of the audience without introducing what is conceptually irrelevant to feeling shame.
>
> (ibid.: p. 59)

To recap, in Sartre's 'example' the feeling of shame came about through a two-stage process: first, the person's awareness of the observer led them to take up a different perspective on their action; and second, the person, on making the switch from participant perspective to an observer perspective, recognises the vulgarity of the gesture and feels shame. For Taylor the first stage need not be invoked. Rather, it is possible that I can make the change from participant to observer perspective without the awareness of *or* the thought that there is an audience to my action. The second step in Sartre's depiction also comes under criticism from Taylor.

She reads it as, first, implying the recognition of the evaluative superiority inherent to the observer's perspective; and second, she takes it to depict the observer's perspective as critical of the agent. Neither of these two implications Taylor finds in Sartre's example are, for her, necessary conditions for feeling shame.

Taylor, therefore, criticises Sartre on three counts. First, Sartre implies the need for an actual audience; second, Sartre depicts the observer perspective as evaluatively superior; and third, Sartre depicts the observer's perspective as always critical of the actor or action. In place of Sartre's alleged requirement for an actual audience and an evaluatively superior critical observer perspective, Taylor offers the *notion* of an audience, which is, further, unencumbered by the evaluative properties given it by Sartre. Taylor's 'notion of an audience' merely serves to differentiate between the observer and participant perspective, or third and first person perspective. For Taylor, the notion of audience is invoked so as to open up the conceptual space for the observer perspective, though she is keen to guard against the oversimplification of the notion.

> The point about the audience is that it occupies an observer and not a participant position. Unlike the agent, the audience is detached. It is reference to just this basic notion of the audience which is primarily needed for an explanation of shame: in feeling shame the actor thinks of himself as having become an object of detached observation, and at the core to feel shame is to feel distress at being seen at all. *How* he is seen, whether he thinks of the audience as critical, approving, indifferent, cynical or naïve is a distinguishable step and accounts for the different cases of shame.
>
> (ibid.: p. 60)

Taylor offers us an understanding of shame in terms of necessary and sufficient conditions; for her the metaphorical audience, in the shape of the observer perspective, is necessary for shame even though it might not *always* be sufficient. While on occasions the thought that one has been seen might well be sufficient for a feeling of shame, at other times the observer's view may invoke an evaluative judgement and this may be an integral part of the feeling of shame. So Taylor's thesis is that a metaphorical audience is necessary to a feeling of shame for it enables the agent to take up another perspective on her actions. She writes,

> To speak of an audience is of course to speak metaphorically. What has been described as seen from different audience points of view

is the content of some of the agent's explanatory beliefs. So on the occasion of an occurrence of shame the person feels she is defective and degraded. This is her identificatory belief. She sees herself in these terms because she is presented with a contrast, where the contrast is between her unselfconscious state, what she thought or hoped or unthinkingly assumed she was, or was doing, and what she has now under the observer-description turned out to be. This comes as a revelation to her. But it need be a revelation only given her initial unselfconsciousness. She may not be making a new discovery about herself; it may just be a reminder. She reaches this judgement by means of her beliefs that what she is doing may be seen under some description (where the description may just be 'object of observation') and that she ought not to be so seen, it is a false position in which she finds herself. What precisely makes it a false position will of course vary according to the circumstances.

(ibid.: p. 66)

3.2. Recalcitrant shame, self-deceit, scepticism

Taylor's thesis is broad in scope and serves to illuminate many instances of shame. However, it meets substantial problems when faced with 'recalcitrant' shame: i.e. shame felt despite beliefs being held that tell one that one has done nothing of which to be ashamed.

If one can, then, feel shame while believing oneself to have no reason to feel shame, this implies the existence of affective shame. This is one of the motivating reasons for much of the focus upon the problem of recalcitrance in the recent emotions literature:[62] The existence of recalcitrance implies that what is essential to emotion is not a set of evaluative beliefs or judgements held by the person but the felt quality, the affect: if our beliefs tell us we have no reason to fear flying yet we do, in fact, fear flying, then what 'fear' is must be something other than what a reason-giving cognitivist account claims it to be. I said earlier that there is no reason to move from this claim about the characteristically affective nature of some emotions, such as fear, to the stronger claim that they are in principle cognitively closed, nor even that they are in some sense essentially pre-cognitive. This is the mistake made by many critics of cognitivism.

It is more difficult to make sense of a recalcitrant higher cognitive emotional episode. This is the problem. If one explains and type-individuates an emotion such as shame by the evaluative beliefs claimed to constitute it, yet at the same time one allows for the possibility that one can feel shame while also believing oneself unworthy of shame, then one is embroiled in something of a paradox. There are three closely related ways in which one might try to overcome this problem; all three in effect involve denying recalcitrance. The first way is just to deny that one can feel shame while *truly* believing or judging oneself to be unworthy of shame. This way denies recalcitrant shame by simply denying that anyone could ever *genuinely* believe themselves to be unworthy of shame while concurrently *genuinely* being ashamed (with respect to the same object). This is the line Robert Solomon, following Sartre, sometimes takes: depicting putatively recalcitrant emotions as instances of self-deceit. On other occasions, Solomon depicts putatively recalcitrant emotions as merely conflicts between emotional ('snap' or 'heated') judgements and ('cooler' or more 'detached') propositional judgements/beliefs. This latter way might be seen as a prototype version of more recent attempts at challenging the notion of recalcitrant emotions. On these later understandings, recalcitrance is denied by denying that the valuations that constitute the emotion are (propositional) beliefs, or, indeed, propositional at all. This dissolves the problem by not granting (propositional) belief authority in the first place; Goldie (2000) and Greenspan (1992) are obvious candidates here.[63]

Taylor must be committed to the first way of denying recalcitrance. She must hold that there is no such thing, and episodes which superficially appear to exhibit recalcitrance are merely cases of self-deceit. In what follows, I will offer a shame scenario which, understood on Taylor's account of shame, understood that is in terms of reason-giving cognitivism, would be a *prima facie* example of recalcitrant shame; thus must, ultimately, for Taylor, be understood as a case of self-deception.

3.2.1. *Primo Levi's shame or the essential 'recalcitrance' of shame*

In *The Drowned and the Saved*, Primo Levi returns to the subject of shame. As I discussed in Chapter 2, he does so in the light of the (at the time) emergent literature on survivor shame (often called survivor guilt). Levi is puzzled by survivor shame, not because he thinks it wrong, as it were, not because he thinks it irrational, but because he cannot find a reason for it:

> Are you ashamed because you are alive in the place of another? And in particular, of a man more generous, more sensitive, wiser, more useful, more worthy of living than you? You cannot exclude this: you examine yourself, you review your memories, hoping to find them

all, and that none of them are masked or disguised; no, you find no obvious transgressions, you did not usurp anyone's place, you did not beat anyone (but would you have had the strength to do so?), you did not accept positions (but none were offered to you...), you did not steal anyone's bread; nevertheless you cannot exclude it. It is no more than a supposition, indeed the shadow of a suspicion; that everyone is his brother's Cain, that every one of us (but this time I say 'us' in a much vaster, indeed universal sense) has usurped his neighbour's place and lived in his stead. It is a supposition, but it gnaws at us; it has nestled deeply like a woodworm; it is not seen from the outside but it gnaws and rasps.

(Levi 1989: p. 62)

The chapter continues in a similar vein. Levi spends much time discussing guilt, why he is not guilty, why he might be thought to be. Levi, with great honesty, explores possible reasons for his shame; none satisfy him. Yet he is left with the emotion, an emotion not only for which he could find no reason, but for which every reason he has entertained, he has dismissed. At the end of the chapter on shame, Levi has good reason to consider himself unworthy of shame: i.e. after much honest deliberation he does not believe he has reason to be ashamed for surviving. But Levi and many other survivors *do feel* shame.

Now a number of thoughts occur to me here. I will briefly address these before progressing to discuss recalcitrance in more detail. First, it is tempting to just deny that this is a genuine case of recalcitrant emotion; we might be tempted to deny such because Levi never arrives at the belief that he should not be ashamed *per se*, but rather has just failed to locate the justificatory beliefs for his shame. This fails as a response, because one could take the same attitude to the scenario, even were Levi to state, categorically, that he believes himself unworthy of shame. That is to say, for the notion of recalcitrance to even make sense, we must be willing—in principle—to accept a person's word for it when they claim to hold beliefs which are in conflict with the emotion. Second, even were Levi to finally arrive at a stage where he considered himself to have found the beliefs (or judgements) that serve to identify and justify his shame, could *these* really be *constitutive* of his shame? Given the process by which they have been arrived at, they are probably rather more akin to *rationalisations* of his shame.

So, we shall take Levi to have here provided us with an instance of recalcitrant emotion. How might Taylor explain this? We saw above three (closely connected) ways that reason-giving cognitivists attempt to meet such a challenge; these are as follows:

1. Levi is suffering self-deceit; he is deceiving himself that he is unworthy of shame for (say) psychological reasons;
2. Levi's shame is based on a snap judgement and his reflections, which give rise to the purported recalcitrance, are more cool and detached; this explains the conflict: they are judgements made in different modes, as it were. This can evolve into the thoughts explained in the next point;
3. The thoughts that constitute Levi's shame are 'evaluative thoughts held in mind by intentional states of comfort or discomfort' (Greenspan), or what is constitutive of Levi's shame is 'his feeling towards an object' (Goldie); and thus there is no tacit commitment to acknowledge the authority of the beliefs in his unworthyness-for-shame.

All these have a degree of plausibility as ways of bypassing the charge of recalcitrance. Which seems most plausible? I am somewhat resistant to accusing Levi of self-deceit. I'm sure that in many putative cases of recalcitrance self-deceit might well turn out to be in play, but to hold that it always is so seems wrong. In any case, Levi's shame seems to be based, first and foremost, in his *feeling* ashamed, not in any belief or judgement. The second option similarly struggles as an account of Levi. The shame felt by survivors, and that felt by Levi, was something that 'afflicted' them over decades (recall the passage from Levi, quoted above, appeared in 1989, some 44 years after liberation). It is hardly likely to be conducive to being characterised, therefore, as borne of snap judgement. This seems to bring us to the third option: recalcitrance doesn't hold because Levi holds no beliefs with which the latter ones might conflict; his shame is not founded on, constituted by, nor explained and type-individuated by (propositional) belief. Here Levi's shame is founded in his feeling towards (we'll follow Goldie's line, rather than Greenspan's here). But feeling towards what? Does shame have an intentional object? And *why* does he have this feeling towards? Is it not just *this* object that Levi is struggling to bring to mind in the above passage? Such problems aside, we already saw the problems that Goldie's account faced (this chapter, Section 2.2.1).

Here's another, world-taking, way to understand Levi's shame, and by extension that felt by survivors of comparable trauma. As an adult, educated Italian, Levi had, in the process of developing his *Bildung*, developed quite sophisticated criteria for what it is to be a good (honourable) person, also for what it is to live with bare human dignity intact. The learning of a language is the learning of a life (with words and with others); Levi learnt not only (as a child and young man) the place the concept of 'shame' took in the lives of those around him, but also the place it should take in his own life (whether he chose to observe its place with respect or treat the place it has with suspicion and derision is of little consequence, either stance implies having learnt its place in the life of the linguistic community into which one is enculturated; acknowledgement is a further step). Levi also learns the significance and the place in a life of words such as dignity, respect, justice, fairness, happiness, goodness, care, compassion, love, fraternity, etc. (the list could go on, and on). Crucially Levi—Primo Levi who chose to title his book on his time in Auschwitz, *If This is a Man*—learnt the place of words, the significance, and the normative, moral significance of words such as 'person', 'human (being)', and 'humanity'. Learning these words is learning their place in the lives of the people with whom you share the world, and their place in the lives of people already gone (through literature, story, memoir, etc.); learning these words is learning the significance these words have, the reactions their employment elicits in those one respects and chooses to be around, and the reactions they elicit in those for whom one has little respect and those one chooses not to be around, in contexts, on occasions; learning these words *is* to become human, is to become a person, and this enables one to acknowledge the humanity of others; learning these words is the learning of the internal relations between them, how (say) shame and remorse in certain contexts and on particular occasions might carry one another—how invoking one can mean invoking the other—and how in some contexts, on some occasions, in a life, these concepts just are not discrete in the manner one might assume.

Auschwitz set about the systematic destruction of this life, the destruction of this person. Shame is felt by Levi, the survivor, because he now sees internal relations of which he never dreamt; moreover these are relations no *man* should perceive. Shame is felt because 'man' has new meaning; it carries with it, for Levi, the capacity for inhumanity, the inhumanity of the perpetrator, and the forced inhumanity of the inmate. In certain contexts, on certain occasions, what 'man' means now carries with it 'unprovoked, unjustified, extreme violence to man'; 'man' is internally related to (carries with it) 'inhumanity'. That is the new place the concept of 'man' has for Levi, and always, despite any subsequent kindness and care of one man for another, will. In certain lights, for the rest of his life (as is reported by many survivors of comparable trauma), these internal relations will be perceived. That aspect of the meaning will be made manifest and shame will be felt. Do you understand? So where does this leave us with regard to recalcitrance? Well there is *no* recalcitrance here. The reason for Levi's shame is also the reason he (as do many in similar positions to him—see Langer (1991)) finds it so difficult to make rational sense of his shame, for his shame stemmed from the radically different world of meanings that Auschwitz imposed upon those who were taken there. In trying to make sense of one's shame, as does Levi, one tries to make sense of it using the pre- and post-Auschwitz (ordinary, learnt-in-the-course-of-a-human-life) meanings. It is part of the magnitude of the crime that one finds it so difficult to make sense of the human consequences of that crime, in terms of the pre- and post-Auschwitz world (of meanings). This is not to advance an ineffabilist thesis (either about meaning in general or about the Holocaust); it is rather to acknowledge how desperately and utterly difficult it can be, after the event, while the shame is forcing itself upon one, to make sense of that shame. Shame is both the residue of the crime and the continuation of the crime. Levi's scepticism about his shame is an ordinary scepticism directed at a *taking of* an extraordinary world, and the emotional responses elicited by that world.[64]

4. Emotions as embodied appraisals: Prinz's psychosemantics

4.1. The Emotion Problem

It seems somewhat inappropriate to move from the discussion of the previous section to the topic of the present one. Though I genuinely feel discomfort at doing so, I am also convinced that a discussion of philosophical accounts of shame done in abstraction from discussion of actual expression of emotion severely disadvantages itself. The last emotion theorist I will examine is Jesse Prinz. Prinz's neo-Jamesian theory employs resources provided by cognitive neuroscience and computational psychology in an attempt to bring about rapprochement between Jamesians and cognitivists and in the process solving what he terms 'the Emotion Problem', which he identifies as follows:

> So we have a serious puzzle. The fact that emotions are meaningful, reason sensitive, and intentional suggests that they must be cognitive. The fact that some emotions arise without intervention of the neocortex suggests that emotions cannot *all* be cognitive. The emotions

that arise in this way seem to be meaningful. This seems to suggest that being meaningful does not require being cognitive. Noncognitive states are explanatorily anaemic and cognitive states are explanatorily superfluous. Noncognitive theories give us too little, and cognitive theories give us too much. Call this the Emotion Problem.

(Prinz 2003a: p. 78)

Well there is a short, and a (few) long, answer(s) to this. The short answer is to merely note that 'the Emotion Problem', or the juxtaposition comprising the problem, is not the whole story. To summarise what Prinz presents us with:

- *On the one hand* we have non-cognitive theories of emotion. These operate in purely **causal**—contentless—fashion; this is what makes them non-cognitive, as it were: the (brute, Given) world has causal impact upon us, resulting in our being availed of sense data,[65] or sense impressions; if, as Prinz suggests, these sense impressions bypass all possible cognitive processes in eliciting emotions, then how can those emotions mean anything? That is, from where does meaning come?
- *On the other hand* we have cognitive theories. These operate in an **interpretive**[66]—i.e. giving conceptual content to the world—fashion; this is what identifies them as cognitive. When we cognise we interpret the sense data/impressions employing our conceptual capacities; it is these interpreted/conceptualised data which are meaningful; the problem is that the 'evidence' suggests (cf. the above paragraph) that some emotions are elicited in the absence of such cognising/interpreting.

4.2. On giving oneself a problem

I see no reason to buy into Prinz's Manichaean picture. Such a view makes a number of presuppositions. It presupposes a disenchanted and non-conceptual world, which stands external to our minds. This world is located outside the space of reasons, is governed by purely causal laws, and thus can *only* have causal impact upon us. It presupposes that our minds are located in our heads (and modelled on, or taken to be, the brain). The world only gains meaning, becomes enchanted, through our cognitively projecting values/meanings on to it, or more accurately, projecting values onto the impressions it causes on our senses. If we assume such a world to be our world, as does Prinz, and if, as Prinz suggests, *not all* emotions involve cognition, how then, indeed, can *all* emotions be meaningful?

Well we do not need to see things thus and so. There are other ways to understand human cognitive powers, the human mind, and the world in which we live with others (cf. Chapter 1, Section 2.3; and the present chapter, Section 2.3). We do not then, as does Prinz, situate the world in some brute Given realm (outside the space of reasons), thus creating for ourselves the problem as to how things caused by this Given realm can give rise to meanings in, and for, us minded animals, operating within the space of reasons. *Of course* if one characterises things in *that* (Prinz's) way, one will have a pretty serious problem and pretty serious trouble in finding the resources to overcome the problem.

We can then rather see the mind as a structured system of object involving abilities; we can see our cognitive powers as our having grasped concepts, learnt how to employ them in contexts, through recognising their significance, for ourselves and for others, recognising their place in a life, and being able to respond to requests for reasons for our actions. We can understand the world and our mental capacities as internally related, rather than externally (causally) so. The world is our world; our minds reach out to meet it, or rather they think of it and act in it.[67]

There is considerable resistance to the alternative view of mind, world, and cognitive powers, which I have suggested here. I'm not quite sure why; this *is* the world *we* inhabit. I do not interpret sense data; I see the world. Furthermore, I convey what I see to you, employing concepts that we both have grasped. Of course saying this will win few arguments, and most likely fewer converts; I say this only because it has been argued in detail, much more detail than I have here, many times, yet still our empiricist interlocutors continue. Let us lay things out syllogistically as we did with Robinson and Goldie:

1. Cognition is absent; put another way, the person is not cognising in the sense of believing or judging something in the world; put yet another—Prinz's—way, nothing is taking place in the brain which involves the intervention of the neocortex;
2. (While 'cognition' is absent), the person is in an emotional state and this suggests that something *akin* to cognition is taking place, i.e. something akin to the perception and evaluation of an object;
3. The conclusion is drawn that something else, other than the involvement of the neocortex, must be *playing the role* of cognition; *something* non-cognitive must *give-forth*—as it were—meaning, and must be

directed onto things in the world. Since cognition-as-neural-activity-involving-the-intervention-of-the-neocortex (what Prinz takes *to be* cognition) is not present, but a meaningful emotional episode is, meaning must emerge from an embodied emotion having semantic properties which enable it to refer in the absence of cognition (in the absence of neocortical intervention).

So what are the assumptions here? Well, Prinz assumes that cognition is a brain process involving the intervention of the neocortex. This assumption is unfounded, unless one takes an extremely narrowly defined, and *a priori*, view of cognition-as-necessarily-involving-the-intervention-of-the-neocortex. (In this respect it is worth noting that it is important not to give up the term 'cognition' to cognitive neuroscience and neuro reductionists; Prinz does so.) We can rather take what it is to cognise to be to perceive, to think, to believe, etc. If the evidence suggests cognition—i.e. something is meaningful for us—yet the neocortex seems to be bypassed, then only prejudice regarding the nature of cognition—perceiving, thinking, believing, etc.—leads you to conclude that no cognising is taking place. Therefore, Prinz is culpable of not only assuming cognition is a process, but that it is a brain process which involves the intervention of the neocortex; in addition he *assumes*—at least he does not give us *reason* to believe this to be so—that neocortical involvement in brain processes gives rise to meaning... How so? Let me put this a little differently. It is one thing for neuroscientists and neuroanatomists to identify the intervention of the neocortex when people claim to be thinking, etc.—i.e. when a person is 'cognising'. It is another thing to conclude that it is the neocortex that does the thinking: that cognition *is* brain-activity-which-involves-neocortical-intervention. It is yet a further thing to then conclude that this 'neocortical intervention' is from where 'meaning' must come. Particularly so, if you then progress to set up your 'Problem' by saying that the mystery that needs solving is that 'something that takes place in the absence of neocortical intervention has the properties of meaning something about something'; i.e. it has all the attributes of cognition![68]

4.3. Psychosemantic emotion modules

So there are a good deal of assumptions in play in Prinz's premises. If we set these aside for now—and only for now—and examine his conclusion/solution to the Emotion Problem, we find him faced with further problems. If we have concepts, the ones we use in our day-to-day transactions in the world with others, the ones through which we read our world, through which we register and acknowledge significant aspects of our world, yet these same public concepts can't give rise to meaningfulness because there is no neocortical intervention in the brain processes taking place, how can our positing 'inner' concepts located in modules do the work denied to our ordinary public concepts? All we've done in claiming to provide a solution to the 'problem' is theorise that we have some concepts inside a module which do the work that we are denying our ordinary (public) concepts can do. What properties do the 'inner' concepts of psychosemantics have that our ordinary concepts do not? All that seems to be clear is that they are, in some sense, inner.[69]

Again, let's be clear about the 'problem' here. We are told by Prinz that cognition does not take place because the neocortex does not intervene in the brain processes; hence, we cannot make sense of our emotions having meaning. The solution is proposed that we have some inner concepts; i.e. the semantically endowed inner concepts of psychosemantics. But if our ordinary (public) concepts were not sufficient for meaning in the absence of neocortical intervention then why are the concepts of psychosemantics?[70] What is the telling difference between our ordinary (public) concepts and those of psychosemantics? The only difference seems to be that the former are public, and the latter are, in some sense, inner; this seems far from sufficient for the latter to have any powers over and above those we might predicate of the former.

Unfortunately, the problems for accounts such as Prinz's do not stop there. There is also, of course, the regress problem. If it is suggested that in order for our public concepts to mean anything, then they must be underpinned by the more basic concepts of psychosemantics, then what underpins the concepts of psychosemantics? Why do our public concepts require underpinning by another more primitive (it is the theorists of psychosemantics that claim them to be more primitive) set of concepts, yet these more primitive concepts do not themselves require underpinning? Again the concepts of psychosemantics differ— on Prinz's own account—from our public concepts only in that they are: (a) 'inner' and (b) more primitive. Does this persuade you that we have a solution?

Ultimately, Prinz effects a similar move to Robinson (and to a much lesser degree, Goldie). The temptation seems to be, when faced with a problem to abstract further and endow something else, something theoretically postulated, with the powers one requires.[71] In fact, I suggest, it is what led to the thought that there was a problem in the first place that is at issue.

5. Concluding remarks

World-taking cognitivism does not face a problem as presented to us in Prinz's 'Emotion Problem', because it does not rest on the same assumptions about mind, world, or the purpose of a philosophical reflection on emotion. It is not a theory of the emotions but an ongoing attempt to make sense of emotional expression; it is a framework for understanding emotion. It is not a rival to scientific studies of the place of the brain or the autonomic nervous system (ANS) in emotion, but it does help us to see why emotion cannot and should not be reduced to the study of the brain or ANS. Similarly, it doesn't face the same problems critics of cognitivism have identified it—reason-giving cognitivism—as being subject. Most importantly, for my purposes it amply provides a way in which to make sense of people struggling with their emotions, without forcing upon them a theory.

4
Shame and World

In the foregoing chapters I have essayed various problems with a number of philosophical approaches to emotion. The scientistic approach, as advocated and exemplified by Paul Griffiths, rested upon a picture of language and meaning that distorted our understanding of ourselves. The theory advocated by Agamben faced structurally similar problems in being wedded to a theory of meaning, which was found to be too abstract. I found much of interest in the version of cognitivism in the philosophy of emotion, which I called reason-giving cognitivism. However, we saw that this faced some serious problems (cf. Chapter 3, Sections 2 and 3). In addition, I briefly turned my attention to a recent influential, neo-Jamesian attempt to overcome (reason-giving) cognitivism's problems, in the work of Jesse Prinz. This too was found to have substantial problems. The problems faced by reason-giving cognitivism and by Prinz's neo-Jamesian approach were traced to their guiding, though unacknowledged, picture of mind and world as externally related, the former being that which bestows meaning on the latter.

Having moved through an analysis of prominent current theories of emotion I proposed my own, delimited version of what I termed, in Chapter 3, world-taking cognitivism. My concern, however, was not to provide another theory of emotions which drew on philosophical and psychological discussions of aspect perception, as for example one finds in the work of Robert C. Roberts (2003). Rather, I sought to provide the tools, such that one might need them, which might assist one to understand emotional expression, thereby hoping to mitigate any desire for a theory of emotion. In doing so, I drew on Wittgenstein's therapeutic employment of (a de-psychologised) aspect seeing, so as to assist us in gaining clarity regarding our conceptual faculties and relation to our world.

However, there are still some questions hanging in the air, as it were. In this chapter I will I hope to address some of these questions.

This chapter takes the following form:

- Section 1 begins by addressing the issue of intentionality and moves onto revisit world-taking cognitivism, seeking to dispel some possible objections.
- Section 2 having discussed world-taking cognitivism, I briefly examine a discussion of shame and approaches to it, put forward by the psychologist Paul Gilbert. The purpose here is to show that what are often presented as competing ways in which one might explain shame are not in fact so.
- Section 3 begins with an examination of the relationship between shame and audience, and progresses to an engagement with Bernard Williams' discussion of shame and autonomy.
- Section 4 much of the ethical and psychological literature on shame has presented it as a purely negative and regressive emotion. While for many instances of shame this is the case, it is not always so. I argue that there is too little shame.
- Section 5 moves towards conclusion by making clear my purpose as author.

1. Emotions and intentionality

In a manner which has striking similarities to the way Prinz presents what he calls 'the Emotion Problem' (Prinz 2003a: p. 78), John Deigh (2004) has identified that the problem facing theories of emotions is their inability to cover both of two facts about emotions.

- **Fact one** is the intentionality of emotion.
- **Fact two** is that, as Deigh puts it, 'emotions are common to both humans and beasts' (p. 9) (with the caveats that (a) humans have a broader set of emotions, and (b) we are not committed to all beasts having emotions).

Deigh continues to write,

A successful theory of emotions must account for both of these facts [Facts one and two]. It cannot skirt them. Yet accounting for both has proven to be surprisingly difficult. Some theories, particularly the cognitivist theories that have been so influential in philosophy and psychology over the last thirty years, use the first fact as their point of departure and leading idea, but they then have trouble accommodating the second. Other theories, particularly those that have developed under the influence of Darwin's seminal work *The Expression of the Emotions in Man and Animals* (1998), take the second fact as their springboard, but then they have trouble accommodating the first. The reason in either case is the way intentional states of mind are typically understood and the way primitive emotions are typically understood. The problem of closing this gap seems to outstrip the resources of these theories. The point is not generally recognised, however. It tends to lie beyond the theories' horizons.

(Deigh 2004: p. 10)

Deigh's is one more way of laying-out a familiar problem faced by those who wish to theorise emotion.[1] On the one side we have the cognitivists, who emphasise (and sometimes essentialise) intentionality and on the other side we have the Darwinians/Jamesians who emphasise (and sometimes essentialise) bodily changes (or how those changes feel).

1.1. Emotion, intentionality, persons and their endowments

The standard way in which both sides of the divide try to bridge the gap, if not initiate rapprochement, is to imbue something sub-personal with cognitive powers. So, as we saw in the previous chapter, Robinson talks of 'subception', which is perception only sub-personally-so; i.e. it is perception taking place without the 'perceiver's' awareness of their perceiving. Prinz invokes computational metaphors to construct a theory of the mind which can account for the existence of perception while there is an absence of any concurrent cognition, as Prinz defines cognition (see ch. 3, Section 4.1, and Prinz 2003a: p. 78). What such moves hope to achieve is the thought that the bodily changes are intentional in that they are borne of, or are, sorts of 'perceptions', just not what we had hitherto understood as perceptions. They are, we are told, the perceptions of something sub-personal.

We find cognitivists employing similar tactics. Of late, even those usually identified as pure, unreconstructed cognitivists have attempted to bridge the divide. For example, in a late paper, Robert Solomon (2003a, b, c) argued that the judgements he takes to be the emotion can be 'pre-linguistic' (p. 15) 'judgements of the body' (p. 14). He writes,

Thus the judgements that I claim are constitutive of the emotion may be non-propositional and bodily as well as propositional and articulate, and they may further become reflective and self-conscious. What is cognition? I would still insist that it is basically judgement, both reflective and pre-reflective, both knowing how (as skills and practices) and knowing that (as propositional knowledge). A cognitive theory of emotion thus embodies what is often referred to as 'affect' and 'feeling' without dismissing these as unanalysable.

(p. 16)

This is a way of retaining his commitment to the intentionality of emotion while accommodating the challenge posed by those who hold that bodily changes are central. But the talk of such 'judgements' being pre-linguistic is unhelpful—Solomon prefers 'pre-linguistic', while the author he draws upon, George Downing (2001), uses 'pre-cognitive'. It is just difficult to grasp what might be meant by a pre-linguistic judgement, such that it raises the question as to the role being played by the 'pre' prefix. What could it be for linguistically endowed beings' bodies to judge pre-linguistically? Do they judge a pre-conceptualised, brute world? Solomon, in a similar manner to Robinson and Prinz, tries to resolve the problem by predicating of something sub-personal what we, in ordinary language, predicate of persons: i.e. that they judge. This said, Solomon is onto something important, at the end of the above quote, when he insists that cognitivists' invocation of affect does not commit them to the invocation of an unanalysable component.

In making this concession, in adapting his judgementalism in this direction, Solomon moves his version of cognitivism in the direction of those we might call the 'hybrid cognitivists', such as Goldie and Greenspan. As we saw in the previous chapter, Goldie argues for the intentionality of feelings, both bodily—with the body or part thereof as object of the feeling—and 'outwards-directed' feelings—that is, feelings directed towards the object of the emotion (see Goldie 2004: p. 92). And Goldie *seems* correct. We do *feel* the pain *in our leg*, or *in our head*, and we do *feel* afraid *of the dog* which stands before us foaming at the mouth and growling; these are the objects of which those feelings are about, they are the objects of those feelings. But, as I noted in the previous chapter, we would like to know more than this. Goldie joins Robinson, Prinz, and Solomon, in trying to resolve the problem by saying of something sub-personal what we would usually say of the person; for it is the *person* that feels the pain in his leg or in his head and it is the *person* who feels—who

IS—afraid of the dog. Thus it is the *'person'* in the sentence which is the locus of our predication of intentionality, not 'feeling'.

In a similar manner to Goldie, Patricia Greenspan writes, 'affect evaluates! Emotional affect or feeling is itself evaluative—and the result can be summed up in a proposition' (Greenspan 2004: p. 132). Now, of course we can raise the same issues, as those that arose in our discussion of Goldie (immediately above), with Greenspan here. For what all those that we have briefly looked at here, Robinson, Prinz, Solomon, Goldie, and Greenspan do in trying to overcome the problem posed is give in to the temptation to commit, what Bennett and Hacker (2003 and 2007) have termed, the mereological fallacy. That is to say, in trying to find a solution to their problem they predicate of a part what is a property or a capacity of the whole.

1.1.1. The formal analysis of thought and theories of mind

Nevertheless, the mereological objection aside, Greenspan makes an important point (following the em-dash in the above quote), which adds to that Solomon makes. Greenspan's point is important to bear in mind so as not to be misled by those critics, such as Deigh, Griffiths, and D'arms and Jacobson, who assume predicating content implies a predication of a propositional stance. As Greenspan alludes to here, invoking evaluation, and thus content and intentionality, does not entail that one must hold to the stronger and more problematic claim that a propositional stance must have been taken to the world. The content can be read-off the world, which can then be represented in propositional form. This is the Fregean thought; and it is something which needs to be kept in mind. Saying with Frege that a thought is expressed in a sentence with propositional form is not to commit oneself to the view that for a person to have a thought is for them to have taken up a propositional attitude towards the world, in the robust sense of them believing or judging that x. It is merely to say that this is how we represent the sense of the thought for the purposes of analysis of *the* mind (as opposed to the study of the minds of individuals).

So why would/do these modifications of intentionality not satisfy Deigh? He writes,

> Standard cognitivist theories, as I observed earlier, explain this feature [intentionality] by attributing propositional thought to emotions, for they take the emotions distinctive of human beings as the

paradigm of their subject and the thought content of these emotions is propositional.

(Deigh 2004: p. 18)

These modifications do not satisfy Deigh because he overstates his case. A cognitivist in the philosophy of the emotions, even a 'standard cognitivist', does not of necessity—i.e. in virtue of being a cognitivist and having intentionality as central to their account—face the problems Deigh claims they do, because they are not *obliged* to attribute propositional thought to emotions, as Deigh claims they are. Sure, there are those who *seem* to so attribute, as does the early Solomon—I say he *seems* to, because I take him at his word that he never held to such a view, despite *appearances* to the contrary—as does Gabriele Taylor (1985) and as does the neoStoic Martha Nussbaum (2001), it seems to most commentators. However, there is nothing in a commitment to the centrality of intentionality that entails a commitment to emotions as propositional attitudes. Deigh's criticism relies on conflating the Fregean formal analysis of thoughts as propositions, which is a commitment to a certain form of philosophical analysis of *the* mind—one which is concerned to resist any temptation to, or slide into, psychologism—with a theoretical position in the philosophy of mind that holds that to have a thought about the world is to have a propositional attitude towards the world, which is a substantive theoretical claim about the nature of the mental content of individuals. Frege was concerned with the philosophical study of *the* mind, not the psychological study of people's minds. Anyway, that's enough said about Frege, we need not labour this point here.[2] Identifying this conflation is enough to demonstrate the misunderstanding at the heart of the criticisms of Deigh and of Griffiths (recall, Griffiths even goes so far as to label cognitivists 'propositional attitude theorists').

However, having rejected the conflation, there is still more work to be done. For, in resisting the identification of a certain form of analysis of thought content with the having of a propositional attitude, in some robust sense of 'having', we need to give an account of content, which can accommodate the intentional character of emotion to which we are committed. This is what I claim for world-taking cognitivism (see Chapter 3, Section 2.3, and this chapter, below, Section 1.3). It does not commit one to the equating of content and intentionality, on the one hand, with the having of a propositional attitude, on the other. Though neither does it commit one to the Fregean analysis of thoughts by representing thoughts in propositions. We can analyse thought in that which it is most ready-to-hand, the language with which we speak, without encoding that language in a *Begrifschrift* or as propositions. It is in analysing thought in this way that we resist the postulation of propositional shadows to thought.[3]

1.1.2. Emotion and object

There is another, somewhat less intellectualist, point regarding the intentionality of emotion, which is captured by the question: 'What about objectless emotions?', that is to say, those states which might be thought of as moods, though not only those. Dread, for example, can be characterised as a sort of 'objectless', global fear. Although, we might keep in mind that those states that we might see as 'objectless' versions of object-directed emotions do not always have distinct names; sadness, for example, can be either intentional or 'objectless', if we are willing to take 'objectless' sadness to be distinct from depression. However, the idea that there are objectless emotions is not as straightforward as it initially seems. The thought that there are such is related to the point just discussed. For the discussions often equate the claim that

    a. an emotion has an object.

    With the commitment to:

    b. The *conscious* directing of a thought onto that object, i.e. having a propositional attitude.

There is no need to equate (a) and (b). We can say that it is part of the *logic* or *grammar* of emotions that they have an (formal) object, without committing ourselves to what strikes me as a patently false claim that the having of an emotional episode always involves the 'having in view' the object of that emotional episode. There are alternative ways of characterising what we might initially take to be objectless emotional states—which way is appropriate, if any, will have to be read-off the phenomenon in its social situation. So some cases of objectless emotion might well have intentional objects, only their objects are diffuse complexes: e.g. it is not the snake which is the object of my fear, nor the 'overwhelming physical danger' which is the formal object of my fear, represented, on this occasion, by the (meaning the) snake (has for us). It is rather that this region, in which I am residing for the next month, is high risk, not only in terms of people receiving snake bites, but also cerebral malaria, various other life-threatening and/or life-transforming illnesses aligned with poor healthcare provision, where receiving blood transfusions can be very dangerous. All these diffuse factors make up the complex object of my emotional state. That state might well be one of dread until the complex, through therapy,[4] is made manifest. At which time it might become fear. The putative lack of intentionality, the lack of aboutness, is not necessarily a lack of aboutness at all, it is a lack of an immediate grasp on the object owing to our, at present, failure to grasp the complexity of the object. The aboutness is there, only it is about what we initially take to be diffuse 'objects', which are seemingly unrelated and taken alone, as discrete, would not seem to us to warrant fear. We later come to see they are aspects or elements of the same complex object.

There are further possibilities; the aboutness might also be global, here the object is (our taking of, our conceptualisation of) the world. This can be understood in a number of different ways. First the world is the complex object of the emotion. Second the world stands proxy for the object of the emotion until I get a grip on the complex object; that is, the world seemed to me to be the object of my emotion because my emotional state coloured the world such that it seemed that the world was playing this role. On registering and acknowledging the object we see that it was not the world, after all. A refusal to acknowledge complex objects can be borne of nothing other than a prejudice in favour of simples. Again, world-taking cognitivism is well placed to avoid being prone to such prejudice through its emphasis on our conceptualisations and the internal relations between concepts.

1.2. Of Beasts and of intentionality

So, Deigh's problematisation of the first fact—of intentionality—can be seen to rest on a number of assumptions. Furthermore, in identifying these assumptions and thus holding to fact one—the centrality of intentionality—we do not necessarily, as Deigh claims we do, face a problem of accepting fact two—that emotions are common to humans and beasts. The thought that fact two causes us a problem is similarly borne of a misunderstanding as to what one is committed to in talking of conceptual capacities, in the way in which I have when laying out the world-taking cognitivist framework. All we need do, to establish that the beast is endowed with intentionality, is establish that the beast exists in a normative context.

What might be the bare minimum required in order that we might predicate of the beast such an endowment? Well, if there is something akin to parental nurturing of the behavioural attributes of the species in the natural history of the species, then we can talk of that species' second nature, i.e. of it having an enculturated nature. Of course, one would want to investigate the scope of that enculturation and thus the scope of the second nature. Linguistic capacity is one distinctive way in which humans have evolved to register, to acknowledge, and to communicate to other humans loci of significance in the world. Saying this does not imply that non-linguistic animals cannot register loci of significance, too. Talking of conceptual capacities is one way in which we can intelligibly talk about an animal's capacity to register, acknowledge, and communicate to other members of the species loci of significance in their world. The specific nature and scope of such registering, acknowledging, and communicating is another matter, which I need not speculate on here. All that needs to be conceded here, for my purposes, is that some species of non-human animals are (a) nurtured (there is something akin to training) by other members of their species in early life, and (b) that they can register, acknowledge and, to some degree, communicate to other members of their species loci of significance in the world. In this sense we might say of the tick that it has no second nature and that it does not exist in a normative context. Of the dog and of the chimp, we can say that they have a second nature and that they exist in a normative context, though in both cases to a degree which falls short of that enjoyed by human animals.

All that needs conceding is that there is something which is appropriate to characterise as the dog or the chimp getting right or getting wrong; i.e., in order to say of Spot the dog that he exists in a normative context we only need to be able to say of Spot, for example, that he mistook some X for food, and that he has now *learned* not to mistake such Xs for food in future, whether that be because his mother guided him away, it tasted foul, or it made him sick. Put another way, we need only show that there is an aspect of the behaviour of the species which cannot be adequately captured, it cannot be adequately explained, by subsumption under strict causal laws, but can be explained in terms of the beast having learnt and acted in accordance with a rule. If we can show such, then we can say of the beast it exists in a normative context and has a second nature.

It is this discrepancy between the scope of (say) the chimp's second nature and the human animal's second nature—why we might feel more ready to refer to the latter's second nature as their *Bildung*—that leads to Heidegger's claim that animals are 'poor in world' in comparison to 'world-forming' human animals.[5] However, while Heidegger's distinction is insightful, it seems too crude in the context of the present discussion (a discussion which is not Heidegger's, so no criticism is necessarily implied here). One should resist the temptation to group all non-human animals (beasts) together; surely we would want to differentiate widely divergent degrees of 'poverty-in-world'. It seems that the tick-in-its-environment is ripe for study in terms of stimulus–response mechanisms subsumable under strict causal laws (with minimal invocation of *ceteris paribus* qualifiers), and even that such studies would likely be exhaustive. Equally, it seems that to restrict oneself to such a form of study when one approaches the chimp-in-its-world or the dolphin-in-its-world is far from perspicacious (see MacIntyre (1999) for philosophical discussion of the latter).

Given the discussion of the last two paragraphs, how might we understand intentionality? McDowell might be of assistance.

> Intentionality or content depends on a normative context. ... [T]he first norm to mention in this connection, it seems to me, is the norm embodied in the so-called identity theory of truth. It is correct or incorrect to judge that something is a chair according to whether or not it is indeed a chair. No doubt when we set about saying what it is for that condition to be satisfied, we shall need to invoke inferential connections.... But going directly to them risks encouraging the thought—which is not one I'm happy with—that insisting on a normative context for the idea of content amounts to undertaking to explain the idea of content in terms of the inference, as in Brandom (1994).
>
> (McDowell 2000b: p. 105)

Now, we should be clear here, one does not need to subscribe to an 'identity theory of truth', know what one is, or even have grasped the concepts of 'truth' and 'falsity' to qualify as having intentionality, on McDowell's account. One needs merely to take something to be a particular or a generic *something* and have the possibility of being corrected if one has mistakenly taken something to be that particular or generic *something*. Indeed, we can adapt McDowell's talk of truth into talk of registering loci of significance, mistakenly taking something to be (a token or instance of) a locus and being corrected by another member of one's species. To repeat, any species that has as part of its nature and its natural history what can be characterised as nurturing and/or training has such a capacity and it therefore makes sense to talk of their thoughts having content and their having intentionality.[6]

1.3. World-taking cognitivism revisited

The force of Deigh's challenge dissipates when looked at closely. He assumed that an account of emotion that had intentionality central to it must subscribe to a particular picture of mind and mental content that thus precluded non-linguistic beasts from the possession of thought content. As we saw, there is no need to subscribe to this picture of mental content. However, we saw that the response of many to the 'problem' posed by Deigh was to merely ascribe intentionality to something sub-personal. Such theorising is of no help in elucidating the way we meet our world. At worst it falls foul of the mereological fallacy. At best it merely theorises into existence shadows of attributes that are actually attributes of persons, which it then progresses to predicate of something sub-personal. My suggestion is that world-taking cognitivism avoids such travails. Let us now revisit this.

1. World-taking cognitivism is offered only as a framework for understanding or as a therapeutic device.
2. World-taking cognitivism is 'world-taking' to the extent that our emotions are, to a significant degree, answerable to the way the meaningful world *is*. Emotions are cognitive.
3. Our emotions are neither truly passive (affective, James) nor plainly chosen by us (Judgements, Solomon and Sartre). They are ways of reading and of taking (grasping) the world; more precisely they are ways in which we acknowledge loci of significance in the world. Our taking of the world is enabled through our conceptual capacities: our second nature. Thus given our nature, our *Bildung*, the loci of significance bear in and down on us. We are both answerable for our emotions and subject to them.
4. I employ the term cognitivism/cognitivist in the sense in which that term is employed in metaethics and *not* in the way it is employed in the contemporary philosophy of mind, cognitive psychology, and 'cognitive science'. The term is not used, therefore, to denote the existence of cognitive processes. When I talk of the cognitive powers, I am talking of the abilities of a person (in the case of human animals).
5. None of this amounts to the advancement of a philosophical theory of emotion. What I here term 'world-taking cognitivism' is merely a suggestion as to a way of seeing our relationship to our world and to others through a reflection upon our conceptual capacities and the internal relations holding between concepts, on occasions of use.

I will elaborate on each of these five points.

1.3.1. A framework for understanding

The content of emotional experience is/can be 'read-off' the phenomena, the phenomena being identified as that expressed by a (enculturated) person, in a social situation. Such reading-off is available to us once we have gained clarity regarding the logic of our language. In this respect I am eschewing an approach to the emotions, found in much of the philosophical literature, which identifies the philosophical task as that of theorising the substantive content of emotions, or defining the meaning of emotion terms through identifying them as natural kinds or in terms of necessary and sufficient conditions. My concern has been to merely provide a framework that might aid to dispel puzzlement and confusion when confronted with emotional expression, which might help one understand, or grasp, the emotion. In this respect world-taking cognitivism is *not* advanced as another philosophical theory of emotion, but rather as a therapeutic device which is designed to aid one to see the yearning for a theory to be borne of a failure to have gained clarity within our domain of enquiry.

Some might object that they suffer no sense of puzzlement and no sense of confusion. One can say in response: Then you do not need the framework. Some might claim that they suffer neither confusion nor puzzlement while still commencing to provide a theory of emotion; in this case we might ask the question: why the need for a theory?

Ultimately the framework for understanding can be cast away. For, once one understands the expression, once one has identified the expression, one has *no* need for the framework. The framework is thus an aid to understanding not an interpretive device; it does not serve to *render* the expression in other terms but serves to aid one's understanding of the expression in its own terms, by merely describing the conceptual resources on which the expression draws.

1.3.2. Takings of the world

World-taking cognitivism is no more than, is mere shorthand for, an attempt to perspicuously present the emotional expression so as to bring to light, by describing the meaning relations in play, the resources which serve to give sense to that expression. The description serves to show that our emotional responses are responses to the meaningful world. At a minimum we can say that emotions, therefore, are a class of modes through which a person's reading of the meaningful world are manifested. Furthermore, membership of this class does not entail anything being common to all members; rather membership merely entails that emotions share, at least, family resemblances as modes that make manifest a person's reading of the world. This is all philosophy should tell us about emotions. Beyond this we should examine the phenomena.

1.3.3. *Neither passion's slave nor sovereign*

The claim that emotions are cognitive as opposed to non-cognitive does not commit us to the problematic view that our emotional responses to the world cannot be wrong (*mistakings*, as it were), in some sense. It merely commits us to the claim that our emotional responses, when understood as responses to the world, are truth-apt. Or rather, it would be better to say that they can be shown to be either appropriate or inappropriate; that they, or better *us* in our emotional state, are answerable to the way the meaningful world is, given our sensibilities as the enculturated person expressing the emotion. In this sense, regarding world-answerability, I largely appeal to the substance of Charles Travis's paper 'The Twilight of Empiricism' while disagreeing with the contrast he draws at the outset. Here Travis uses an example of being disgusted at Sid's food-smeared face as a case of something which is not answerable to the world; I have contended here and in the previous chapter that such disgust *is* answerable to the world, in the sense that it is a response to the way the world is under an aspect, seen by a being with certain enculturated sensibilities.

The contrast class to the world of which I am talking here, we might say, following to an extent Heidegger's discussion of 'the open' in *Parmenides*, is the 'environment' (*Umwelt*).[7] What are called reflex actions can be understood on the model of physiological reactions of an animal to the causal impact of certain triggers in its environment. In contrast, emotional responses to the world are responses of an enculturated being to loci of significance in its meaningful world.

Empiricism always sees before it an animal in its environment, a disenchanted material environment governed by causal laws. The relationship between the animal and the environment is one of cause and effect, stimulus and response. This model therefore drives the tendency to theorise into existence modules in an attempt to explain from where meaning comes (cf. Chapter 3, Section 4). By contrast, an enculturated being lives in a meaningful world, a world to which it responds in a manner which makes manifest the significance of aspects of that world for that enculturated being.[8]

The difference, therefore, is that for enculturated beings, such as, but not exclusively, humans, there is a central role for the concept of *acknowledging* the loci of significance it finds in its world. For the animal in its

Umwelt, [9] there is no place for acknowledgement; the animal's loci of significance trigger its responses, it is not open to the animal to deny, turn away from, nor choose to acknowledge those loci. The loci of significance in the animal's environment stand in a relationship to the animal which can be subsumed under law-like explanations with minimal *ceteris paribus* clauses, which, all things considered, might be species-world specific. For the enculturated being explanations which abstract from the crucial role of that being, explanations which abstract from that being's ability to acknowledge or turn away from the loci of significance in its world, fail to capture the distinctive nature of that being's relationship to the world.

1.3.4. Cognition as world-answerability (not as a process)

There are two prominent uses of the term cognitivism in contemporary analytic philosophy. One is that found in cognitive science and the contemporary philosophy of mind. Here 'cognition' is generally used to denote, or used in a manner which implies, mental (sometimes brain) processes. The other use is that found in metaethics. Here there is no commitment to distinctively mental processes, nor to the thought that brain processes *explain* our mental capacities. In metaethics the term 'cognitivism' denotes a commitment to the view that ethical claims are truth-apt. The use to which I put the term cognitivist/cognitivism in 'world-taking cognitivism' invokes this latter use. Emotions are answerable to the world, given that the world is understood as the conceptualised world and, further, that we do not consider that world as externally related to the enculturated being that is having the emotion.

How such a position cashes out is that when we are faced with a person expressing, say, shame we identify the meaning of their expression through identification of the internal relations holding for them such that they might see the event that gives rise to their emotional episode as meriting that emotional response (which can involve dispositions to act, patterned changes in the ANS, etc.), as meriting their emotion in this situation. That is to say, their grasp of the concept of shame is also, in this context, to grasp the meaning, the conceptualisation, of this event. For the event under this conceptualisation and shame are internally related. This means, as I said in the previous chapter, simply that that person *has* the emotional response to that event (under that aspect); they simply have the emotion. In other words, we ask what holds true about the person's grasping of the event such that the event merits shame for this person, given their enculturated, second nature. The world-taker expresses shame if and only if the event—which encapsulates the world-taker—is characterised as (the internal relations hold such that it is) shameful. Put another way, it is correct or incorrect to feel shame in relation to some object—some conceptualised shame scenario—according to whether or not that object is indeed shameful: i.e. do the internal relations hold between the concept of shame, as grasped by this person with these sensibilities (this *Bildung*), and the conceptualised state of affairs, as taken by (as bears down on) this person, such that the latter is correctly taken to be a shame scenario?

1.3.5. Resisting theorising emotion

Identifying the relations holding between concepts, such as those between shame and remorse, is not to propound a theory. It is to describe how the grasping of one concept might carry with it, in a particular context, another. That is to say, grasping shame entails, on some occasions, in some contexts, also having grasped the concept of remorse, maybe the concept of human being, etc. Similarly we could work with the concepts of disgust, dignity, etc. (see Chapter 3, Section 2.3.1). There is nothing mysterious, much less theoretical, about the invocation of concepts being internally related. It is simply to note, to describe, the nature of our conceptual capacities. For example, saying of someone that they have grasped the concept of 'fire' entails that we predicate of them that they have also grasped the concepts of, say, 'heat' and of 'burning'. For a person who employed the word 'fire' while unable to demonstrate that they knew that fire burns and that fire generates heat would not be able to make standard linguistic moves with the word 'fire'; in the absence of a grasp of the concepts of 'heat' and of 'burning' a person is not correctly described as having grasped the concept of 'fire'. Again, we here merely invoke the truism that goes somewhat grandiosely by the name of the identity theory of truth. One has grasped the concept of fire if and only if one has in fact grasped the concept of fire. Not knowing that fire is hot, that fire burns, is to fall short of fulfilling one side of the equation, thus one has failed to grasp the concept.

Now, one can employ the word 'fire' in some contexts and on some occasions whereby the internal relation between it and, say, 'heat' does not hold, to the extent that the relation is not active on that occasion of use. One significant difference between a concept such as 'fire' and one such as 'shame' is the level of cultural specificity demanded, the number of concepts with which it can be internally related and the level of occasion sensitivity demanded for the internal relations to hold or be active. The internal relations that might hold on an occasion between 'shame' and other concepts such as 'disgust', 'dignity', 'human being', 'justice', 'care', 'love', 'remorse', or 'world' do so only given a high level of cultural specificity: a specificity regarding the enculturation of the expresser of shame. This is one reason why we often talk of an audience or an honour group being central to the experience of shame (see the previous chapter, Section 2.3).

2. Exploring shame

In his introductory chapter to *Shame: Interpersonal Behaviour, Psychopathology, and Culture* , the psychologist (and co-editor of the collection), Paul Gilbert, writes the following,

> Not only are there different schools and theoretical approaches to shame, but it can also be conceptualised and studied in terms of its components and mechanisms (Tangney 1996). It can be examined in terms of *emotion* (e.g. as a primary affect in its own right, as an auxiliary emotion, or as a composite of other emotions such as fear, anger, or self-disgust); *cognitions and beliefs* about the self (e.g., that one is and/or is seen by others to be inferior, flawed, inadequate, etc.); *behaviours and actions* (e.g., such as running away, hiding and concealing, or attacking others to cover one's shame); *evolved mechanisms* (e.g. the expression of shame seems to use similar biobehavioural systems to those of animals expressing submissive behaviour); and *interpersonal dynamic interrelationships* (shamed and shamer; Fosum and Mason, 1986; Harper and Hoopes, 1990). Shame can also be used to describe phenomena at many different levels, including internal self-experiences, relational episodes, and cultural practices for maintaining honour and prestige.
>
> (Gilbert 1998: pp. 3–4)

One does not need to spend too long on this paragraph to see that the list with which Gilbert furnishes us is not so much a taxonomy of mutually exclusive conceptualisations and modes of study, but a set of interweaving perspectives we can take on an expression of shame so as to make it intelligible. Gilbert tells us that we can conceptualise and examine shame in terms of: *emotion; cognitions and beliefs; behaviours and actions; evolved mechanisms;* and *interpersonal dynamic interrelationships.* Let us examine the list.

Well first of all, when Gilbert employs 'emotion' as his first category, he does so in a rather specialised and restricted way. He already has in play a particular account of emotion, i.e. emotion-as-affect, as found in the affect program research (see Chapter 1, Section 1.2.1). As we saw in Chapter 1, while Griffiths thought the affect program research strong on certain basic emotions, such as fear and disgust, he rejected it as an account of emotions such as shame, which he termed a 'higher cognitive emotion' (though he now prefers the term 'complex emotion'). Griffiths seems right, on this. However, let us entertain the thought that we might correlate shame expressions with specific patterned changes in the ANS, and thus hold that this differentiates it from other states. However, this is still to fall short of a conceptualisation of shame. For, we need only accept the *possibility* that such changes in the ANS could be induced through the administration of drugs. Would the resultant state be a case of shame? Would we not want to differentiate between drug-induced 'shame' and life-world-induced shame? Indeed, if we are to take the veracity of the Method actor's claim to experience the emotion at face value and we want to then differentiate this from 'genuine' shame, do we not then see that to identify the emotion with the affect program, with the patterned changes in the ANS correlatable with that emotional expression, is to actually identify shame in a way which leaves us with no resources to differentiate between a drug-induced manifestation of some aspects of an episode of shame (drug-shame), a practice-induced controlled manifestation of some aspects of shame (Method-shame, which we can even concede might involve patterned changes in the ANS) and life-world-induced shame (shame).

Identifying the emotion with specific patterned changes in the ANS is borne of fetishising a certain form of explanation, and in doing so fails as a useful explanation. It has striking similarities to a problem with the natural kinds literature, identified by Avrum Stroll, which I discussed in Chapter 1 (Section 2.2). There, following arguments made by Stroll (1998), I wrote,

> Stroll suggests that there is an un-argued for neglect of the phenomenological differences between natural kinds sharing the same microstructure but having a different phenomenology: such as (e.g.) between water, steam, and ice; all have the same microstructure, but all are not sensically called water, and for good reason. The phenomenological differences are not only crucial to people in their day-to-day lives, but the understanding and harnessing of such differences has led to scientific advance: such as steam power, to employ

a somewhat dated though socially, historically, and scientifically significant example.

Identifying an emotion with a specific configuration of changes in the ANS is to make a similar mistake. It is important to us that we differentiate between drug-induced facsimiles of aspects of shame, practice-induced facsimiles of aspects of shame, and life-world-induced lived shame. In saying this, therefore, we come to see that the other items on Gilbert's list all have a role to play. What weight the role of each plays in our enquiry depends on our purpose, but all, I would suggest, have a role to play.

This is the key. It is not that we have to choose a methodology or a way of conceptualising shame from the list on offer. Rather, we need to identify our purpose, what it is we wish to understand. First-off we will have to identify the emotion; that is, what counts for us as a case of shame? How do we answer this question? Should we not look at expressions of shame and try to find some relevant, non-accidental, commonalities? I would argue so. What we are likely to find is that the commonalities we observe can be placed into those categories that Gilbert lists. So, expressions of emotion will often be supported by the identification of certain other beliefs held (see, for example, Taylor's (1985) account, and Chapter 3, Section 2.2 (above)), they will often be accompanied by, or better the full expression will include, dispositions to act in certain ways (Ryle, 1949), if not actions themselves; and those actions might well strike us as akin to the behaviour of social animals from other species, such that we take there to be strong grounds for telling an evolutionary story (see Darwin); furthermore, we might find that making sense of these beliefs and actions can only be done by embedding them in the context of interpersonal dynamic interrelationships, i.e. their social situation.

But let's pause here for a moment. Is this list all it seems? For example, there is no reason to accept the 'cognitions and beliefs' – 'behaviours and actions' dichotomy; we can rather talk of takings of the world *as* dispositions to act; i.e. as another, more perspicuous, way of talking of dispositions to act. For, someone who takes an event thus takes that event conceptualised, with all the normative richness to which their moral sensibilities, their *Bildung*, afford them. Talking of a person's taking of the world, that taking being of a conceptualised world, those concepts having normative properties, the taking of which merits, under the right conditions, certain actions helps us guard against any thought that we have an inner–outer dichotomy in play, with cognitions being necessarily inner and actions being outer and caused by those inner cognitions.

Rather we can talk of our taking the world, in all its normative richness, and our actions finding both reason and motive in those takings. Put another way, we make sense of our actions by embedding them in our takings of the world, as enculturated beings. Furthermore, that we are enculturated beings acting on our takings of a meaningful world is likely to capture what Gilbert means by the last term on his list: interpersonal and dynamic relationships. The taking of a meaningful world includes others in that world and the meanings we read-off their actions, the meaning of those actions, and how we react to those actions. While, further, our sensibilities are formed through our interactions with others and our learning a public language (see Chapter 3, Sections 2.3 and 3.2.1). Actions have meaning in a social situation. Furthermore, in talking of our second (enculturated) nature, our *Bildung*, we invoke—not deny—our first nature. Therefore, our nature as evolved animals, with certain evolved traits, will take its place in our understanding of some of our characteristics.

World-taking cognitivism accommodates all these perspectives on emotion, while guarding against seeing them as exclusive and competing categories. We describe the meaning relations which hold such that a person sees the world in this way, as meriting this response.

3. An audience to shame

3.1. The inhumanity of humanity

One way in which a taking of the world which merits shame can be manifest in action is in the disposition to hide oneself from others. This can be because those others, in their attitudes, can embody the meaning relations one is acknowledging in one's shame: *'I feel ashamed before another'*. However, this should not lead us to believe there is a requirement for an audience or honour group, actual or imagined. Consider the following passage from Léopard, a perpetrator of heinous violent crimes against innocent individuals during the Rwandan genocide. Léopard is one of Jean Hatzfeld's interviewees in *A Time for Machetes*. In this book Hatzfeld relays testimony of perpetrators of the Rwandan genocide,[10] gathered through interviews conducted in a Rwandan prison. In the chapter titled 'Remorse and Regrets' Léopard says the following:

> Some try to show remorse but tremble before the truth. They sneak around it, because of too many conflicting interests, and wind up flung backwards.

It was in a camp in Congo that I first felt my heart ache. I prayed, hoping to find relief, but in vain. After prayers or hymns, shame waited for me, without fail. So I began being sorry out loud, paying no attention to the mockery spewing from my comrades' mouths. In prison I told my whole truth. It came out freely. Ever since then, whenever someone asks me for it, it flows the same way.

> (Léopard, in Hatzfeld 2005b: 154)

Léopard's shame comes as he acknowledges his crime. It comes despite the mockery of his comrades who have yet to, or who do not, acknowledge their crime. Those mocking comrades are Léopard's immediate audience; they stand as strongest candidate for being his (most immediate) honour group. Yet it is not before their gaze that he feels his shame, so to speak. Léopard feels shame despite those around him mocking him for the way his shame makes him act. So, how do we make sense of Léopard's path to shame, on its own terms?

Let's try, here. Léopard has over time acknowledged his crime; this might have emerged as the anti-Tutsi propaganda of the months that preceded the genocide and the months of the genocide began to ebb. As Léopard again began to see those people he murdered, those Tutsi, as human beings, as neighbours, as people. As his moral sensibilities begin to return he begins to see the actions he carried out with his machete, the crimes he committed, for the moral crimes they are. The true meaning of those crimes bears down upon Léopard. His first awareness is his aching heart, which he tries to absent through prayer. But to no avail. Shame follows every prayer he offers and hymn he sings.

The way, I suggest, that we can make sense of Léopard's crime and his emerging remorse and shame is only through talking of his seeing and not seeing his crime for the moral crime that it is at different points. I would suggest that in perpetrating his crimes, during the genocide, Léopard is aware of the objective status of his actions as a crime under international and domestic law. However, he had turned away from, had denied, that which would force him to acknowledge his moral crime; he had denied, turned-away-from, that which would allow him to acknowledge the true meaning of his actions. Léopard's denied that in carrying out those actions he had not merely violated a code to which he was bound by an external authority, but that he had done violence to the very fabric of human existence (and, therefore, his own).

In the perpetration of his crime, Léopard refused to acknowledge the humanity of his victims. It was not that he refused to admit that the extension of human being is 'member of the species *Homo Sapiens*'. It was rather that he had refused to acknowledge, had turned-away-from, the meaning of human being as a moral concept, he had denied it to those he subjected to brutality, suffering, and death; in doing so, in being able to do so, he had also denied it to himself. This is what creeps-up on Léopard. This said, we can make sense of Philip Gourevitch's comment (reprinted on the front cover of Hatzfeld's book) that 'Hatzfeld's harrowing documentation of the voices of Rwandan killers reminds us once again how perfectly human it can be to be perfectly inhumane'. The first 'human' in the sentence denotes, I suggest, 'member of the species *Homo Sapiens*' and the second, in the locution 'inhumane', invokes the moral concept human being. This latter, I should like to suggest, is to what Léopard's shame testifies; that is, his inability to fully escape the moral meaning of human being.[11]

3.2. Shame: heteronomy and autonomy

Another point raised by our reading of Léopard's testifying to his shame is that of the audience. The notion of the audience taken as central to shame, on many accounts, can mislead us. For not only can shame come upon one in the absence of an audience but it can come upon one in the face of an audience which would have one deny one's shame. The audience, therefore, is simply a metaphor that can serve to illustrate the shift in meanings which occur as shame comes upon one. It should not be taken as more than a metaphor and as thus implying the necessarily heteronomous nature of shame; that is, of shame *requiring* our acceding to the judgements of others.

In Chapter 4 of his book *Shame and Necessity* Bernard Williams (1993) concerns himself with this question regarding the nature of shame: whether shame is heteronomous or autonomous.[12] Let us put this in less philosophically technical language; to illustrate, let us say, for now, that some instances of shame can involve the thought that one has failed to uphold a value or set thereof, and feels shame because of this; one feels one's status and/or value as a person diminished in one's shame. When one is so ashamed is one so because one accepts the judgements of others regarding the values one must uphold and whether or not one has so done? Or, is one ashamed because one acknowledges the meaning of those values oneself and recognises oneself as failing to uphold those values? Williams argues the latter. Shame can be autonomous. He is not arguing that shame can never be heteronomous, but rather he is arguing against the thought that it need be so, that it *is* a heteronomous emotion. I agree. At the start of Chapter 5, Williams writes,

The Homeric, tragic, in particular Sophoclean, characters are represented to us as experiencing a necessity to act in certain ways, a conviction that they must do certain things.... We should understand this in terms of mechanisms of shame. The source of the necessity is in the agent, an internalised other whose view the agent can respect. Indeed he can identify with this figure, and the respect is to that extent self-respect; but at the same time the figure remains a genuine other, the embodiment of a real social expectation. At the extreme, the sense of this necessity lies in the thought that one could not live and look others in the eye if one did certain things: a thought that may be to varying degrees figurative but can also be in a deadly sense literal, as it was with Ajax. These necessities are grounded in the *ēthos*, the projects, the individual nature of the agent, and the way he conceives the relation of his life to other people's.

(Williams 1993: p. 103)

Now, as I said, I agree with Williams's argument that shame can be autonomous. But we need to do more to clarify the nature of that autonomy than merely invoke metaphors of 'internalised others'. For, it is not too difficult to imagine the response of someone committed to the heteronomy of shame, on reading Williams's invocation of an 'internalised other'. We need to show how the role played by the 'other' in a heteronomous account can be replaced by something else. In other words, how the aspect shift in evaluation takes place in the absence of an act of acceding to the value-claims of others. For our shame is heteronomous if our shame comes upon us owing to our desire not to have our status or value diminished in the eyes of others. In this case it is not that we see an event involving us as shameful that merits our shame but rather it is our desire not to be diminished in the eyes of our honour group, who judge us so diminished.

Again I think there is no need to accept the dichotomy, such as it is presented. Let us look at Ajax's shame. 'On Achilles' death, his armour was awarded, by common consent, to Odysseus rather than to Ajax. In his rage at this decision, Ajax launches an attack on what he thinks to be his comrades in arms; it transpires that he had actually attacked and slaughtered a herd of cows and sheep. Ajax's shame at his actions leads him to suicide. He believes that in suicide he will both escape his shame and demonstrate that he has the courage to acknowledge his shame. As Dilman puts it, 'in his suicide he thus *separates* himself from his disgrace by repudiating his own behaviour—without evading shouldering responsibility for it—and in the courage it takes to kill himself he regains his honour' (Dilman 1999: pp. 314–315).

Williams (and Dilman in his comment on Williams' discussion of Ajax) both want to argue that one can make perfect sense of Ajax's shame as being autonomous, as not being heteronomous. I would like to argue that it is something of both, neither exclusively one nor exclusively the other. Ajax's taking of his failure to be awarded Achilles' armour and his slaughter of sheep and cattle rather than the warriors who were his intended targets is a taking which, we might say, is under the aspect afforded him by his *ēthos*. Put another way, the normative content of Ajax's taking of these events is both independent of him: it is down to the way the world is; and dependent on him: Ajax's seeing the world under that aspect—i.e. seeing the state of affairs conceptualised as internally related to the concept of shame—is dependent on his moral sensibilities, his *Bildung*. We can illustrate the latter's role by talking of honour groups or, as in Ajax's case, talking of his father, Telamon, who serves as a concretisation of that honour group. As Ajax speaks,

What countenance can I show my father Telamon?
How will he bear the sight of me
If I come before him naked, without any glory,
When he himself had a great crown of men's praise?
It is not something to be borne.
                    (Sophocles 1957: 462, seq. cited in Williams 1993: p. 85)

We need not be led astray by talk of honour groups and audiences into thinking of shame as necessarily heteronomous. For, as we saw in the discussion of Diogenes of Sinope, in the previous chapter, one can deny the judgements of one's honour group; indeed, one can, with work, refuse to acknowledge their judgements. What one cannot do is escape ones own *ēthos*. Because one's character is not simply a cloak one wears or baggage one carries, one's character is oneself to the extent that one is a human being, in the moral sense (as discussed above). And, one's character is formed through the living of a life with others, learning a language, which is to learn about the significance of things to one, to one's peers, and to one's enemies.

To take an event (involving us) as shameful is to read it as such. We *acknowledge* it as such, for ourselves; as seen under that aspect that event has that meaning for *us*. It is *us* that read it so, given the way the world is and the way our sensibilities are, given our moral character. In this sense it fulfils the criteria for being autonomous.

Having this meaning for us, it does so through the meanings of which we are availed in our learning of a language, a public language; in turn this is to learn to register, acknowledge, and communicate the loci of significance in our world. In this sense we can see the heteronomous sources of shame. The event is shameful because it has that meaning for us. It has that meaning in virtue of our reading it this way, seeing it as shameful. We can do so, we can see it under this aspect, in virtue of our *Bildung*, our conceptual capacities. Our *Bildung* is formed in and through our life with others.

4. Shame: regressive or progressive?

One figure that takes a place in the literature on the Holocaust is the figure of the bystander. They are those who knew what was going on but stood by and stayed silent. So while not perpetrators they are in some sense complicit in the perpetration of the crime. Norman Geras (1998) has argued that we should not comfort ourselves that this figure is comfortably distant from us. In his book *The Contract of Mutual Indifference* he suggests that in contrast to the social contract invoked in much normative political theory there is reason to hold that there is in practice another contract, which appears to be binding as regards the actual relations of people in the world: the contract of mutual indifference. There is something striking about Geras's suggestion. It does seem to capture, if the invocation of any form of contract might so capture, the predominant way in which much of the global population relate to one another.

While much talk of shame in the philosophical and psychological literature focuses on individuals experiencing shame, in contrast, relatively little argues that shame is sadly lacking where it should be present. Of course, in ordinary parlance the locution 'shame on you' or 'you should be ashamed of yourself' are not uncommon. However, it is uncommon to find a psychologist or philosopher writing on shame and arguing that there should be 'more of it about', as it were. One reason for this is the widely held assumption that emotions are passive; for if we accept that emotions are essentially passive, then imploring one to be ashamed would be akin to imploring someone to catch the common cold. However, such a response we can set aside. I have already given good reason not to accept the passivity of shame. Another reason, to which I want to address myself here is, I suggest, that shame is seen as a regressive emotion, one that does not serve any useful purpose, does not help one make progress in one's life. Shame, it is generally thought, 'weighs one down'. Therefore, on this understanding, one might well claim that certain states of affairs are shameful, correctly understood, but that one should not conclude from that one ought to feel shame, for that is not to make progress. So, for example, one might hold that for a world as affluent as ours to also be a world where millions suffer and die through easily-avoided poverty is correctly characterised as shameful but that we should not, therefore, feel ashamed. However, as I have argued, seeing a state of affairs that involves us as shameful and being ashamed are not externally related. To correctly apprehend a state of affairs that involves one as shameful is to be ashamed. The admonishment that one should be ashamed, therefore, is not analogous to wishing on one's interlocutor an affliction (such as an illness) but rather one which demands of them that they see the state of affairs for what it is (one that merits shame).

So is shame necessarily regressive? Should we be followers of Diogenese of Synope and deny, turn away from, the relations that lead one to shame? Should we refuse to see the world this way on the grounds that shame is a regressive emotion and restricts our individual freedom to live as we choose, unfettered, as it were, by the baggage of shame? Indeed, to feel shame is not to make progress, in terms of absenting the conditions that give rise to one's shame. However, this does not mean that feeling shame at a shameful state of affairs is regressive.

Gaining clarity helps us move in the right direction, once we begin to move. To feel shame at the avoidable suffering, radically curtailed and miserable lives that are common to our world is to have gained clarity about that world and about one's nature as a human being. The relations that hold between the concepts of human being and of human world are such that shame presses in on one, it is our due, because of the way the world is and the way one conceptualises human being (as a moral concept). It is in this way that shame connects us, and reminds us of our connection, to our fellow human beings.[13]

Sure shame can be characterised as baggage, but only ideologically induced prejudice regarding our self-understanding implores us to see such connections as baggage to be shed through denial of its (shame's) claim on us. So, we might therefore turn away from shame, deny the relations holding between our concepts of 'shame', 'human being', and 'human world' through a refusal to conceive of human being as anything other than, say, essentially atomised egos. But to do so, to conceive of 'human being' in such a way, is to deny our essentially dependent nature.[14]

The survivor of extreme trauma who feels shame for surviving while others died, or who feels shame at having borne witness to the inhumanity present in humanity continues to be subject to the crime they are said to have survived. In this sense shame is baggage one should dearly like to help those survivors shed.

On the other hand, to deny one's shame, to not see the relations between 'shame', 'human being', and 'human world', in a world where technological advance has brought the possibility of health and comfort for all but has brought the actuality of suffering and misery for vast numbers, and the real possibility of the destruction of life on Earth through anthropogenic global warming, is to take Cynicism too far.[15] It is to take the experiment lived by Diogenese of Sinope in the Athenian marketplace to a level of absurdity and detachment that, I venture, even Diogenes would have baulked at.

Sure one can characterise shame as baggage, but to talk of baggage is to deal in analogy, and in doing so we should subject the analogy to scrutiny. It is internal to the grammar of the term 'analogy' that analogies only reach so far. Drawing an analogy is not to make an identity claim. The purpose of drawing an analogy is to draw attention to, 'throw light on' or to illustrate, an aspect of that under discussion. Indeed, showing the analogy's limitations can help throw light, too. Hence: 'Life's baggage' as an analogy only reaches so far. For, we neither choose our baggage, nor its contents. Similarly, how we 'carry' our baggage is not always of our choosing and it is certainly not always carried with the minimum possible effort. We cannot unpack our bags on arrival home, putting their contents away, in drawers and in cupboards. We accumulate life's baggage despite our best efforts to 'travel light': shedding our load is not achieved through a mere decision to 'travel light' henceforth. It is shed, *if* it can be so at all, through deep personal psychological transformation. The '*if*' in the previous sentence is significant, for there are no guarantees of achieving liberation from life's baggage.

The shame experienced by survivors of extreme trauma is a continuation of the moral crime perpetrated upon them and about them because it bears down on and bears in on them, and it does so from a world which was not theirs but to which they were forcibly subjected. The shame one might argue that many inhabitants of the early twenty-first-century Western world ought to feel is a step towards changing that world.

5. Notes towards conclusion

In moving towards conclusion I shall focus upon the ethical point of my work as author. This will begin by picking up on a point of Raimond Gaita's, by way of trying to clarify my aims. I will then progress to summarising why the philosophical engagements with shame were unsatisfactory. I finish with a long passage from Lawrence Langer's book

Holocaust Testimonies, which serves to refocus the discussion, bringing together the various strands that I have tried to interweave throughout these lectures.

5.1. Gaita against ethical reductionism

A French woman was interviewed in a television programme called *The World at War*. She had witnessed, over a long period, a young Nazi officer sending trainloads of (mainly) children to the death camps. She said that every day since then she had asked herself how it were possible for him to do it. Hers is not a question which invites an answer. It expresses a sense of mystery at that kind of contact with evil, and that sense of mystery is connected with a sense of the reality of evil as something *sui generis*. But that depends on her sense of what he did being informed by concepts which allow for more substantial elaboration than that he violated the inalienable natural rights of the children he sent to be murdered. 'How could he violate their natural rights?' 'How could he fail to see that these children had natural rights?' Such questions cannot express the kind of bewilderment she expressed and they invite no elaboration which could express it.

(Gaita 1991: p. 5)

In the above passage, Raimond Gaita draws attention to the impotence of rights discourse when one is attempting to convey one's sense of the evil of certain acts. Gaita's point sheds light upon what I have been engaged in throughout this book. However, before I progress to say how, I shall just offer a few words of clarification, in the main to make clear what I am *not* arguing here. I am not seeking to critique the moral efficacy of legally ascribing rights to individuals. Nor am I advancing or endorsing (here) an argument against theories of rights; such critiques, as we saw in Chapter 2, are not uncommon. However, my point here is that if we allow rights discourse to be our only moral discourse then we lose something of fundamental significance to our moral and self understanding.

Saying that those children had their rights violated is a little like saying that Rwanda was depopulated in 1994; it is euphemistic and crassly so, though, of course, in some sense true. In contrast, the fact that such descriptions are true is important, because it is part of the content of the crassness of such a description that it is, at one level, true: i.e. it being true is what makes it insidious. It is therefore important, if we are to be able to make sense of our lives, not to allow our moral language to be reduced to the language of rights.

5.2. On prejudice and abstraction

This book has been concerned with questions similar to this on two levels. On one level, by discussing shame and by providing a way of making sense of shame, we have found a non-reductive way to make sense of the effects of the crimes of (say) the Holocaust on individuals who bore witness to those crimes. Thus, in the numerous engagements with Primo Levi's remarks on shame and my suggestion of a—world-taking— framework for understanding his shame, I hope to have contributed a little to our understanding of ourselves, and our moral nature.

On another level, throughout this book, I have tried to bring to the fore philosophical prejudice; prejudice that not only leads us to philosophical confusion, but also leads to a propensity to (theoretical) abstraction, in trying to overcome that confusion. In Griffiths the prejudice was manifest in his scientism, leading to his eliding of normativity. In Agamben the prejudice stemmed from his post-structuralist foundations, and led to him misrepresenting Levi's shame; for Agamben shame was the awareness of inhumanity's trace in humanity and, while one is prepared to accept this might sometimes be the case, we are not driven to see it as necessary to understanding humanity, by the logic of potentiality.

In structuring the book in this way, my intention was to set up two philosophical positions; the thought is that one's rejection of one of these might well incline one to recoil to an embracing of the other. However, both contain, on a structural level, similar flaws. As we saw in Chapter 1, scientism is committed to an attempt to determine meaning through a theory of natural kinds; here meaning is determined by the extension of the kind term. In Chapter 2 we saw how post-structuralist linguistics claims to show that meaning is always deferred because it is always disrupted by the trace of previous events of communication. Both views treat meaning (and language) in a too abstract manner, while arriving at their—seemingly—opposing conclusions. Neither position will satisfy us.

Those I discussed in Chapter 3, in various ways, operated with a disenchanted picture of the world, the picture of the world as found in the natural sciences. It is the hold of this picture which leads emotion theorists to the 'Emotion Problem' (cf. Chapter 3, Section 4) and cognate 'problems': e.g. how to account for meaning in the absence of cognition? Well, of course, if one thinks of cognition as a process in the head then things will become mysterious when one can detect no process, yet things have meaning. On this level, therefore, our emotional experiences—and a fundamental way in which we meet our world—become puzzling to us.

We should therefore take as the bedrock of enquiry the conceptualised world; we conduct our enquiry wholly within the space of reasons, not 'below' or 'outside' this world/space. People have emotions in, and in response to, a world of meanings; indeed, *people* exist in the world of meanings. Consider what Ilham Dilman has to say in this regard:[16]

> The life we live is a life of the language we speak; and the world in which we live is a world of that life—the life of our language. The structures inherent to its dimensions of reality reflect the grammatical forms of our language—'grammar' in the sense in which Wittgenstein uses the term. That language has evolved in the course of men's adaptation to and engagement with their environment; and that environment itself, in turn, comes to be increasingly permeated by the forms of significance originating in the course of the evolution of their language. It is in this sense that the human world, the world in which we live, is the world of the life we live with language.
>
> (Dilman 2002: pp. 218–219)

The evolution spoken of here is not the (reductionist) biological notion of evolution, found in evolutionary psychology; it is rather how we evolve (in the ordinary sense) with the language we speak—not merely the natural language, but any meaningful communication. I think the resistance to this view is based in the thought that it results in a form of linguistic idealism. This is incorrect.[17] One does not have to reject the disenchanted world view of the natural sciences; the physical world is their subject-matter. It is only that in noting this, and in noting their predictive success, we should not allow ourselves to assume that this is the world we inhabit as persons. As persons the world has significance for us; in contrast the pressing of the *return key* on my laptop computer does not have significance for my laptop computer, however many pro-cesses are triggered by the button being so depressed. In order that we can understand ourselves and others we need to understand *how* things become significant for us, *what* is significant for us, how some people *see* the significance while others *deny* and/or *fail to acknowledge* it. We can only begin such an investigation if we decline invitations to discuss our emotions and morality in narrow terms.

If, with Hillel Steiner (1994), we re-describe all freedom-claims in extensional terms do we not lose something in the process of claiming to have solved the problem of needing to adjudicate between competing freedom claims within discussions of distributive justice?[18] If we translate all atrocities committed by person upon person into talk about the violation of one person's rights, do we not lose something in the process of claiming to have identified the foundations of morality and translating this crime into those terms? If we translate the emotional experience of shame into the language of having a propositional attitude towards a—formal—object, do we not lose something in the process of trying to provide a rational theory of shame? My claim is that in each case we do lose something.[19]

Such abstractions tell us little about what it is that those people making their freedom claims are doing, i.e. the place the concept of 'freedom' has in their lives; they tell us little about what it is that people take to be evil, when they come upon a heinous—evil—crime being perpetrated, i.e. they tell us little about the place of the concept of 'evil' has in their lives; and they tell us little about what it is that people feel and experience when they are overcome by recurrent episodes of shame, i.e. what place the concept of 'shame' has in their lives.

In accepting that we live our lives within the space of reasons, within a meaningful world, one commits oneself to being alive to the ethical importance of understanding the place of concepts such as 'freedom', 'evil', and 'shame' (and a very many others) in the lives of people.[20] What it is to acknowledge such concepts and their place, what it is to turn one's back—as it were—on such concepts and their place. Furthermore, one begins to understand how such concepts can be related to other morally significant concepts such as 'person' or 'human being'.

5.3. On the refusal to conclude

One way of understanding the place of shame in the lives of those who have survived extreme trauma is as the continuation of the trauma, as its refusal to conclude. The crime—as I noted in Chapter 2, Section 4.1.1, and in Chapter 3, Section 3.2.1—continues into the present in the shape of shame (and anguish). One finds this characteristic relationship between the experience of extreme trauma and shame often referred to as the 'scar' left by the event, or how a person has been 'tainted' by the event. Langer (1991: p. 92) rightly corrects these metaphors. He notes that if we acknowledge that the shame, anguish, humiliation, etc. are continuations of the crime then the more perspicuous metaphor is that of the 'festering wound'. The oral testimony of Edith P.[21] brings this into stark relief; I quote, at length, Langer's reconstruction:[22]

Throughout her testimony, Edith P. alternates between a fierce insistence that 'There's one thing that they didn't do to us. They didn't break our spirit. I was very proud', and frank descriptions of episodes undermining that pride. Neither triumphs over the other; neither cancels the other. But because circumstances in Auschwitz had little respect for individual pride, one's evidence does not always confirm one's conviction. Edith P., for example, tells of an instance of when she was suffering severely with dysentery but had enough 'humanity' in her, as she reports, to prevent her from relieving herself inside the barracks. She was too ashamed. But she could not go to the latrine, because an order for *Blocksperre* had been issued, a temporary sealing of the barracks while a search was carried out for two missing inmates. She violated the order and left anyway, only to meet a particularly brutal SS woman guard who, learning of her mission, on the spot told her to turn around and gave her ten lashes on the back with her whip. Although she managed not to cry, Edith P. admits that she was humiliated. She explains that the pain was not the problem. 'Physical pain you can stand', she says, 'but how can you bear the emotional pain?'

Edith's public loss of dignity and the attendant emotional pain imply a complex system of motive and effect largely beyond her control. 'My body healed', she confesses, 'but it never healed my soul, that I had been humiliated this way, in front of my family'. (Her sister-in-law and the sister-in-law's three sisters had witnessed the whipping from the barracks)... When the 'rules' changed in Auschwitz, when Edith P. discovered that shame made no difference because it was not allied to dignity as she had supposed (all of this having nothing to do with her, of course, but with her persecutors), then humiliation replaced pride.

After arriving in Auschwitz, she says, 'you don't think what goes through your mind. You say to yourself, "Well, here I am in Auschwitz. And where am I, and what's going to happen to me?"' You lose the ability to think about yourself in the situation in which you find yourself. For example, she reflects, one can say 'When I get married', or 'If I die', or 'If someone I love dies', or 'If I have a child', or 'When I get a job', or 'If I have some money', creating certain theoretical probabilities and then imagining oneself into those situations because we know how to think about them—they have precedents in our own and other people's experience. But no one before has ever said 'When I get to Auschwitz, I . . .'; therefore, the mind remains blank. There is no way, she maintains, of imagining it in advance or thinking about it when you're in the midst of it, because mental process functions not in a vacuum but in relation to something that happened previously, that you had felt, thought, read, seen or heard about.

Thus when Edith P. confesses that in Auschwitz you didn't feel and you didn't think, she is recording not a mental and emotional numbness endemic to the place but a totally foreign atmosphere inhospitable to the responses that normally define a human being.

(Langer 1991: pp. 103–104)

As I noted in Chapter 3, Section 3.2.1, Auschwitz creates a whole new set of relationships between concepts and in doing so serves to disrupt the settled relations of the pre-Auschwitz world—and later the post-Auschwitz world. This is what Edith P. means by her soul not healing; basic human functions such as going to the toilet are now related to episodes of deep humiliation. As Langer writes: 'When the "rules" [norms] changed in Auschwitz, when Edith P. discovered that shame made no difference because it was not allied to dignity as she had supposed (all of this having nothing to do with her, of course, but with her persecutors), then humiliation replaced pride.' It seems brutal to even write it, but the point is that there is no shame in relieving oneself in the barracks because there is no dignity in the alternative—a public beating/humiliation. When dignity is deprived one at every turn then shame is everywhere and thus, in a sense, nowhere. When the post-Auschwitz rules (norms) are established, in the years following liberation, shame can return because the meaning relation between shame and dignity holds, and thus can be perceived, once more. We see lack of dignity as shameful.[23]

Auschwitz, like many other sites of extreme violence and trauma, subjected the concept of 'dignity'—and by extension, 'shame'—to violence, as well as subjecting people's bodies to violence. It is the forced removal of Edith P.'s dignity at Auschwitz that continues to fester; it does so in that when the post-Auschwitz norms allow dignity and thus (this sort of) shame the possibility, then shame can be felt about the complete deprivation of dignity and shame while forced to live by the rules of Auschwitz.

One job for moral philosophers therefore, alongside (or even instead of) theorising what one ought to do, how one ought to live and the metaphysical status of value, is to help us see the moral, the human significance, of certain concepts in our lives. How what our lives are, their very meaning, our self-understanding as beings is interwoven with our understanding of our world and the concepts through which we gain that understanding. We must be alive to the full extent of the violence that events of extreme trauma, whether they be genocidal or individual on individual, inflict upon those who are subject to that violence. We must not turn away from addressing their shame, borne of that to which they have been subject, for that is to fail to see the crime for what it is. We must also be alive to the poverty of our own view of our world, if we view that world (from a vantage point of comfort, security, and affluence) without shame. For that is to view the world but not to see it. We should not turn away from our own shame, borne of our seeing our world as it is, for that is to stand by while others suffer.

We can only be so alive by regaining our concepts, i.e. investigating the place moral—very broadly construed—concepts have in our lives, and how this is disrupted, denied, and sometimes annihilated by crimes which are perpetrated upon us, and by us, as persons.

Notes

Introduction

1. In addition to ethical works which are expressly concerned with moral psychology (e.g. Deigh 1992), there are also those which are not expressly, nor even obviously so. Nevertheless, one can gain insight into moral psychological issues and have one's own moral sensibilities worked on by such work, even though they might be more obviously classified as History, Testimony, Aesthetics, etc. Works that I see as being of this sort are—and are as diverse as—Browning (2001), Des Pres (1976), Diamond (1988), Gaita (1991), Gourevitch (2000), Hatzfeld (2005a, 2005b) Langer (1991), Levi (1989, 2000), Mulhall (2001b), and Todorov (1996). Some of these are very far away from being works in ethics, as traditionally conceived, or works in moral psychology, undertaken in the conventional sense; what admits works to my list is their ability to engender reflection on (the moral nature of) humanity on the part of the reader. I have omitted works of literature from the list, only for reasons of space.

2. For a very clear statement of this view, see Rosalind Hursthouse's (2002) paper 'Virtue Theory and Abortion'. The three approaches are: deontology—which is, strictly speaking, concerned with the logic of duty; consequentialism—which is, of course, concerned with the consequences of acts; and virtue ethics—which one might characterise as concerned with virtuous character and human flourishing.

3. Such an aspect shift cannot be forced on one's interlocutor by mere force of argument. One needs to *see*, to acknowledge, the new aspect as one's own. See Baker (2004, chapters 1 and 9), and Hutchinson and Read (2008) 'A Perspicuous Presentation of "Perspicuous Presentation"'.

1. Experimental Methods and Conceptual Confusion: Philosophy, Science, and *What Emotions Really Are*

1. Some will be surprised to see Peter Goldie on this list. Philosophers of emotion such as Goldie, Patricia Greenspan, and Michael Stocker are often explicitly critical of (pure) cognitive accounts. In Chapter 3 I give some reasons for Goldie being understood as a cognitivist. Indeed, Goldie writes that this is the view he favours, while criticising certain tendencies of the view (see Goldie, 2004: p. 91). In addition, and most importantly for his taking his place on *this* list, I believe that Griffiths, in *WERA*, would certainly have taken Goldie as one of his targets (Goldie's book appeared 3 years after publication of *WERA*); he would have done so by identifying Goldie, alongside Michael Stocker and

Robert Nash, as a late sophisticated, hybrid entrant into the research program (see *WERA*: Section 2.6). There is often a distinction made between
pure cognitivism (e.g. Solomon) and hybrid theories (e.g. Greenspan,
Stocker, Nash and Goldie); again, there is further discussion of this in
Chapter 3.

2. To talk of a 'blistering attack' might strike some as a hyperbolic depiction
   of Griffiths' criticisms. However, in addition to some of the passages I quote
   below from Griffiths, consider Robert Solomon's depiction of Griffiths' book
   as 'polemic' and his criticisms of cognitivism therein as 'ferocious abuse'
   (Solomon, 2003c: pp. 132 and 178; respectively).

3. Almost all work in the philosophy of the emotions—of which I am aware—
   that has appeared subsequent to the publication of Griffiths' book has, to
   some degree, had to contend with his critique; whether taking (significant)
   time and space to argue against his critique (e.g. Roberts 2003), or through
   the positioning of their own work with reference to his claims (e.g. Goldie
   2000), or—not in a wholly uncritical manner—building upon his claims (e.g.
   Prinz 2003b).

4. As we shall see below, much of the disdain he exhibits for propositional attitude theorists is based on what he considers to be their ignorance of current
   science.

5. The motivation for his advancing his own causal homeostatic theory is founded in his understanding of what was wrong with Putnamian natural kinds:
   their metaphysical nature. Griffiths explicitly claims to avoid such recourse
   to metaphysics.

6. He claims to be doing more than this, and must do more in order to sustain his
   critique of propositional attitude theorists as only ever being able to provide
   us with the stereotype of an emotion.

7. Though neither developed nor refined (in the direction Griffiths takes the
   theory), by Putnam or Kripke, it is important to note. Kripke has not contributed (in print at least) to the subject since he delivered, what appeared
   as, *Naming and Necessity* and Putnam has explicitly distanced himself from
   the (popular) reading of his original MoM; i.e. as advancing that which Griffiths takes it to (see Section 2.1). Putnam has also gone into print (1990:
   Chapter 5; 1994: Chapter 14) critiquing the 'Cornell realists', and Richard
   Boyd in particular—Boyd's theory of natural kinds is the theory that Griffiths follows most closely in advancing his own theory. I discuss these issues
   in more detail below.

8. Griffiths' account is somewhat general and I suspect he papers-over some
   quite substantial cracks. That there is anything here that warrants the term
   'research program' attaching to it is unclear. Even if we allow him to characterise these philosophers as 'propositional attitude theorists'—which it is
   questionable that we should—it is a further step to the identification of a
   research program in which they are all participants. To say that they all
   inherit and apply the same methodology is somewhat tendentious. Take just
   two of those whom Griffiths identifies as exemplars of the 'research program':
   Solomon and Kenny; I would suggest from the most rudimentary glance at

the respective work of these two that one might be *sceptical* that they can serve as two exemplars of one methodology.

9. For the uninitiated the term 'affect program' might be somewhat puzzling. 'Affect' is the standard way in which 'sub-cognitive' states are characterised; a paradigm case being disgust, where no belief in the disgusting nature of an object *need* be available to the person undergoing the emotion. 'Program' invokes the metaphor of a computer software program (a mental state) running on computer hardware (the brain).

10. See also various books and papers by Ekman (some co-authored, see Bibliography for details) 1969, 1971 (x2), 1973, 1980, 1983, 1985, 1992. A more extensive list can be found in Griffiths (*WERA*; Bibliography).

11. I say 'largely' because Griffiths does not see the higher cognitive emotions as needing to be supervenient upon affect programs, or on the same underlying causal homeostasis. This, he suggests, others such as Frank (1988) and Damasio (1994) do. Griffiths sees the higher cognitive emotions as having a causal homeostasis distinct from that underlying the affect program emotions; hence the requirement for, at least, two distinct kind terms and the elimination of the vernacular concept. In this sense, for all his 'abuse' (to coin Solomon's term), Griffiths is actually closer to agreement with cognitivists/propositional attitude theorists, on the higher cognitive emotions at least, than are many other recent critics, such as Prinz (2003b).

12. It is not clear to me that 'loyalty' is an emotion. Griffiths expresses no such qualms. It strikes me that loyalty is better characterised as a *moral virtue* or a *character trait*, rather than as an emotion.

13. I put the word 'findings' in scare quotes here because it is far from established as to what status such 'findings' have. This is not so much a criticism as a question: what *status* do the 'findings' of game theory have? The Euthyphro dialogue (and the beginning of a headache) looms when considering such matters; but such considerations will have to wait for another occasion.

14. It is important not to take Ekman *et al.* as depicting the affect program emotions as reflexes. Ekman, Friesen, and Simons (1985) rule out 'startle', not admitting it to their list of affect program emotions because it is *too* reflex-like (see *WERA*: p. 241). See also Chapter 3 for discussion of the reflex/affect distinction.

15. The classic statement is found in Harré (ed.) (1986).

16. In the seriousness with which he takes social construction of MPS Griffiths seems to unwittingly backtrack on his overall scientistic agenda in *WERA*. The current psychiatric orthodoxy is to give an account of MPS closer to the sort of account Griffiths favours for the affect program emotions, or to medicalise it completely (i.e. give a physicalist explanation). Social-psychological accounts of MPS have been on the retreat (at least in terms of adherents in the medical professions) for a couple of decades now. I say this not by way of criticism, but only by way of noting how it is uncharacteristic given the otherwise scientistic agenda.

17. This claim, as it stands, would obviously, if merely assumed as true, beg the question of those such as Sartre, Solomon, and others who set out with the intent of precisely denying such a claim.

18. Indeed, it is important for Griffiths to show that philosophers and folk psychologists offer the same account; that is to say they do so when philosophers rely upon conceptual analysis, as do the propositional attitude theorists.

19. I have quoted a number of instances of Griffiths employing such 'arguments'; if the reader would like to see more, see the following: pp. 4, 24, 171, 172, 173, 244 of *WERA*.

20. Griffiths stipulates that a number of philosophers are participating in a *research program*; he claims that those research programs are **degenerating**; and he identifies *core commitments*—i.e. conceptual analysis as a methodology—as being flawed in order to show that the research program *has* to fail. This is an application of Imre Lakatos's (1978) Methodology of Scientific Research Programs (MSRP) *all but declared*. There are many problems with an analysis such as that proposed by Lakatos. Simply put, progress and degeneracy are evaluative terms. Thus, in an extreme case, one man's degeneracy might well be another's progress. Other judgements we have to make are *when* to 'call it a day', so to speak. The answer that will usually be offered to this question is 'when the core commitments of the research program have been shown to be flawed'. But which commitments are core and which commitments are a part of the protective belt are questions, once again, that are open to judgement. Furthermore, who are these 'metascientists' who can judge which commitments are core and which periphery (protective belt)? Who is to judge when a core commitment should be acknowledged as flawed? We might well infer from Griffiths' writing that he sees this as a role for philosophers such as him.

   These are problems, to which the Lakatosian MSRP cannot respond in its own terms; is *it* then a degenerative research program? Furthermore, I suggest that one does not need to be a 'card-carrying' Feyerabendian to recognise the dismantling of Lakatos's MSRP in *Against Method* (Feyerabend 1975).

   Eliminativists, it seems, are fond of invoking Lakatosian method (albeit undeclared in name)—see, for example, Churchland's, now famous, paper 'Eliminative Materialism and the Propositional Attitudes' reprinted in Rosenthal (ed.) (1991).

21. I here list a minute (and somewhat methodologically diverse) sample: Bennett and Hacker (2003, and their contributions to Bennett, Dennett, Hacker and Searle (2007)); Button, Coulter, Lee, and Sharrock (1995, particularly chapter 3); Hutto (1999; and particularly his *Folk Psychological Narratives* (2008)); Putnam (1988, 1994, 1999); Searle (1992, 2004: pp. 84–95) and Meredith Williams (1999a,b,c,d,e). These are a small number of books and papers, which to my mind offer criticisms of computational psychology to which that project has yet to give an adequate response. One could add to this list some of the literature which draws upon work in natural kind semantics (Putnam 1988, 1994: chapter 24, Burge 1979, 1986, etc.), which has done much to draw in to question the possible content of narrow content.

22. Griffiths is silent about this. Williams (1999c,d) does, however, show that in remodelling his position Fodor retreats to a point where he ends up arguing for very little, and less than a little if taken in comparison with what he had originally claimed to be arguing.

23. Putnam 1975d: p. 227.

24. More recent natural kind theorists tend to equivocate on what should at first appear as a fundamental axiom of their project. We find Griffiths on occasion conceding that the distinctions are no longer to be found in nature: i.e. the distinctions are not to be identified with laws of nature (see Section 1.3).

25. I have reconstructed the thought experiment in my own words in a somewhat compressed form for considerations of brevity. I take my recounting to be true to Putnam's (1975d: pp. 223–227) original thought experiment.

26. Dupré's critique is, therefore, made more powerful with Putnam's (relatively) recent (1992) claim that all he was seeking to do in MoM was effect a 'mild rational reconstruction of scientific practice' (quoted above): simply put, Dupré shows him to be simply wrong. An essentialist thesis, such as Kripke's, might be seen to be less susceptible to Dupré's criticisms.

27. Stroll (1998) advances a number of related arguments: the compositional and the function arguments (pp. 46–52); the isotope argument (pp. 89–92); the category-mistake argument (pp. 92–95); and the argument from isomers (pp. 95–97). Stroll's book is a much overlooked devastating critique of the whole program of natural kind semantics.

28. We might say—coining and extending Dan Dennett's terminology—that the pump is constructed in such a manner that our intuitions are pumped in the desired direction.

29. This series, to which Putnam refers, includes what are now reprinted as Chapters 3, 4, and 8 of McDowell (1998a). One might also add to this list, Chapters 2, 5, 7, and 9; and, of course, his *Mind and World*.

30. It will serve to pay attention to the clauses in this passage. For example, 'a **good account** of **certain elements** of scientific practice' and 'an **important aspect** of the formation and use of concepts by humans **in general**' (my emphases). I will argue below that we should pay more attention to these clauses than does Griffiths; in doing so we should recognise the potentially mundane and ineffectual nature of his claims. Indeed, my arguments below indicate that Griffiths can be read at turns as both a pre-theoretic pragmatist and metaphysical realist.

31. A phenotype is an evolved trait. It is also instructive to observe the drift from 'pattern of reasoning' through re-description of this pattern of reasoning as 'neural organisation' and then to positing of a 'psychological phenotype'.

32. This is another instance of what I referred to (above) as the tendency to equivocation in the 'late' natural kinds literature. If kinds are differentiated according to their evolutionary descent then are not the distinctions 'in nature', as it were? However, while we find this claim made here, alongside the claims about experiments—such as Keil's—which allegedly demonstrate

that it is in our—human—nature to define organisms according to these distinctions, we also find remarks such as the following: 'Natural kinds are no longer conceived as the subjects of the fundamental laws of nature. They are *simply nonarbitrary ways of grouping phenomena*. These kinds are nonarbitrary (or 'natural') because they have <u>some</u> *degree of projectability*' (p. 213; emphases mine).

I am trying to think of an example of an *arbitrary non-projectable* term; I cannot. Maybe the contrast-class Griffiths has in mind here is something along the lines of the categories and classification depicted by Jorge Luis Borges in his (fictional and satirical) Chinese Encyclopaedia. However, I am not convinced that we need a causal homeostatic theory of natural kinds to show us the folly of such arbitrary classifications; and of course, even these are not non-projectable.

Furthermore, regarding the move to classifying kinds in accordance with evolutionary descent, Griffiths fails to note that Dupré (1981: Section V, pp. 83–90) anticipates this move in his 'Natural Kinds and Biological Taxa', giving good reason to see it as just as problematic as he found Putnam's and Kripke's accounts to be. Indeed, Griffiths fails to note this, despite approvingly citing Dupré's criticisms from the same paper, when he takes them to support his own story of the evolution of the theory of natural kinds.

33. Even this might be too strong. I do not wish to invoke any theoretical agenda here. I mean 'pragmatic' in a pre-theoretical sense.

34. It is, I suggest, significant that Griffiths chooses to refer to 'causal laws' as 'causal *mechanisms*' thus invoking an ontological status where otherwise one might have assumed no more than pragmatic inference of a law.

35. Here I invoke a point made by Cora Diamond in her paper 'Rules: Looking in the Right Place' in discussing the purpose of Wittgenstein's—so called—private language argument (Diamond 1989: pp. 20–21).

36. This line of questioning owes much to Wittgenstein, particularly *On Certainty* (1975: Section 308).

37. Griffiths does not give us the figures. So we do not know if the results were unanimous or majority, and if the latter what were the percentages? It is also of crucial importance to know—we are not given such information—whether the children were allowed to confer or see/hear each other's answers. Otherwise we might just find out something about how susceptibility to peer pressure is learnt. It is, I venture, an identifying characteristic of his book that Griffiths simply presents certain theories (and activities) as proffering-forth scientific fact; he does so with no hesitancy and no critical appraisal. As with the computational theory of mind, he merely presents such theories as unproblematically science.

38. 'Infers' might be too strong a term here. As I noted above Griffiths takes Keil's conclusions to demonstrate a 'pattern of reasoning'; he then slides from this to predicating 'neural organisation' and thus the existence of a 'psychological phenotype'. In one effortless move we 'progress' from observing a pattern to positing the existence of something.

39. Of course the (subsequent) move to prioritisation (the ascribing of a status of ultimate justification) of the theoretically postulated over the observable is the move that, retrospectively, 'justifies' the theorist's own move to metaphysics in the first place.

40. Another concern that leads to such 'passive' constructions presumably would be that talk of 'children learning' is contingent talk, as it were.

41. Or, as is more likely, deny the existence of such a gap by denying normativity in general.

42. If this is not what his argument amounts to then one is apt to find what Griffiths' writes just plain peculiar. One should be forgiven for being unsure whether or not this is his argument, however. As we have seen, he remarks late in his book (p. 213) that 'natural kinds are no longer conceived as the subjects of the fundamental laws of nature. They are simply nonarbitrary ways of grouping natural phenomena.' This sounds like a thoroughgoing normative claim. In any case, think about this claim and about his employment of the 'results' of Keil's experiments for a moment... *You* are being asked to accept a theory of natural kinds—i.e. a theory of how we ought to conceptualise nature—on the grounds that some children between the ages of 8 and 10 have been observed to conceptualise nature in this way. There is also something peculiar in the thought that our ordinary ways of conceptualising things is arbitrary—I touch on this point in more detail in the following section. Also, one might note again Griffiths' propensity to see-saw between metaphysical realism and a domain-specific (pre-theoretic) pragmatism.

43. In a recent article Avner Baz (2003) says something that ties in with the point I am making here: 'In Cavell's Wittgenstein, the philosophical work of leading words back to their everyday uses is a constant struggle against the temptation to think, or fantasise, that the words might somehow *speak for us*, over our heads as it were, independently of our *investing* them with meaning. Cavell describes that fantasy as the idea that 'I must empty out *my* contribution to words, so that language itself, as if beyond me, exclusively takes over responsibility for meaning' (Cavell 1989: p. 57). This human tendency to renounce our responsibility to the meaningfulness of our words, which is the tendency to reject *conditions* under which our words can be meaningful—and hence, in particular, be in touch with reality— Cavell often presents as (an allegory for) the human tendency to renounce, or reject, the human. (see Cavell 1979: pp. 109,207,355)' (Baz 2003: pp. 483–484). I would only like to add here that I think there is every reason to drop the qualification 'Cavell's' in the opening sentence; 'in Wittgenstein' would have been more accurate, of course one might then add that Cavell has been foremost in bringing this aspect of Wittgenstein to general attention.

44. If one does not meet this attack as it is executed by Griffiths then one will be merely dismissed as reproducing the current stereotypical understandings of phenomena. Bennett and Hacker's recent *Philosophical Foundations of Neuroscience* (2003) would be open to such a charge from Griffiths. This book is co-authored by a prominent neuroscientist (Bennett) and prominent

philosopher of language (Hacker). Unlikely to be two people that Griffiths could charge with antipathy for the recent findings of science, and unaware of (any) progress made in the philosophy of language. However, the section on the emotions would be simply dismissed by Griffiths as missing the point. Differentiating, according to grammatical rules, between emotions, appetites, agitations, and moods, as do Bennett and Hacker, is to do no more than give us the stereotype of these terms. In this respect, their critique of cognitive neuroscience of the emotions would be simply seen as itself question begging: asking their cognitive neuroscientist 'opponents' to assume the truth of the approach which they have already eschewed.

45. That is to say, aside from asking what 'exactly akin' as opposed to (say) *merely* akin might mean. Saying exactly akin is like (akin we might say) saying there was a precise family resemblance.

   Furthermore, regarding the whale/fish example, John Dupré (1981: p. 75) shows that the ability of this oft-cited example to do the work authors such as Griffiths intend it to do is not borne out by examination of the terms 'fish' and 'whale'. Dupré notes that 'fish' is a prescientific category and might well not be a genuinely 'postscientific' one, while 'mammal' is 'more a term of biological theory' (ibid.). We do not generally *assume* that the concept 'mammal' is something we can ascribe on sight but rather we assume it is something we need to have *learnt* 'quite sophisticated' criteria for in order that we can employ the concept correctly. (Not) Incidentally, I understand that whales are referred to (quite correctly) as fish in Polish (I owe my knowledge of this (latter) fact to Richard Hamilton).

46. I italicise *must* here to make the point that for Griffiths to make his claims it must be a description, it cannot function in any other way.

47. See footnote 29.

48. This is all very compressed. I return to these matters in more detail in Chapter 3.

2. To 'Make Our Voices Resonate' or 'To Be Silent'? Shame as Fundamental Ontology

1. Agamben neither discusses MacIntyre nor situates his account with reference to MacIntyre's. My reason for employing MacIntyre in Section 1 is merely to illuminate Agamben's work, through similarities and differences with MacIntyre's account in *After Virtue*.

2. I say 'his', as in Heidegger's Kant, for the Kant of *Kant and the Problem of Metaphysics* is not generally accepted as Kant, by Kant scholars, rather as a Heideggerian distortion of Kant. Such exegetical disputes will not be my concern here.

3. There is much discussion as to the clearest translation of this term: see Annas (1998: pp. 37–55), Hursthouse (1999: pp. 9–10), and McDowell (1998a: pp. 3–22), for contributions to the discussion that I have found helpful.

4. I follow contemporary notational orthodoxy in using 'ϕ' to generically denote an act-token.

5. This is most clearly stated by Aristotle in the *Nicomachean Ethics* book I, ch. 7, 1097^{a}15—1098^{b}15.

6. I have quoted the Barnes translation, which departs somewhat from that printed in *HS*. However, it does not depart in substance, only in style. I choose to quote the Barnes as opposed to the translation found in *HS* because the latter comes third hand, as it were. Heller-Roazen translates Greek quotes from Agamben's Italian, these were originally translated by Agamben from the Greek.

7. MacIntyre identifies Diderot, Hume, Kant, and Adam Smith as exemplars of Enlightenment philosophers who pursued this project of rationally justifying morality by recourse to human nature; he identifies Kierkegaard as the first philosopher to acknowledge the failure of the project and dispense with any attempt to rationally justify morality. Instead, in *Either/Or*, Kierkegaard shows that living a moral life is the product of pure choice and not the product of a rationally informed and justified decision.

8. Recent modern moral philosophers, at least the deontological/contractarian/contractualist ones, tend to dispense with any claim to have a conception of the human as their axiom. The axiom is often no more than an idealised rational chooser.

9. For MacIntyre they are *logically* doomed, in that at the core of modern moral reasoning is a fundamental contradiction. For Foucault they are *practically* doomed, in that the modern predominance of biopolitics will lead to human catastrophe. Agamben sees himself completing the work, left unfinished by Foucault on his death, in linking the notion of biopolitics to the notion of the camp, culminating in Auschwitz.

10. Recall, without participation in the polis one cannot develop *phronesis*; exclusion from the life of the polis carried with it exclusion from living a life in a state of *bios*.

11. I do not imply any identification between Foucault's project and MacIntyre's here. I only wish to highlight that Agamben's own project has striking similarities with both. Agamben cites Foucault; there is no evidence that he is familiar with MacIntyre's work.

12. Levi refers explicitly to the lacuna at the heart of testimony in an interview. The quote is cited in Agamben and translated from the Italian by Agamben's translator Daniel Heller-Roazen: 'There is another lacuna in every testimony: witnesses are by definition survivors and so all, to some degree, enjoyed a privilege ... No one has told the destiny of the common prisoner, since it was not materially possible for him to survive ... I have also described the common prisoner when I speak of 'Muslims' [musselmänn, musselmänner] but the 'Muslims' did not speak' (Levi 1997: pp. 215–216 cited in Agamben 1999: p. 33).

13. This is why there is said to be a 'lacuna' at the heart of testimony. Those who *fully* experience the event of Auschwitz cannot bear witness to it.

14. Note: I have amended the page numbering of Agamben's reference to Levi's *The Drowned and the Saved* here as this quote appears at p. 43 in the English language version of Levi's book not at p. 60, as is stated in *RA*. All

references to Levi's text, unless otherwise stated, are to the English (not US) translations.

15. Muselmänner (muselmänn) is thought by the vast majority of scholars to come from 'muslim', and was a term employed at Auschwitz. The term was not employed in all the Nazi camps, though those exhibiting the symptoms associated with muselmänner are documented in all the camps. The term is, to say the least, unfortunate. There is some question as to whether the term did in fact have as its root the Persian plural for the Arabic 'Muslim': *Musulman*. The alternative, though not a widely subscribed to alternative, is that it is a perversion of the German *Muschelmann*.

16. The final sentence here might strike those unfamiliar with Améry's text as brutally dismissive of an important aspect of the camp. However, it should be noted that Améry is not writing a testimony as such but is engaged in a reflection upon the experience of the intellectual in Auschwitz. The merits or otherwise of such an endeavour are open to question, though this not a question I will ask here.

17. Here the similarity with MacIntyre's thesis transfers from a similarity in diagnosis of the problem to a similarity in identification of the problem. Both Agamben and MacIntyre see modern moral philosophy (contemporary liberal political theory) as floundering owing to its invocation of juridical categories to ethical ends.

18. It concerns me that this diagnosis is based upon a somewhat a-historical way of thinking about Auschwitz—and oddly-so given Agamben's orientation. Why not see the Nuremberg trials as the law effectively being applied to Auschwitz?

19. One might ask the question here, 'But who ever said shame was that?'; rather, is it not that this is a thought that seems to be correlated with a feeling of shame in cases of the survival of extreme trauma.

20. In contemporary parlance, it is not *analytic*.

21. Agamben has 'modified' the translation of the passages from Heidegger's text that make up this quotation. Following is Richard Taft's and then James S. Churchill's English translations of Heidegger's text.

As pure self-affection, time is not an acting affection that strikes a self which is at hand. Instead, as pure it forms the essence of something like self-activating.... But if [the attempt] cannot succeed in showing the self as temporal, does the opposite way perhaps have a chance of success? How does it stand with the proof that time as such has the character of selfhood? Its chances of failure are just as slight as of the claim, which indeed is undisputed, that time 'apart from the subject is nothing'. This indeed implies that in the subject, it is everything.
(Heidegger 1997: pp. 132–131, Taft translation)

As pure self-affection, time is not an active affection concerned with the concrete self; as pure it forms the essence of all auto solicitation.... But if the attempt to prove that the self is temporal will not succeed, perhaps the opposite procedure will have a better chance of success. In short, what about a proof that time as such has the character of selfhood? The chance of its being unsuccessful is the less because it is incontestable that time 'apart from the subject, is nothing', and this implies that in the subject it is all.

(Heidegger 1962: pp. 194–192, Churchill translation)

The somewhat odd page numbering of these quotes indicates the somewhat odd nature of the 'passage' as it is 'quoted' by Agamben. The section of the quote prior to the ellipsis comes from later in Heidegger's text—from the following page—than the section that *follows* the ellipsis.

22. Here the first ellipsis in brackets [ ] is mine and denotes an omission and a continuation to the following paragraph in Heidegger's text. The second ellipsis, not in brackets, is Heidegger's text. In quoting from Heidegger's text I will follow Taft's translation, in doing so what Agamben's translator renders as auto-affection I render as self-affection. Nothing, I think, hangs on this difference. When not quoting I will stick with Agamben's favoured term. I quote the above passage below as translated by Churchill:

Time as pure self-affection is that finite, pure intuition which sustains and makes possible the pure concept (the understanding) as that which is essentially at the service of intuition.

Hence, it is not in the second edition that Kant first introduces the idea of pure self-affection, which last, as has now become clear, determines the innermost essence of transcendence. It is simply that the idea is for-mulated more explicitly in this edition, and characteristically enough, appears [at the beginning of the work] in the transcendental aesthetic. [. . .]

'Sense' means 'finite intuition'. The form of sense, therefore, is pure receptivity. The internal sense does not receive 'from without' but from the self. In pure receptivity, internal affection must arise from the pure self, i.e. be formed in the essence of selfhood as such, and therefore must constitute the latter. Pure self-affection provides the transcendental ground-structure [*Urstruktur*] of the finite self as such. Therefore, it is abso-lutely untrue that the mind exists in such a way that, among other beings, it relates certain things to itself and in so doing posits itself [*Selbstsetzungen ausübt*]. Rather, this line of orientation from the self toward . . . and back to [the self] first constitutes the mental character of the mind as a finite self.

(Heidegger 1962: pp. 195–196; Churchill translation)

23. 'Emotive Tonality' is standardly translated as 'mood' in English translations of Heidegger's work.
24. It should be recalled that the writer of camp testimony then falls between *testis* and *superstes*, not the former because not impartial and not the latter because not having fully experienced the camp.
25. Recall the title of Antelme's book, *L'especie Humaine*, translated into English as *The Human Race*. Also Levi's *Se questo è un uomo*, translated as *If this is a*

man (I ignore the somewhat crass US non-translation of the title as *Survival in Auschwitz*). I do not wish to imply either Antelme or Levi were consciously taking up humanist or anti-humanist positions in their choice of titles. I wish only to draw attention to the fact that in titling their books the question of what it is to be human, or a member of the human race, was central.

26. This ties-in with my discussion of Cora Diamond in the final section of Chapter 1.
27. We can stay agnostic on this here.
28. I find myself hesitantly using the word 'crime' here for fear of being dismissed as invoking juridical categories in an ethical context.
29. When I invoke the 'Wittgensteinian' term 'grammar' in this way, I might just as well say 'meaning of the term "shame"'. The purpose of using the quasi-technical term 'grammar' is to emphasise that I am saying no more than this is how we use the term 'shame' in our language, for these purposes, etc. Using the term 'grammar' as opposed to 'meaning' merely serves to emphasise that I am not predicating of words or concepts that they have certain properties when I talk of their meaning, nor am I saying that speakers project meanings onto words. The idea is that when we have rid ourselves of certain (metaphysical) pictures of meaning, the quasi-technical term can be cast away, as *it* will have no further role for us. Because we will no longer have to guard against the thought that in talking about what a word means we are talking about a property of the word (or intentions of the speaker, etc.)
30. I feel I should have put Levi's name in scare quotes in this reference. I think there is a question of intellectual honesty here (as there is even more so with the Antelme omission, I discuss below). In omitting a significant clause in the Woolf quote (and the Italian original), it is no longer the Woolf translation, even if one does enter the caveat that it is 'modified'. If one quotes a translation and modifies it slightly, that is one thing; if one modifies it (omits a whole clause) and does so solely to suit one's own purposes, then one needs to offer an account as to why one is warranted to do so.
31. I should quote the full passage in Italian:

> Non salutavano, non sorridevano; apparivano oppressi, otre che da pieta, da un confuso ritegno, che sigillava le loro bocche, e avvinceva I loro occhi allo scenario funereo. Era la stessa vergogna a noi ben nota . . . quella che il giusto prova davanti alla colpa commessa da altrui, e gli rimorde che esista, che sia stata introdotta irrevocabilmente nel mondo delle cose che esistono.
>
> (Levi 1997: vol. I: p. 206)

I know of one other English translation of this passage, which is by Robert S. C. Gordon in his (excellent) book *Primo Levi's Ordinary Virtues*:

> They neither greeted us, nor smiled; they seemed to be suffering not only from pity but also from a confused restraint that sealed their lips and drew their eyes to the funeral scene. It was that shame we knew so well . . . the

shame of the just man when faced with the guilt committed by others, whose existence he regrets, the fact that it has irrevocably entered the world and all that exists in it.

(Gordon 2001: p. 83)

The clause omitted by Agamben is rendered by Gordon as indicating Levi's regret at the crimes committed by others: 'whose existence he [the survivor who feels shame] regrets, the fact that it ["the guilt committed by others"] has irrevocably entered the world and all that exists in it' (ibid.).

32. One only has to look at much work in Jurisprudence and the philosophy of law to see how the 'contamination' could just as easily be said to work the other way round.

33. The ordinary virtues are usually, love, honesty, care, and the like, and are often posited in contra-distinction to the heroic virtues. See Todorov (1996) for an excellent study of the ordinary and heroic virtues in the context of the concentration camps.

34. Bettelheim constructs psychiatric theories in the light of reflections on the Nazi camps in general, and the muselmänner in particular. For a clear statement of Levi's hostility towards Bettelheim's theorising, see the interview with Levi in *The Voice of Memory: Interviews 1961–1987* (2001: pp. 233–238; I was directed to this by Robert S. C. Gordon's writing on the subject in his *Primo Levi's Ordinary Virtues* (2001: p. 122)). Améry spends some time at the beginning of *At the Mind's Limits* defending phenomenology as a philosophical approach in order that he can apply it to his meditation upon the intellectual's experience of Auschwitz. While Levi conveys a respect for Améry, not present in his references to Bettelheim, he has misgivings regarding Améry's approach. For a discussion of this, see Levi's chapter 'The Intellectual in Auschwitz' in *The Drowned and the Saved* (1989: pp. 102–120); N. Wood (1998), 'The Victims Resentments'; and the 'Introduction' to the US edition of Améry's *At the Mind's Limits* (1990: pp. vii–xv) by A. Stille. Again, I owe my knowledge of these to Robert S. C. Gordon (ibid.: p. 69).

35. Indeed, I quoted Josh Cohen (p. 16) above saying as much, though he did so with approval.

36. I leave to one side the separate question as to Derrida's reading and criticisms of Austin.

37. This is important, for one might offer a Searlesque response and say that the 'iterability thesis' is irrelevant to a 'Robinson Crusoe', drawing from this that Derrida's thesis, if it applies at all only does in the delimited domain of one person sending a message to another where both are in separate locations. Derrida meets this, as part of a response to an objection of this sort put by Searle, who invokes a shopping list he writes for himself:

Why would I bother about a shopping list if the presence of the sender to the receiver were so certain? And why, above all, this example of the memorandum [*pense-bête*]? Why not some other example? It would have been no less pertinent, or no more: even in the extreme case of my writing something in order to be able to read (reread) it *in a moment*, this moment is constituted – i.e. divided – by the very iterability of what produces itself *momentarily*. The sender and the receiver, even if they were the self-same *subject*, each relate to a mark they experience as made to do without them, from the instant of its production or of its reception on; and they experience this not as the mark's negative limit but rather as the positive condition of its possibility. Barring this the mark would not function and there would be no shopping list, for the list would be impossible. Either I wouldn't need one or it would be unusable as such. This necessitates, obviously, a rigorous and renewed analysis of the value of presence, of presence to self or to others, of difference and of *différance* [differing and diferring].

(Derrida 1988: p. 49)

Again Searle is shown to have missed the point, and somewhat dramatically. The point, to be clear, is that Derrida is making a *structural* point about 'writing', and writing means communicable elements in general, a wink, a wave, a smile just as much as words of a natural language written on a page. Searle seems to assume that either Derrida's claim is an empirical claim *or* that one can refute a structural/logical claim by empirical provision of a counterexample; hence, Searle provides what he takes to be a counterexample such as both author and recipient being present to each other on an occasion when a note is passed from one to the other.

38. I **do not** intend this to be taken as a criticism. Derrida's use makes perfect sense, to me at least, though one does have to learn to use the word in this way when one begins to read Derrida.

39. There are small quotes from Derrida in this passage from Glendinning; I have left the single quotation marks to indicate these to the reader. I have omitted the citations, and refer the reader to Glendinning's text for the location of the Derrida passages.

40. I employ scare quotes here as it should be obvious that Agamben's *modus operandi* is much more than a theory of language, it is a theory of being, an ontological thesis that emerges from a meditation upon language.

41. Indeed, one might argue in the light of his inventive 'citing' of Levi and Antelme that Agamben does this in any case.

42. I have chosen to follow this metaphor further than one might usually do, so as to highlight the similarities between etymology and the sort of investigations Victorian 'explorers' undertook in Africa in searching for the source of the Nile, hardly a radical form of investigation.

43. Derrida (1973) *Speech and Phenomena and other Essays on Husserl's Theory of Signs*.

44. In less charitable voice one might even say it is to commit the genetic fallacy.

45. It is important to be clear here; the argument is not that a blush-as-a-physiological-reaction is meaningless, or that the reaction is not *triggered* by the blusher's seeing something as worthy of embarrassment, and thus

blushing. It is only to say that there is a distinction to be drawn here between reactions of this sort and intentional actions.

46. In this respect, note Derrida's use of the modal terms, 'must', 'always', and 'necessarily' in the quotation from him in Section 5.1.

47. I, of course, paraphrase here Wittgenstein's closing remark of the *Tractatus Logico-Philosophicus* (Wittgenstein 1922: Section 7).

3. Emotion, Cognition, and World

1. 'Judgement theory' is the term favoured by Jenefer Robinson (2004) to denote these theorists. 'Judgementalism' is employed by Greenspan (2004: p. 128), though she does not include herself in the category picked out by the term. 'Quasi-judgementalism' is the term favoured by D'Arms and Jacobson (2003), who employ it so as to include Greenspan and Roberts (Greenspan rejects the label, 2004: p. 133).

2. The 'quasi' prefix might be seen to serve two roles here: (a) it allows evaluative beliefs to be captured by the term and thus can be applied to theories where the theorist does not employ the word 'judgement'; and (b) it allows that the judgements need not be manifest to the agent at the time of the emotion. D'Arms and Jacobson (2003) use it in the sense of (b); I think they do so to confusing effect. What results from their definition of quasi-judgementalism is the collapsing-together of two distinct variants of cognitivism: reason-giving and world-taking. I show below that these differ enough to make one question the perspicacity of treating them together and as one.

3. Recall Griffiths' reason for rejecting the term in favour of propositional attitude theory was that cognitivism would be too easily confused with cognitive science, something which he, in contrast to cognitivism in the philosophy of the emotions, admires. Of critics of cognitivism, Deigh (2004) employs this term.

4. Where, one might ask, is the possibility of 'rational feelings'? Is the term 'rational feeling' a category mistake?

5. Some theorists, indeed most, take the term and employ it as it is used in cognitive psychology, as capturing a set of mental processes. I do not use the word in this way when I employ it in the term 'world-taking cognitivism'. More is said on this below and in the following chapter.

6. This is still to go into more detail than do critics of cognitivism such as Griffiths and D'Arms and Jacobson.

7. It is this latter claim which is crucially important, because to say, by way of criticism of cognitivism, that one can have an emotion without awareness of cognition (or manifest believing that x) actually leaves many cognitivists untouched. Cognitivists surely do not deny unconscious action and reaction? For if it is intelligibility of the emotion which interests us, we can make sense of it in terms of the beliefs of the agent without making the stronger claim that those beliefs must have been present to the agent (ready-to-hand, as it were) on experiencing the emotion. For example, in reaching into my pocket for the keys to my office when I arrive at work every morning, I do

not believe propositionally and manifestly that the keys are in my pocket, etc. However, one way of making sense of the action involves attributing to me the belief (albeit unconscious) that the keys were in my pocket; if they are not there I act with surprise (sometimes anger and maybe regret). This is one defence cognitivists in the philosophy of the emotions might mount: identifying beliefs is merely a way of making (say) 'fear' intelligible to us and type-individuating it (I discuss this in more detail in Chapter 4, Section 1). In talking this way they do not commit themselves to theorising unconscious processes or processes in an unconscious. Theorising such amounts to no more than theorising shadows cast by one's theory of conscious processes; see, for a critique of such errors in cognitive science, Sharrock and Coulter's 'Revisiting "The Unconscious"' in Moyal-Sharrock (2007).

8. Both Cheshire Calhoun (1984) and Robert C. Roberts (1988, 2003) have advanced cognate accounts. Patricia Greenspan's (1992) account also shares *some* similarities. The criticism frequently levelled at such theories is that they are too metaphorical or too sketchy in their invocation of 'seeing as'. I will endeavour to paint the full picture, as it were, of what is meant by invoking 'seeing as'.

9. A similar, though less sophisticated attempt, can be found in D'Arms and Jacobson (2003).

10. As will transpire, I do not find the division of emotions into affective and higher cognitive helpful; indeed, the division, however characterised, is misleading. Shame can be felt in an affect-type way, just as disgust can arise in a manner captured by calling it a higher cognitive emotion. More below.

11. For the uncultured amongst us, Mr Spock is the character from the original *Star Trek* TV series; he is from the planet Vulcan, where they have culturally evolved to a stage whereby they live their lives without emotion, acting only in accordance with logic. So the story goes.

12. I think this owes much to the early context, where such theorists, in self-consciously advancing a corrective to feeling-theories, tended to down-play feeling's role a little too strongly.

13. As we saw in Chapter 1, the way the affective emotions are characterised in psychology is on the model of a computer program running; hence the name: 'affect program emotions'.

14. We need to tread cautiously, hereabouts. There is some equivocation on the nature of the sub-personal mechanisms which populate theories advanced by cognitive science. Are these mechanisms physical—part of the biological furniture of the creature—or not? Some explicitly claim them to be so, others (such as Griffiths, as we saw in Chapter 1) merely refer to them as psychological, leaving their ontological status open. In a paper which discusses Dan Dennett's work in cognitive science, John McDowell writes,

> What could an information-processing device *really* tell *anything* (including another component in a sub-personal or 'sub-personal' informational system)? It is essential to realise that the answer to this question can be—in

fact is—"Nothing", without the slightest threat being posed to the utility, or even theoretical indispensability, of cognitive science.

(McDowell 1998b: p. 350)

I have to disagree; or rather I do agree with McDowell's answer to his own question ('Nothing'), but do not agree with the conclusion he draws regarding the lack of threat to cognitive science. For most of those working in and drawing on cognitive science, the acceptance of McDowell's answer would pose the greatest of threats to the utility and theoretical indispensability of cognitive science. It would, for example, render otiose almost everything Jesse Prinz has written on the emotions (one book and half a dozen papers at time of writing), if he were to accede to McDowell's answer to this question. McDowell is led to make this remark by assuming that the sub-personal informational system 'is a physical mechanism' (ibid.) as it, indeed, is for Dennett, though not for many of those who invoke them in their theories. For McDowell to be correct in his claim regarding the implications of his answer for cognitive science, he must work with a severely restricted definition of the discipline— e.g. he must bracket-out all work done by Jerry Fodor and his followers. (I discuss Prinz below in Section 4.)

15. Though, to be sure, one would want to approach Ekman *et al.*'s 'findings' with more than a little caution. A smile is a smile in a context, a social situation, and of course, on a human face. Ekman often writes as if a smile could be extensionally described in terms only of 'its' physical components taken in abstraction from these.

16. Even Solomon, who on most people's account offers the most basic and pure of the cognitivist theories, readily acknowledges the important role affect plays in emotion (2003a: p. 12).

17. Of course, in certain respects embarrassment and shame are, rightly, seen as indiscrete emotions, at least they seem to intersect; in other respects, such as when we focus on the relative degree of affect constitutive of each, embarrassment can seem a long way away, in virtue of its (generally) affective nature. This is in contradistinction to the (generally) cognitive nature of shame.

18. As we saw in Chapter 1, this is the claim Paul Griffiths advances.

19. This is Jenefer Robinson's (1995) claim.

20. This all-too-ready acceptance of the affective–cognitive distinction is ubiquitous in the emotions literature, both philosophical and psychological.

21. In Agamben's terms, we might say that those who argue for the essentially affective nature of emotion (or a class or kind, thereof) ignore the distinction between *zoe* and *bios*, thinking only of our nature in terms of the former. See Chapter 2, above.

22. See Hutchinson (2007) and Hutchinson and Read (2005b, 2008) for details as to why appeal to grammar-as-stock-of-uses (or grammatical rules) cannot do the work some think it can.

23. For Griffiths to merely accept Ekman's 'belief' here is somewhat striking when one considers what he has written a little earlier in his book about

Lazarus, a cognitive psychologist, who makes the same decision as Ekman—i.e. to not admit startle to his list of emotions. With respect to Lazarus, Griffiths writes,

> Another interesting parallel between cognitivists in psychology and propositional attitude theorists in philosophy is a tendency to use a priori arguments for their view. Lazarus is prone to stipulate that cases that don't involve his preferred form of cognition can't count as emotion: 'Those who are less sanguine than I about the causal role of cognition in emotion often point to the startle response, since cognition is obviously absent or negligible in this reaction. I do not consider startle an emotion. Emotion results from an evaluative perception... Startle is best regarded as a primitive neural reflex process' (Lazarus 1982: p. 1023). This tendency to argue for 'cognitivism by definition' may reflect the same linguistic intuitions that drove conceptual analysts to the propositional attitude view.
>
> (*WERA*: p. 26)

In what sense, one might ask, is Ekman's decision sound and Lazarus's not so?

24. In order to deny this, one must hold that cognition must always be manifest to the cogniser to be such: i.e. to be cognition. There is no reason to hold this to be so. My account below fleshes this out in a non-modular and non-computational way.

25. It is, of course, important in such matters to be clear about which are **experimental results** and which are **extrapolations from those results**. So often one finds these collapsed together.

26. This is the dominant view in psychology and neuroscience.

27. Robinson also discusses and draws on the 'subception' experiments in her (2004) 'Emotion: Biological Fact or Social Construction?' p. 33.

28. Usually, in the former claim holding—absence of *manifest* cognition—the latter (stronger) claim—*no possibility* of cognition—is assumed; the latter is, of course, a more difficult claim to sustain.

29. This theme recurs throughout this chapter; it also appeared in Chapter 2, Section 4.1.

30. I take this to be uncontroversial. Ekman (1984) takes openness to cognitive overcoming to be an essential characteristic of affect program emotions; this is one of the reasons why he doesn't admit startle to the list of these emotions, because it is, according to him, not amenable to cognitive overcoming (I disagree; more below). Indeed, many human practices simply would not exist unless one could absent fear.

31. The specifying of the gun as a 'submachine gun' is crucial. If one were to react with startle with every shot the machine gun releases, as one holds down the trigger, then one would end up blindly (for one's eyes would be if not constantly closed, then almost constantly) shooting into the ground (or into one's feet). In the absence of the ability to cognitively overcome reflexes, the greatest danger a submachine gun would pose is to its firer.

32. In this sense, although apparently divergent, Griffiths and Robinson can be seen to share the same prejudice. Griffiths sees the affect program emotions as cognitively closed and thus of a different natural kind to the higher cognitive emotions; Robinson sees them as cognitively closed but takes them as essential to all emotions, i.e. what Griffiths calls higher cognitive emotions (for Robinson) supervene upon the cognitively closed affect program emotions, the cognition is merely window dressing, as it were. Griffiths and Robinson both share the assumption that the affect program emotions are cognitively closed.

33. The example is taken from Taylor's (1985) rendition of Davidson's (1976) 'Hume's Cognitive Theory of Pride'.

34. I cite Taylor rather than Davidson here because, remarkable as it might seem given the title of Davidson's paper ('Hume's Cognitive Theory of Pride'), Davidson, as Solomon notes (2003a: p. 6), *never* actually discusses pride, the emotion.

35. I find something problematic about identifying such a belief as universal, in the first place. Is all that it has to be is for the holder of the belief to consider it universalisable? Both Taylor and Davidson say merely 'universal' and leave things there.

36. 'Feeling' in this sense, therefore, is not the delimited notion invoked by feeling theorists: i.e. awareness of sensation or patterned changes in the autonomic nervous system. Rather it is the *whole* of what it feels to be in an emotional state of one kind or another. It is, I think, in this respect misleading to call such theories 'add-on' theories as does Goldie (2000, ch. 2, 2004).

37. This is crucial to acknowledge. It is unfortunate that many critics of cognitivism mistakenly assume that the cognitive constituents suggested by the particular theorist must be manifest to the agent of the emotion at the time of the emotional episode. This would be, if true, not merely incredibly crude as a theory, but also widely divergent with the phenomenology of much emotional experience. Fortunately it is not true.

38. Robert Solomon (2003a: p. 12) complains that authors such as Stocker (1996) and Goldie (2000), in arguing against cognition and in favour of affect, ultimately smuggle in quite a lot of cognition. Such a complaint is broadly-speaking consonant with my criticism of Goldie here.

39. Their content only differs because Goldie takes *cognitive* content to be always propositional, whereas the content of the perceptions afforded by 'feeling towards' is non-propositional. As I have noted, this is neither a necessary thought on his part nor is it something that many cognitivists would argue for (though some might seem to imply it, on occasion). Their phenomenology differs in that feeling towards, as feeling, comes upon one, so to speak: you *feel* it. One doesn't tend to feel a belief, so the story goes. One might just question the assumption that these concepts are discrete; if one rejects this assumption, then one might just say that some non-propositional beliefs about the world come over one with felt qualities. Some don't. It depends on the situation, your history, your hopes for the future, etc.

40. Calhoun proposes the notion of 'seeing as' by way of a constructive critique of (reason-giving) cognitivism. Lyons' theory is a causal 'seeing as' theory. Roberts's theory is the closest to that I shall advance here. However, what is crucially different is that I do not provide an account of emotions which theorises the *substantive content* of emotional expression or provides the necessary and sufficient conditions for the applicability of emotion terms. I am concerned to offer a framework for understanding emotion. The substantive content ought to be 'filled-out' 'empirically', case by case.

41. The charge is often levelled in a somewhat hand-waving type way. The critic will often just dismiss such accounts by saying they are too metaphorical while progressing to later talk of underlying mechanisms and modules: do they, one wonders, talk literally when they talk of mechanisms and modules? This is not to suggest it is only Griffiths and his like who so readily dismiss such accounts. Solomon (2003a) also says that Roberts's notion of 'concern-based construal' is in need of clarification.

42. I do this not merely for Wittgensteinian reasons but also following to a degree Amelie Rorty's remarks on theorising emotions (see Rorty 2004). In short, understanding emotions can only be done by embedding them in an economic, political, and cultural context and by gaining an understanding of the place of emotions in the lives of people.

43. Wittgenstein de-psychologises the notion, however. (See Hutchinson and Read (2008) 'A Perspicuous Presentation of "Perspicuous Presentation"'.)

44. This, of course, has more than a passing similarity to the world of which Husserl is talking when he talks of the 'life-world' and Heidegger when talking of 'Being-in-the-world'. Husserl's and Heidegger's notions are fuller than that of McDowell, i.e. they imply more. McDowell seeks only to practice therapy, he is not engaged in fundamental ontology. (See above, Chapter 2 (Section 3.2) for more on Heidegger. And Chapter4, below.)

45. The invocation of 'acknowledgement' is important to keep in mind here. It guards against (mis-)reading of this as a behaviourist thesis. One can 'turn away' from those normative properties. In doing so one has still registered them, though refused to acknowledge them. For explication of this notion of acknowledgement, see Cavell (1976, ch. IX, 1979, Part Four) and Stephen Mulhall's (2001a) excellent reading of Ridley Scott's *Blade Runner* as being a meditation on this Cavellian theme. Also, see below (this chapter, Section 2.3.1) for a discussion of a refusal to acknowledge.

46. It is of crucial importance not to read this as implying such characterisations as supervening upon, nor as being characterisations of, a disenchanted/Given world outside the space of reasons.

47. For those who think this is a clear case of guilt rather than shame, on account of it implying the omission of an act of intervention, we can merely replace the example with 'helplessly-witnessing-an-unprovoked-and-violent-attack-on-an-innocent-individual'. And call this 'helpless-witnessing*'. As already noted, there is clear overlap between shame and guilt. What Karl Jaspers

calls metaphysical guilt just is what most people understand as shame. Similarly, what Primo Levi calls shame is discussed by many others as 'survivor guilt'.

48. Let us say (for our purposes here) that my complicity is based on my voting and my tax-paying, which have supported such policies, and my failure to give enough time to protesting, campaigning, and letter-writing. While only potentially contributing to the reduction or end to such policies, such actions would have served to reduce the moral taint I feel in virtue of being British at this time.

49. Or one can simply refuse to acknowledge the dawning; you refuse to convey upon the aspect the significance it claims of you. You see it, you perceive the internal relation, but it clashes with others and you treat it with scepticism: you deny it. Hence: 'being in denial'.

50. It also makes sense of the role beliefs and/or judgements play in much emotional experience.

51. Owing to the huge volume of literature on rule-following, some readers will be bursting with detailed and narrowly focused questions. It is beyond my remit to engage in a detailed discussion of rule-following here. I largely endorse, and draw upon, John McDowell's (1998a, b) 'Wittgenstein on Following a Rule'; Warren Goldfarb's (2002) 'Kripke on Wittgenstein on Rules'; Cora Diamond's (1988) 'Rules: Looking in the Right Place'; and Rupert Read and James Guetti's (1999) 'Meaningful Consequences'.

52. And on *this* point, they are at one with the neo-Jamesians, such as Prinz, for all identify some*thing* having the property of meaningfulness with it having been interpreted. The difference between reason-giving cognitivists and neo-Jamesians—in the context of this particular discussion—is in *what* they take it to be that is being interpreted: in the case of the former it is the object of the emotion and in the case of the latter it is the sensation or patterned change in the autonomic nervous system.

53. I choose to stay with Griffiths' (1997) terminology here for convenience and so as to avoid confusion, following Chapter 1. One could just as easily employ the term 'sophisticated emotions of self assessment' (as Taylor (1985) refers to these emotions), or 'complex emotions' (as Griffiths (2004) later decides to refer to them). The terms carry no baggage; one can treat them purely as place-markers.

54. Just to reiterate, shame can be experienced in both 'affective' and 'cognitive' modes, as can fear; though the latter does seem to more frequently occur in 'affective' mode and the former more frequently in 'cognitive' mode. While this suggests to us why categorisation of *emotion terms* into 'affective' and 'higher cognitive' is so pervasive, it should also indicate one reason to reject a categorisation of *emotion terms* as opposed to *emotional episodes*, which is so often found in literature on emotions as otherwise diverse as Taylor (1985) and Griffiths (1997).

55. This helps us to make sense of shame cultures, such as those of the Homeric texts, where affective shame seems far more common; also why moderns, such as Primo Levi, grapple with their shame, recognising it but also trying

to resist and understand it in terms of guilt—the latter (guilt) is amenable to purely legal (non-emotional, non-moral) understanding.

56. This ties in with my discussion of Cora Diamond on the concepts of 'human being' and of 'member of the species Homo sapiens' (see Chapter 1, Section 4.2, above).

57. This is to be distinguished, therefore, from what one might call the 'Kaspar Hauser' sense of shamelessness, i.e. shamelessness as a product of the absence of a fully-formed *Bildung*. Such shamelessness results from an inability to perceive the internal relations between concepts, through not having been availed of those concepts, not having learnt the place of those in concepts in persons' lives. This is not the same as Diogenes' shamelessness.

58. The original source of our knowledge of Diogenes of Synope is to be found in Diogenes Laertius. In relaying the story, Geuss provides his own account of shame; I do not subscribe to this, for reasons I discussed above (Section 2.2). Michel Foucault also discussed Diogenes' public masturbation in an as yet unpublished, late (1983) lecture series on the cynics.

59. Though public eating is often frowned upon in societies where food is scarce. However, generally speaking, it is just that: frowned upon, and not taboo.

60. This is from where the name 'cynic' is said to come. It comes from the Greek 'kynikos', which is literally translated as 'dog-like'. There is some dispute as to whether this has its origins in the cynics' desire to attain shamelessness being likened to the shamelessness of a dog, or whether it has as its origins 'Grey Dog', which a was the name of the gymnasium in ancient Athens where the founder of the cynics, Antisthenes (student of Socrates and tutor of Diogenes), taught. For my own part, I do not think it was beyond the Greeks in general or the cynics in particular to be aware of, and exploit, both connotations.

61. I can find no reason to read Sartre's 'example' as committing him to the thought that an actual audience is *required*, as does Taylor.

62. D'Arms and Jacobson (2003), Deigh (1994), Griffiths (1997: pp. 28–30), Prinz (2003a: p. 74), and Zajonc (1984) all identify recalcitrance as *the* problem faced by cognitivist accounts.

63. Some might attempt to dismiss such a move as merely playing semantics while eliding the genuine problem, in that it plays on the meaning of 'recalcitrance' as 'a refusal to acknowledge authority'. This denial of recalcitrance therefore hinges on refusing to grant authority to belief in the first place; if belief is not granted its explanatory or constitutive sovereignty, if it has no authority in the explanation, then neither can certain other beliefs be said to be recalcitrant. Of course critics of cognitivism will be quick to point out that this defence works only at the expense of giving up on one's commitment to cognitivism, neither Goldie nor Greenspan would object. However, critics such as D'Arms and Jacobson are still dissatisfied.

64. In this sense this is the mirror image of philosophical scepticism, where the sceptic merely pushes on one, tries to persuade one of, the possibility of the extraordinary by way of disrupting one's assumptions and beliefs about

the ordinary, everyday, world in which we live. Levi's scepticism is an ordinary scepticism as to the meanings forced upon him, and which elicit his emotion, by the extraordinary world of Auschwitz.

65. Sense data as a term is somewhat unfashionable now; I suspect because it was Ayer's preferred term and thus the term with which Austin (1962) had so much sport in *Sense and Sensibilia*.

66. My discussion of interpretation and grasping, above, is relevant here (cf. Section 2.3).

67. The alternative picture I here offer as a prophylactic to the empiricist picture of mind and world of mind and world is variously found in the works of Aristotle, Wittgenstein, (recent) Putnam (1994, 1999), and McDowell (1994).

68. For extended discussion of these issues, see Bennett *et al.* (2007).

69. One could go into much detail on this. I shan't. For pretty devastating critiques of such theories, see Austin (1962) and Travis (2005). It is also pertinent, following Austin and Wittgenstein, to question in what sense the concepts of psychosemantics and the modules that encapsulate them are 'inner'; briefly, if I say the book is in the drawer, or the pig is in the sty, then we can be expected to be able to respond to basic questions such as 'If we open the drawer/sty will we find the book/pig?' Can one say cognate things about thoughts and the head? It might be objected that it is another use of 'inner' that is in play here, say, such as 'John is in the Army' or 'John has a hole in his trousers'. But John joined the Army, he left the Army after his six-year stint, his parents watched him marching with his platoon at his passing-out parade, etc. 'John being in the Army' does not imply location. Is this the use of 'in' our theoreticians of psychosemantics invoke? Does it make sense to talk of psychosemantic concepts being *in* modules in this way?

70. Calling them *bio*-semantics and telling an evolutionary story doesn't help. Why do they evolve in a way that our public concepts don't? And if you feel inclined to retort that our public concepts do evolve (and I have no objection to speaking this way), then why the need for the inner concepts of biosemantics?

71. I have already conceded that this runs the risk of been unfair to Goldie. I take him to be embroiled in a similar bind to Robinson and Prinz, but to be less scientific in his proposed solution to the problem. Unfortunately while this is to be applauded, it doesn't ultimately get him out of the bind.

4. Shame and World

1. It is common for papers on the emotions to begin with a version of this problem/dilemma. In addition to Prinz and Deigh, see Hatzimoysis (2003b) and Robinson (2004). Furthermore, one might ask why we need a theory in the first place, Deigh merely assumes that we do.

2. I mean only that it is not my purpose to argue over what Frege achieved. For those who want to look into this area more, I recommend Cora Diamond's *The Realistic Spirit* (1992) and Charles Travis's Thought's Footing (2006). Furthermore, I am not concerned to defend Fregean analysis, here.

3. See Travis (2000) *Unshadowed Thought* for an excellent critique of 'shadows'.
4. I do not necessarily invoke a psychoanalytic, or even formal, therapeutic procedure here. All I mean to suggest is a process whereby one brings to consciousness the object. Therapy can be practised on oneself, with an interlocutor, with a book, or with a professional therapist.
5. And stones, for example, are world-less. It should not be assumed from these remarks that Heidegger argues that the human animal's world-forming nature is borne of its capacity for reason, or of it being a beast with the added capacity for language. Heidegger was keen to provide an alternative to such a view.
6. Of course our scientistic interlocutors will want more; they will want to know what it is that does the intending. We can here respond simply that it is the beast. We do not need to acknowledge the pertinence of their question which demands of us that we locate the capacity for intentionality somewhere in the beast's brain.
7. This is sometimes translated as 'subjective world' or 'subjective universe'. This is misleading. It is better rendered as 'species-specific world', meaning 'the world as specified by the natural attributes of the species to that species'.
8. I here allude to Heidegger's discussion of environment—*Umwelt*—and world in *Parmenides* (1992: Part 2, Section 8). Agamben (2004) discusses the relation in his *The Open: Man and Animal*, see particularly chapters 12 and 13. There is a parallel discussion to be found in McDowell (1994), see particularly p. 115 for a parallel with animal-*Umwelt* and his discussion of second nature and *Bildung* throughout.
9. When I talk of the animal in its *Umwelt*, I do not denote by 'animal' all non-human animals, but rather the animal-in-*Umwelt*, the *locus classicus* of which is the tick (see, for example, Uexküll (1957)).
10. The Rwandan genocide was perpetrated over a 100-day period, beginning in April 1994; in that time over 800,000 Rwandans were murdered. There are numerous books and documentaries on the genocide. That which I have found most helpful is Mamdani (2001) *When Victims Become Killers: Colonialism, Nativism and the Genocide in Rwanda*.
11. As I noted in the previous chapters (2 and 3), this is, arguably, the topic of both Primo Levi's *If This is a Man* and Robert Antelme's *Human Race*. I also come close here to agreeing with Agamben. Note, however, I am not claiming that this *is* shame. I am saying here that this is how one makes intelligible Léopard's shame, as expressed in the quotation.
12. Williams chooses to employ Kantian terminology here. He does so because one of his purposes in this work is to rebut the thought, which he attributes to Kantian moral philosophy, that the Greek conception of 'good' was heteronomous, and thus not genuinely moral. Ilham Dilman's (1999) insightful discussion of Williams on this topic is what first drew my attention.
13. One could give a similar argument here regarding our relations to non-human animals.
14. See MacIntyre (1999) *Dependent Rational Animals*.

15. See Mark Lynas (2007) *Six Degrees: Our Future on a Hotter Planet* for a recent account of the projected effects of anthropogenic global warming. The science changes rapidly, so I refer the reader the IPCC's (Intergovernmental Panel on Climate Change) website for the most up-to-date data: http://www.ipcc.ch/.

16. While I concur with most of what Dilman writes in the book from where this quote is taken, I do have some misgivings; for details of these, see Hutchinson and Read (2005b).

17. Dilman's book is principally concerned to show this accusation to be false.

18. See Hutchinson (2004) for a detailed critique of Steiner.

19. We can allow that there might well be cases for engaging in such abstractions, in well-defined (practical) contexts—maybe such as law courts.

20. Of course, one cannot merely assert this picture of the world. It is the burden of this book to have given reason to accept this picture of the world as, at the least, better off than those with which other authors discussed in previous chapters have worked. It is a piecemeal process, engaging with one's philosophical interlocutors, identifying the problems to which they are prone, and persuading them that these problems stem from being in thrall to a particular picture of how things must be, by way of persuading them that things do not have to be thus and so: e.g. one does not *have* to work with the unconceptualised world.

21. Langer's book takes as its subject the oral testimonies of survivors of the Holocaust, as these are recorded in video-taped interviews held at the Fortunoff Video Archive, Yale. All the interviewees are referred to by first name and the first initial of their last name only.

22. The directly quoted passages from Edith P.'s testimony are in double quotes.

23. This is not meant to be *in any sense* a definition; I now hope that it is clear that such a goal is not mine. This is merely another exercise in understanding shame; here with respect to it being internally related to 'dignity'.

Bibliography

Agamben, Giorgio (1998) *Homo Sacer: Sovereign Power and Bare Life*, trans. Daniel Heller-Roazen. Stanford: Stanford University Press.

——(1999) *Remnants of Auschwitz: The Witness and the Archive*, trans. Daniel Heller-Roazen. New York: Zone Books.

——(2000) *Potentialities: Collected Essays in Philosophy*, trans. Daniel Heller-Roazen. Stanford: Stanford University Press.

——(2004) *The Open: Man and Animal*, trans. Kevin Attell. Stanford: Stanford University Press.

Améry, Jean (1999) *At the Mind's Limits*. London: Granta.

Annas, Julia (1998) 'Virtue and Eudaimonism.' In Paul, E., Jaul, J. and Miller, F. (eds) *Virtue and Vice*. Cambridge: Cambridge University Press.

Anscombe, Elizabeth (2000 [1957]) *Intention*. Cambridge MA: Harvard University Press.

Antelme, Robert (1992) *The Human Race*, trans. Jeffrey Haight and Annie Mahler (1998). Evanston, IL: The Marlboro Press.

Aristotle (2002) *The Collected Works of Aristotle* (2 Vols). Oxford: Oxford University Press.

Austin, J. L. (1962) *Sense and Sensibilia*. Oxford: Oxford University Press.

Baker, Gordon (2004) *Wittgenstein's Method: Neglected Aspects*. Edited and Introduced by Katherine Morris. Oxford: Blackwell.

Baz, Avner (2003) 'On When Words are Called for: Cavell, McDowell, and the Wording of the World.' *Inquiry*, 46, 473–500.

Bennett, M. and Hacker, P. M. S. (2003) *The Philosophical Foundations of Neuroscience*. Oxford: Blackwell.

Bennett, M., Dennett, D., Hacker P. M. S. and Searle, J. (2007) *Neuroscience and Philosophy: Brain, Mind and Language*. New York: Columbia University Press.

Bettelheim, Bruno (1979) *Surviving and Other Essays*. New York: Knopf.

Blackburn, Simon (1998) *Ruling Passions: A Theory of Practical Reasoning*. Oxford: Oxford University Press.

Boyd, Richard (1991) 'Realism, Anti-foundationalism and the Enthusiasm for Natural Kinds.' *Philosophical Studies*, 61, 127–148.

Brandom, Robert (1994) *Making it Explicit*. Cambridge MA: Harvard University Press.

Browning, Christopher (2001 [2nd edn]) *Ordinary Men: Reserve Police Battalion 101 and the Final Solution*. London: Penguin.

Burge, Tyler (1979) 'Individualism and the Mental.' *Midwest Studies in Philosophy*, 4, 73–121.

——(1986) 'Individualism and Psychology.' *Philosophical Review*, 45, 3–45.

Button, Graham (ed.) (1991) *Ethnomethodology and the Human Sciences*. Cambridge: Cambridge University Press.

Button, Graham, Coulter, Jeff, Lee, John R. E. and Sharrock, Wes (1995) *Computers, Minds and Conduct*. Cambridge: Polity Press.

Calhoun, Cheshire and Solomon, Robert (eds) (1984) *What is an Emotion: Classic Readings in Philosophical Psychology.* New York: Oxford University Press.

Cavell, Stanley (1976) *Must We Mean What We Say* Cambridge: Cambridge University Press.

——(1979) *The Claim of Reason.* Oxford: Oxford University Press.

——(1989) *This New Yet Unapproachable America: Lectures after Emerson after Wittgenstein.* Albuquerque: Living Batch Press.

Cicioni, Mirna (1995) *Primo Levi: Bridges of Knowledge.* Oxford: Berg.

Cohen, Josh (2001) 'Review of Giorgio Agamben: *Homo Sacer* and *Remnants of Auschwitz.*' *Textual Practice*, 15 (2), 379–385.

Coulter, Jeff (1991) 'Cognition: Cognition in an Ethnomethodological Mode.' In Button, G. (ed.).

Crary, Alice and Read, Rupert (2000) *The New Wittgenstein.* London: Routledge.

Curtis, Mark (2002) *Web of Deceit.* London: Abacus.

D'Arms and Jacobson (2003) 'The Significance of Recalcitrant Emotions (Or Anti-QuasiJudgmentalism).' In Hatzimoysis, A. (ed.).

Damasio, Antonio R. (1994) *Descartes' Error: Emotion, Reason and the Human Brain.* London: Macmillan.

Davidson, Donald (1976) 'Hume's Cognitive Theory of Pride' *Journal of Philosophy*, 73 (19), 744–757.

Davidson, D. and Harman, G. (eds) (1970) *Semantics of Natural Language.* Dordrecht: Kluwer Academic Publishers.

Deigh, John (ed.) (1992) *Ethics and Personality: Essays in Moral Psychology.* Chicago: Chicago University Press.

——(1994) 'Cognitivism in the Theory of Emotions.' *Ethics*, 104, 824–854.

——(2004) 'Primitive Emotions.' In Solomon, Robert C. (ed.), pp. 9–27.

Derrida, Jacques (1973) *Speech and Phenomena*, trans. David B. Allison. Evanston: Northwestern University Press.

——(1988) *Limited Inc.*, trans. Alan Bass and Samuel Weber. Evanston: Northwestern University Press.

Des Pres, Terrence (1976) *The Survivor: An Anatomy of Life in the Death Camps.* New York: Oxford University Press.

Diamond, Cora (1988) 'Losing Your Concepts' *Ethics*, 98, 255–277.

——(1989) 'Rules: Looking in the Right Place.' In Phillips and Winch (eds) *Wittgenstein: Attention to Particulars: Essays in Honour of Rush Rhees.* London: Macmillan; New York: St. Martin's Press.

——(1992) *The Realistic Spirit.* Cambridge MA: MIT.

Dilman, İlham (1999) 'Shame, Guilt and Remorse.' *Philosophical Investigations*, 22 (4), 312–329.

——(2002) *Wittgenstein's Copernican Revolution: The Question of Linguistic Idealism.* Basingstoke: Palgrave.

Downing, George (2001) 'Emotion Theory Revisited.' In Wrathall, M. and Malpas, J. (eds).

Dupré, John (1981) 'Natural Kinds and Biological Taxa.' *The Philosophical Review*, 90 (1), 66–90; also in Dupré (2001a).

——(1983) 'The Disunity of Science.' *Mind*, XCII, 321–346; also in Dupré (2001a).

——(1993) *The Disorder of Things: Metaphysical Foundations of the Disunity of Science.* London: Harvard University Press.

——(2001a) *Human Nature and the Limits of Science.* Oxford: Oxford University Press.

——(2001b) *Humans and Other Animals*. Oxford: Oxford University Press.

Edkins, Jenny (2000) 'Sovereign Power, Zones of Indistinction, and the Camp.' *Alternatives*, 25 (1), January–March, 3–25.

Ekman, P. (1971) 'Universals and Cultural Differences in Facial Expressions of Emotion.' In Cole, J. K. (ed.) *Nebraska Symposium on Motivation*, 4. Lincoln: University of Nebraska Press.

——(1972) *Emotions in the Human Face*. New York: Pergamon Press.

——(1973) *Darwin and Facial Expressio: A Century of Research in Review*. New York: Academic Press.

——(1980) *The Face of Man*. New York: Garland.

——(1984) 'Expression and the Nature of Emotion.' In Scherer and Ekman (eds).

——(1992) 'Are There Basic Emotions' *Psychological Review*, 99 (3), 550–553.

Ekman, P. and Friesen, W. V. (1969) 'The Repertoire of Nonverbal Behavior: Categories, Origins, Usage, and Coding.' *Semiotica*, 1, 49–98.

——(1971) 'Constants Across Cultures in the Face and Emotion.' *Journal of Personality and Social Psychology*, 17 (2), 124–129.

——(1975) *Unmasking the Face: A Guide to Recognizing Emotions from Facial Clues*. Englewood Cliffs, NJ: Prentice-Hall.

Ekman, P., Levenson, R. W. and Friesen, W. V. (1983) 'Autonomic Nervous System Activity Distinguishes Among Emotions.' *Science*, 221, 1208–1210.

Ekman, P., Friesen, W. V. and Simmons, R. C. (1985) 'Is the Startle Reaction an Emotion' *Journal of Personality and Social Psychology*, 49 (5), 1416–1426.

Elliott, Ward (1968) 'Guilt and Overguilt: Some Reflections on Moral Stimulus and Paralysis' *Ethics*, 78 (4), 247–254.

Evans, Dylan and Cruse, Pierre (eds) (2004) *Emotion, Evolution and Rationality*. Oxford: Oxford University Press.

Feyerabend, Paul (1975) *Against Method*. London: Verso.

Fodor, J. A. (1983) *The Modularity of the Mind: An Essay in Faculty Psychology*. Cambridge MA: MIT Press.

Fossum, M. A. and Mason, M. J. (1986) *Facing Shame: Families in Recovery*. New York: Norton.

Foucault, Michel (1978) *History of Sexuality Vol. II*. London: Penguin.

——(1984) 'Right of Death and Power over Life.' In Rabinow, P. (ed.) *The Foucault Reader*. New York: Pantheon Books, p. 265.

Frank, R. H. (1988) *Passions Within Reason: The Strategic Role of the Emotions*. New York: Norton.

Gaita, Raimond (1991) *Good and Evil: An Absolute Conception*. Basingstoke: Macmillan.

Geras, Norman (1998) *The Contract of Mutual Indifference: Political Philosophy After the Holocaust*. London: Verso.

Geuss, Raymond (2001) *Public Goods, Private Goods*. Princeton: Princeton University Press.

Gilbert, Paul (1998) 'What is Shame? Some Core Issues and Controversies.' In Gilbert, P. and Andrews, B. (eds).

Gilbert, Paul and Andrews, Bernice (eds) (1998) *Shame: Interpersonal Behaviour, Psychopathology, and Culture*. Oxford: Oxford University Press.

Glendinning, Simon (1998) *On Being With Others: Heidegger–Derrida–Wittgenstein*. London: Routledge.

Goldfarb, Warren (2002) 'Kripke on Wittgenstein on Rules.' In Miller, A. and Wright, C. (eds).

Goldie, Peter (2000) *The Emotions: A Philosophical Exploration.* Oxford: Oxford University Press.

——(2004) 'Emotion, Feeling and Knowledge of the World.' In Solomon, Robert C. (ed.).

Goodenough, Jerry and Read, Rupert (eds) (2005) *Film as Philosophy: Essays on Cinema After Wittgenstein and Cavell.* Basingstoke: Palgrave.

Gordon, Robert S. C. (2001) *Primo Levi's Ordinary Virtues.* Oxford: Oxford University Press.

Gourevitch, Philip (2000) *We Wish To Inform You That Tomorrow We Will Be Killed With Our Families.* London: Picador.

Greenspan, P. S. (1988) *Emotions and Reasons.* London: Routledge.

——(1992) 'Subjective Guilt and Responsibility' *Mind*, 101, 287–303.

——(1995) *Practical Guilt: Moral Dilemmas, Emotions and Social Norms.* Oxford: Oxford University Press.

Greenspan, Patricia (2004) 'Emotion, Rationality and Mind/Body.' In Solomon, Robert C. (ed.), pp. 123–135.

Griffiths, Paul E. (1989) 'The Degeneration of the Cognitive Theory of Emotion.' *Philosophical Psychology*, 2 (3), 297–313.

——(1997) *What Emotions Really Are.* Chicago: Chicago University Press.

——(1999a) 'Author's Response.' *Metascience*, 8 (1), 49–62.

——(1999b) 'Squaring the Circle: Natural Kinds with Historical Essences.' In Wilson, R. A. (ed.) *Species: New Interdisciplinary Essays.* Cambridge MA: MIT Press.

——'Is Emotion a Natural Kind' In Solomon, Robert C. (ed.), pp. 233–249.

Harré, Rom (ed.) (1986) *The Social Construction of Emotions.* Oxford: Basil Blackwell.

Guetti, James and Read, Rupert (1996) 'Acting from Rules: 'Internal Relations' versus 'Logical Existentialism'.' *International Studies in Philosophy*, XXVIII (2), 43–62.

Guignon, Charles (2003) 'Moods in Heidegger's *Being and Time.*' In Solomon, Robert C. (ed.).

——(ed.) (1993) *The Cambridge Companion to Heidegger.* Cambridge: Cambridge University Press.

Hacking, Ian (1995) *Rewriting the Soul: Multiple Personality and the Sciences of Memory.* Princeton: Princeton University Press.

Hager, J. C. and Ekman, P. (1985) 'The Asymmetry of Facial Actions is Inconsistent with Models of Hemispheric Specialization.' *Psychophysiology*, 22 (3), 307–318.

Hale, Bob and Wright, Crispin (eds) (1997) *A Companion to the Philosophy of Language.* Oxford: Blackwell.

Harper, J. C. and Hoopes, M. H. (1990) *Uncovering Shame: An Approach Integrating Individuals and Their Family Systems.* New York: Norton.

Hatzfeld, Jean (2005a) *Into The Quick of Life: The Rwandan Genocide: The Survivors Speak.* London: Serpent's Tail.

——(2005b) *A Time For Machetes: The Rwandan Genocide: The Killers Speak.* London: Serpent's Tail.

Hatzimoysis, Anthony (ed.) (2003a) *Philosophy and the Emotions: Royal Institute of Philosophy Supplement: 52.* Cambridge: Cambridge University Press.

——(2003b) 'Emotional Feelings and Intentionalism.' In Hatzimoysis, A. (ed.).

Heidegger, Martin (1962) *Kant and the Problem of Metaphysics*, trans. James S. Churchill. Bloomington: Indiana University Press.
——(1992) *Parmenides*, trans. André Schuwer and Richard Rojcewicz. Bloomington: Indiana University Press.
——(1997) *Kant and the Problem of Metaphysics* (5th edn), trans. Richard Taft. Indianapolis: Indiana University Press.
Hill, Christopher, S. (1992) *The Philosophy of Hilary Putnam: Philosophical Topics*, 20 (1).
Hursthouse, Rosalind (1999) *On Virtue Ethics*. Oxford: Oxford University Press.
——(2002) 'Virtue Theory and Abortion'. In LaFollette (ed.).
Hutchinson, Phil (2004) 'Steiner's Possession: As it Were.' *European Journal of Political Theory*, 3 (3), 245–265.
——(2007) 'What's the Point of Elucidation.' *Metaphilosophy*, 38 (5), 691–713.
Hutchinson, Phil and Read, Rupert (2005a) 'Memento: A Philosophical Investigation.' In Goodenough, J. and Read, R. (eds), 72–93.
——(2005b) 'Whose Wittgenstein' *Philosophy* 80 (3), 432–455.
——(2005c) 'An *Elucidatory* Interpretation of Wittgenstein's *Tractatus:* A Critique of Daniel D. Hutto's and Marie McGinn's Reading of *Tractatus* 6.54.' *International Journal of Philosophical Studies* 13 (4), 1–29.
——(2008) "A Perspicuous Presentation of 'Perspicuous Presentation'." *Philosophical Investigations*, 31 (2), 140–160.
Hutto, Dan (1999) *Beyond Physicalism*. Amsterdam: John Benjamins.
——(2008) *Folk Psychological Narratives*. Cambridge MA: MIT Press.
James, William (1884) 'What is an Emotion' *Mind*, 9, 188–205.
Kafka (1994) *The Trial*. London: Penguin.
Kant, Immanuel (1929) *The Critique of Pure Reason*, trans. Norman Kemp-Smith. Oxford: Blackwell.
Keil, F. C. (1989) *Concepts, Kinds and Cognitive Development*. Cambridge MA: MIT Press.
Kenny, Anthony (1963) *Action, Emotion and Will*. London: Routledge.
——(1989) *The Metaphysics of Mind*. Oxford: Clarendon Press.
Kincaid, Harold (1996) *Philosophical Foundations of the Social Sciences: Analyzing Controversies in Social Research*. Cambridge: Cambridge University Press.
Kitching, Gavin (2004) *Wittgenstein and Society: Essays in Conceptual Puzzlement*. London: Ashgate.
Kripke, Saul (1972) 'Naming and Necessity.' In Davidson, D. and Harman, G. (eds).
——(1980) *Naming and Necessity*. Oxford: Blackwell.
LaFollette, Hugh (ed.) (2002) *Ethics in Practice: An Anthology*. Oxford: Blackwell.
Lange, C. G. (1885) *Om Sindsbevaegelser: et Psyko-Fysiologisk Studie*. Kjbenhavn: Jacub Lunds.
Langer, Lawrence L. (1991) *Holocaust Testimonies: The Ruins of Memory*. New Haven: Yale University Press.
Lakatos, Imre (1978) *Collected Papers* I and II. Cambridge: Cambridge University Press.
Lazarus, R. S. (1982) 'Thoughts on the Relations between Emotion and Cognition.' *American Psychologist*, 37, 1019–1024.
Levi, Primo (1988) *Ad ora incerta in Opere*, Vol. 1. Turin: Einaudi.
Levi, (1989) *The Drowned and the Saved*. London: Abacus.
——(2000) *If This is a Man/The Truce*. London: Everyman's Press.

——(2001) *The Voice of Memory: Interviews 1961–1987*. Edited by Belpoliti and Gordon. Cambridge: Polity.

Levinas, Emmanuel (1982) *De l'evasion*. Montpellier: Fata Morgana.

Lynas, Mark (2007) *Six Degrees: Our Future on a Hotter Planet*. London: Fourth Estate.

Lyons, William (1980) *Emotion*. Cambridge: Cambridge University Press.

MacIntyre, Alasdair (1985) *After Virtue*. London: Duckworth.

——(1988) *Whose Justice? Which Rationality?* London: Duckworth.

——(1999) *Dependent Rational Animals: Why Human Beings Need the Virtues*. London: Duckworth.

Mamdani, Mahmood (2001) *When Victims Become Killers: Colonialism, Nativism, and the Genocide in Rwanda*. Princeton: Princeton University Press.

McDowell, John (1992) 'Putnam on Mind and Meaning.' In Hill, Christopher S. (ed.); also in McDowell (1998b).

——(1994) *Mind and World*. Cambridge: Cambridge University Press.

——(1998a) *Mind, Value and Reality*. Cambridge MA: Harvard University Press.

——(1998b) *Meaning, Knowledge, & Reality*. Cambridge MA: Harvard University Press.

——(2000a) 'Experiencing the World.' In Willaschek (ed.) (2000).

——(2000b) 'Responses.' In Willaschek (ed.) (2000).

Miller, Alexander and Wright, Crispin (2002) *Rule-Following and Meaning*. Chesham: Acumen.

Moyal-Sharrock, Daniele (ed.) (2007) *Perspicuous Presentations: Essays on Wittgenstein's Philosophy of Psychology*. Basingstoke: Palgrave.

Mulhall, Stephen (2001a) *Inheritance and Originality: Wittgenstein, Heidegger, Kierkegaard*. Oxford: Oxford University Press.

——(2001b) *On Film*. London: Routledge.

Murphy, G. L. (1993) 'A Rational Theory of Concepts.' *Psychology of Learning and Motivation*, 29, 327–359.

Nash, R. A. (1989) 'Cognitive Theories of Emotion', *Nous*, 23, 481–504.

Newman P. L. (1964) ' "Wild Man" Behaviour in a New Guinea Highlands Community.' *American Anthropologist*, 66, 1–19.

Norris, Andrew (ed.) (2005) *Politics, Metaphysics and Death: Essays on Giorgio Agamben's* Homo Sacer. Durham: Duke University Press.

Nussbaum, Martha (2001) *Upheavals of Thought*. Cambridge: Cambridge University Press.

Prinz, Jesse (2003a) 'Emotions, Psychosemantics, and Embodied Appraisals.' In Hatzimoysis, A. (ed.).

——(2003b) *Gut Reactions: A Perceptual Theory of Emotion*. Oxford: Oxford University Press.

——(2004a) 'Embodied Emotions.' In Solomon, Robert C. (ed.).

——(2004b) 'Which Emotions are Basic?' in Evans and Cruse (eds.)

Putnam, Hilary (1975a) *Mind, Language and Reality*. Cambridge: Cambridge University Press.

——(1975b) 'Explanation and Reference.' In Putnam, H. (1975a).

——(1975c) 'Is Semantics Possible.' In Putnam, H. (1975a).

——(1975d) 'Meaning of 'Meaning'.' In Putnam, H. (1975a).

——(1988) *Reclaiming Reality*. Cambridge MA: Harvard University Press.

——(1990) *Realism with a Human Face*. Cambridge MA: Harvard University Press.

——(1992a) 'Response to Gary Ebbs.' In Hill, Christopher S. (ed.).

——(1992b) 'Response to John McDowell.' In Hill, Christopher S. (ed.).
——(1994) *Words and Life*. Cambridge MA: Harvard University Press.
——(1999) *Threefold Cord: Mind, Body, World*. Columbia: Columbia University Press.
Read, Rupert and Guetti, James (1999) 'Meaningful Consequences' *Philosophical Forum*, XXX (4), 289–315.
Roberts, Robert C. (1988) 'What an Emotion Is: A Sketch.' *Philosophical Review*, 97, 183–209.
——(2003) *Emotions: An Essay in Aid of Moral Psychology*. Cambridge: Cambridge University Press.
Robinson, Jenefer (1995) 'Startle.' *Journal of Philosophy*, 92 (2), 53–74.
(2004) 'Emotion: Biological Fact or Social Construction' In Solomon, Robert C. (ed.).
Rorty, Amélie Oksenberg (2004) 'Enough Already With "Theories of the Emotions".' In Solomon, Robert C. (ed.).
Rosenthal, David M. (1991) *The Nature of Mind*. Oxford: Oxford University Press.
Ryle, Gilbert (1949) *The Concept of Mind*. London: Hutchinson & Co.
Sartre, Jean-Paul (1957) *Being and Nothingness*. London: Routledge.
Schachter, Joseph (1957) 'Pain, Fear, and Anger in Hypertensives and Normotensives: A Psychophysiological Study.' *Psychosomatic Medicine*, 19(1), 17–29.
Scherer, K. and Ekman, P. (eds) (1984) *Approaches to Emotion*. Hillsdale, NJ: Erlbaum.
Schiller, Claire H. (ed.) (1957) *Instinctive Behaviour: The Development of a Modern Concept*. New York: International Universities Press.
Schwartz, Gary E., Weinberger, Daniel A. and Singer, Jefferson (1981) 'Cardiovascular Differentiation of Happiness, Sadness, Anger, and Fear Following Imagery and Exercise Psychosomatic Medicine.' *Psychosomatic Medicine*, 43 (4), 343–364.
Searle, John (1980) 'Minds, Brains and Programs.' *Behavioural and Brain Sciences*, 3, 417–457.
——(1992) *The Rediscovery of Mind*. Cambridge MA: MIT Press.
——(2004) *Mind: A Brief Introduction*. New York: Oxford University Press.
Sellars, Wilfrid (1956) 'Empiricism and the Philosophy of Mind.' In Feigl, H. and Scriven, M. (eds), *Minnesota Studies in the Philosophy of Science, Volume I: The Foundations of Science and the Concepts of Psychology and Psychoanalysis*. University of Minnesota Press, 253–329.
Sharrock, Wes and Coulter, Jeff (2007) 'Revisiting 'The Unconscious'.' In Moyal-Sharrock (ed.).
Sherova, Charles M. (1988) *Heidegger, Kant and Time*. London: University Press of America.
Sluga, Hans and Stern, David (eds) (1996) *The Cambridge Companion to Wittgenstein*. Cambridge, UK: Cambridge University Press.
Solomon, Robert C. (1976) *The Passions*. Garden City, New York: Anchor/Doubleday.
——(2003a) 'What is a 'Cognitive Theory' of the Emotions' In Hatzimoysis, A. (ed.).
——(ed.)(2003b) *What is an Emotion: Classic and Contemporary Readings*. New York: Oxford University Press. (This is the——significantly changed——2nd edn of Calhoun and Solomon (eds) (1984).)
——(2003c) *Not Passion's Slave*. Oxford: Oxford University Press.

——(ed.) (2004) *Thinking About Feeling: Contemporary Philosophers on Emotions.* Oxford: Oxford University Press.

de Sousa, Ronald (1987) *The Rationality of Emotion.* Cambridge MA: MIT Press.

Steiner, Hillel (1994) *An Essay on Rights.* Oxford: Backwell.

Stocker, Michael (1987) 'Emotional Thoughts.' *American Philosophical Quarterly,* 24 (1), 59–69.

Stocker, Michael with Hegeman, Elizabeth (1999) *Valuing Emotions.* Cambridge: Cambridge University Press.

Stroll, Avrum (1998) *Sketches of Landscapes.* Cambridge MA: MIT Press.

Tangney, J. P. (1996) 'Conceptual and Methodological Issues in the Assessment of Shame and Guilt.' *Behaviour Therapy and Research,* 34, 741–754.

Taylor, Gabriele (1985) *Pride, Shame, and Guilt: Emotions of Self-Assessment.* Oxford: Oxford University Press.

Todorov, Tzvetan (1996) *Facing the Extreme.* New York: Henry Holt.

Travis, Charles (2000) *Unshadowed Thought.* Cambridge MA: Harvard University Press.

——(2005) 'The Twilight of Empiricism.' *Proceedings of the Aristotelian Society,* XII.

Uexküll, Jakob von (1957) 'A Stroll Through the Worlds of Animals and Men: A Picture Book of Invisible Worlds.' In Schiller, Claire H. (ed.), pp. 5–80.

Wall, Thomas Carl (1999) *Radical Passivity: Levinas, Blanchot, and Agamben.* New York: SUNY.

Weatherston, Martin (2002) *Heidegger's Interpretation of Kant: Categories, Imagination and Temporality.* Basingstoke: Palgrave.

Wiesel, Elie (1985) *Against Silence* (3 Vols). New York: Holocaust Library.

——(1996) *The Night Trilogy: Night, Dawn & Day (The Accident).* New York: Hill and Wang.

Willaschek, Marcus (ed.) (2000) *John McDowell: Reason and Nature.* London: Lit Verlag.

Williams, Bernard (1993) *Shame and Necessity.* Oxford, UK: University of California Press.

Williams, Meredith (1999a) *Wittgenstein, Mind and Meaning.* London: Routledge.

——(1999b) 'On the Representational Theory of Mind.' In Williams (1999a).

——(1999c) 'Postscript to Chapter 4.' In Williams (1999a).

——(1999d) 'Social Norms and Narrow Content.' In Williams (1999a).

——(1999e) 'Wittgenstein's Rejection of Scientific Psychology.' In Williams (1999a).

Winch, Peter (1992) 'Persuasion.' *Midwest Studies in Philosophy,* XVII, 123–137.

Wittgenstein, Ludwig (1922) *Tractatus Logico-Philosophicus.* London: Routledge.

——(1958) *Philosophical Investigations* (2nd edn). Oxford: Blackwell.

——(1967) *Remarks on the Foundations of Mathematics* (2nd edn). Oxford: Blackwell.

——(1969) *The Blue and Brown Books: Preliminary Studies for the 'Philosophical Investigations'.* Oxford: Blackwell.

——(1975) *On Certainty.* Oxford: Blackwell.

——(1978) *Philosophical Grammar.* Oxford: Blackwell.

Wrathall, M. and Malpas, J. (eds) (2001) *Heidegger, Coping and Cognitive Science: Essays in Honour of Hubert L. Dreyfus* (Vol. 2). Cambridge MA: MIT Press.

Zajonc, Robert (1984) 'On the Primary of Affect,' *American Psychologist,* XXXIX: 117–123.

Index